KU-169-950

CHALLENGING TIMES, CHALLENGING ADMINISTRATION

Manchester University Press

IRISH SOCIETY

The Irish Society series provides a critical, interdisciplinary and in-depth analysis of Ireland that reveals the processes and forces shaping social, economic, cultural and political life, and their outcomes for communities and social groups. The books seek to understand the evolution of social, economic and spatial relations from a broad range of perspectives, and explore the challenges facing Irish society in the future given present conditions and policy instruments.

SERIES EDITOR
Rob Kitchin

ALREADY PUBLISHED

Public private partnerships in Ireland: Failed experiment or the way forward for the state?   *Rory Hearne*

Migrations: Ireland in a global world
Edited by Mary Gilmartin and Allen White

The domestic, moral and political economies of post-Celtic tiger Ireland: What rough beast?   *Kieran Keohane and Carmen Kuhling*

Challenging times, challenging administration

The role of public administration in producing social justice in Ireland

Chris McInerney

MANCHESTER UNIVERSITY PRESS
Manchester and New York

*distributed in the United States exclusively
by Palgrave Macmillan*

Copyright © Chris McInerney 2014

The right of Chris McInerney to be identified as the author of this work has been asserted by him in accordance with the Copyright, Designs and Patents Act 1988.

Published by Manchester University Press
Oxford Road, Manchester M13 9NR, UK
and Room 400, 175 Fifth Avenue, New York, NY 10010, USA
www.manchesteruniversitypress.co.uk

Distributed in the United States exclusively by
Palgrave Macmillan, 175 Fifth Avenue, New York,
NY 10010, USA

Distributed in Canada exclusively by
UBC Press, University of British Columbia, 2029 West Mall,
Vancouver, BC, Canada V6T 1Z2

British Library Cataloguing-in-Publication Data
A catalogue record for this book is available from the British Library

Library of Congress Cataloging-in-Publication Data applied for

ISBN 978 07190 8829 2   hardback

First published 2014

The publisher has no responsibility for the persistence or accuracy of URLs for any external or third-party internet websites referred to in this book, and does not guarantee that any content on such websites is, or will remain, accurate or appropriate.

Typeset in Minion by
Servis Filmsetting Ltd, Stockport, Cheshire
Printed in Great Britain by
CPI Antony Rowe, Chippenham, Wiltshire

Series editor's foreword

Over the past twenty years Ireland has undergone enormous social, cultural and economic change. From a poor, peripheral country on the edge of Europe with a conservative culture dominated by tradition and Church, Ireland transformed into a global, cosmopolitan country with a dynamic economy. At the heart of the processes of change was a new kind of political economic model of development that ushered in the so-called Celtic Tiger years, accompanied by renewed optimism in the wake of the ceasefires in Northern Ireland and the peace dividend of the Good Friday Agreement. As Ireland emerged from decades of economic stagnation and The Troubles came to a peaceful end, the island became the focus of attention for countries seeking to emulate its economic and political miracles. Every other country, it seemed, wanted to be the next Tiger, modelled on Ireland's successes. And then came the financial collapse of 2008, the bursting of the property bubble, bank bailouts, austerity plans, rising unemployment and a return to emigration. From being the paradigm case of successful economic transformation, Ireland has become an internationally important case study of what happens when an economic model goes disastrously wrong.

The Irish Society series provides a critical, interdisciplinary and in-depth analysis of Ireland that reveals the processes and forces shaping social, economic, cultural and political life, and their outcomes for communities and social groups. The books seek to understand the evolution of social, economic and spatial relations from a broad range of perspectives, and explore the challenges facing Irish society in the future given present conditions and policy instruments. The series examines all aspects of Irish society including, but not limited to: social exclusion, identity, health, welfare, life cycle, family life and structures, labour and work cultures, spatial and sectoral economy, local and regional development, politics and the political system, government and governance, environment, migration and spatial planning. The series is supported by the Irish Social Sciences Platform (ISSP), an all-island platform of integrated social science research and graduate education focusing on the social, cultural and economic transformations shaping Ireland in the twenty-first century. Funded by the Programme for Research in Third Level Institutions, the ISSP brings together leading social science academics from all of Ireland's universities and other third-level institutions.

Given the marked changes in Ireland's fortunes over the past two decades it is important that rigorous scholarship is applied to understand the forces at work, how they have affected different people and places in uneven and unequal ways, and what needs to happen to create a fairer and prosperous society. The Irish Society series provides such scholarship.

Rob Kitchin

This book is dedicated to my mother, May, and my daughter, Nia, who have taught and continue to teach me that an awareness of social justice begins in our everyday interactions with each other.

Leabharlanna Poiblí Chathair Bhaile Átha Cliath
Dublin City Public Libraries

Contents

Figures and Tables

Figures

Tables

Acknowledgements

I would like to express my sincere thanks to a number of people whose support made the completion of this book possible. Writing a book about public administration benefits hugely from the insights of those who work in, have worked in or closely engage with the public administration system. I am grateful therefore to those who took the time to so openly share their experiences and perspectives. I trust that I have faithfully represented your views.

I would also like to thank my colleagues in the Department of Politics and Public Administration at the University of Limerick, those who commented so constructively on earlier drafts but, more broadly, the entire staff of the Department who together create such a collegial and supportive working environment.

Thanks also to the staff at Manchester University Press for their guidance and support.

Finally, I am truly grateful to my family and friends who have been supportive of this endeavour, most especially, to my daughter Nia for her patience, forbearance and continued interest in how many pages I had left to write.

Pembroke Branch Tel. 6689575

Introduction

We need a scholarship that is genuinely centred on originality rather than imitation: one that rejects the notion of inevitabilities supinely accepted; that restores the unity between the sciences and culture in their common human curiosity, discovery and celebration of the life of the mind; and that encourages and enables not only new visions to emerge, but new forms of inclusive, warm and celebratory forms of life to be experienced, in conditions of real freedom including affective freedom, freedom from the deprivation of the essentials of life, and the obstacles to participation in society. (President Michael D. Higgins, Address to the Royal Irish Academy, 2012)

Why a book on public administration and social justice

The use of the term crisis has now become so commonplace in Irish society that it has almost become accepted as the natural state of being, however uncomfortable. Crisis in the public finances, crisis in the financial system, crisis in health care, crisis of confidence in politics, the church, the banks, perceived crisis in public order – all pervade the pages of the nation's newspapers and threaten to overwhelm the airwaves. Consequently, there might be a temptation to view this book on the role of public administration in social justice as the product of crisis, motivated by the need to add another layer of analysis to explain why it is we are where we are. The book however is not simply a child of contemporary crisis and instead signals a longer term concern to interrogate and understand the role of public administration in national development. Clearly however, the current state of the nation provides both an unfortunate backdrop as well compelling evidence in favour of many of the proposals explored in the chapters that follow.

Beyond crisis then, the key purpose of the book is to explore the premise that public administration in Ireland should embrace the promotion and protection of social justice as one of its central tenets, alongside the more traditional responsibilities of enabling effective and efficient government

(Frederickson, 2010). As such, it argues that the civil and broader public service, the machinery underpinning the functioning of government and governance, should integrate social justice as an overarching priority that guides the design and implementation of a range of policies – economic, social, cultural and others. The book is not simply about the making of public policy but is specifically concerned with the role of public administration in the policy process. It is neither purely about government nor governance but about how public administration facilitates and underpins them. It is not only about social justice, but specifically about what public administration does about it. In making the argument that public administration needs to play a more proactive social justice role, there is no suggestion that public administration should act autonomously of the democratic system, without reference to elected representatives. In reality though, beyond the narrow confines of formal and procedural democratic processes, it is clear that the public administration system is a significant and influential actor in the policy-making process. As such it can be argued that it has a duty and an obligation to live up to and stand up for the human development and emancipatory demands that have informed the rhetoric of democracy for hundreds of years. Unfortunately, within the sometimes self-serving boundaries of representative democracy, a preoccupation with the short term and the expedient can frequently obscure the search for substance, depth, equality and justice. Public administration, this book suggests, needs to consider its role as a counterbalance to short-term thinking and rent seeking behaviours, consideration not confined to moments of crisis but to be addressed over sustained, longer time horizons.

The presentation of these arguments draws both on conceptual material and new primary research and is offered in a small way to meet the challenges laid down by President Michael D. Higgins, quoted above, and some years earlier by Tom Barrington, one of Ireland's leading public administration scholars. Barrington (1980: 11) in particular posed fundamental challenges to the study of public administration, an endeavour described by him as being in a very 'backward condition indeed'. He advanced a number of reasons for studying public administration, all of which still hold true today and which have provided a significant measure of guidance for this book. Barrington firstly suggested that given the significance of 'government' in our society, there is need for 'a continuing, lively scrutiny of old ideas and assumptions and their replacement where that is appropriate'. If ever such a challenge to old ideas and assumptions were needed, it is surely now, though the space for such lively thinking appears elusive. His second reason for studying public administration related to the increasing role of government in addressing social problems, providing services such as health, education and transport and the redistribution of resources. Successful involvement in these areas, he argued, 'makes heavy demands on the skill, intelligence and imagination of those concerned', demands to which public administration scholarship needs to contribute. Barrington further emphasised the importance of the study of public administration in supporting understanding amongst practitioners of the world in which they operate on the basis that for the average administrator, 'the less the world seems to be mysteriously unpredictable or irrational – the less it represents a Kafka novel, the more likely he is to feel at home in it and make the best possible contribution to it'. Finally, he suggested, public administration scholarship should support a capacity for reflection and in the process 'contribute to the triumph of orderly thought over the random, disorderly and the unpredictable' (Barrington, 1980: 11–12). Several decades on, we might well ask whether the study of public administration is now, more than ever, in need of challenge and new thinking that goes beyond simply describing what public administration looks like and instead seeks to explain how it operates and why it acts the way it does.

One of the frequently suggested benefits of crisis is the potential it offers us to think differently about things we take for granted, whether it be public administration or any other discipline. Curiously though, the severity of the economic crisis and the Europe wide orthodoxy of response to it seem to have stifled the type of challenging, transformative thinking that is needed to guide us towards a new reality, politically, economically, socially and indeed, administratively. Instead, debate remains bounded by preconditions and mantras of inevitability. Our ability to scrutinise old ideas and assumptions and consider their replacement seem to have deserted us, not least in public administration. So, just as the economic responses to crisis appear trapped within the confines of 'old economics', so too thinking about public administration is constrained by tired and unimaginative responses to the challenges of the moment. As a consequence, the acknowledged weaknesses that have been identified in public administration over many years will simply persist and may even deepen, albeit within a slimmed down public sector. This will happen because the only significant items on the current agenda of public administration reform in Ireland appears to be how can we have less administration and how can we pay less for that which remains. Current public sector reform in reality is not about reform, it is about retrenchment and reduction, about economics and efficiency, about performance and productivity. As a result, there is little time taken to fundamentally review the purpose of public administration, nor to review its role in the wake of an economic crisis which was both created and facilitated by decisions taken not just by politicians but also by officials.

A number of these broader challenges for public administration are explored in Chapter 1. The first challenge concerns the role of the administration system in the economic and social crisis currently confronting Ireland, including the relative merits of arguments about the intellectual complicity or intellectual timidity of officials. Related to this is the further challenge of managing the politics-administration dichotomy and assessing whether the division of roles between elected representatives and public officials is as clear cut as might sometimes be thought. The chapter also reflects on current levels of confidence in public administration which have been deteriorating in Ireland over the past number of years and questions whether a retreat from governance and more progressive forms of civic engagement will do anything to stem this dilution of confidence. Finally, Chapter 1 reflects on issues of capacity in public administration, contrasting the current exclusive emphasis on building technical, bureaucratic capacity at the expense of the additional types of transformative and relational capacity needed to imagine a different future beyond crisis.

In his review of the Irish administrative system in 1980, Barrington specifically identified the importance of the state's role in addressing social problems and acknowledged that this makes heavy demands on the skill, intelligence and imagination of those concerned. Following Barrington, this book seeks to focus on the renewal of ideas, thinking and attitudes within public administration on the issue of social justice. As such, the book is unashamedly normative in as much as it takes the unambiguous position that public administration should play a stronger leadership role in promoting and pursuing social justice objectives. Chapter 2 provides a conceptual rationale for such a normative position. It firstly situates the administrative function within a broader set of perspectives on the role of state, on its size and its role in the delivery of supports and services to citizens, perspectives that clearly impact on the shape of the administrative system. In the same vein, it promotes the public administration system as a basic institution of democracy, one that has a consequent responsibility to create the conditions for a socially just state. Seen in this way, it is challenged to play a role in leading and facilitating citizens to establish the basis for fair co-operation and 'a well-ordered society' (Rawls, 2001). However, it is recognised that not all perspectives on public administration assume such a starting point and consequently Chapter 2 also explores the war of ideas that exist between the more social justice oriented ideas of New Public Administration (NPA) and the more efficiency oriented views associated with New Public Management (NPM).

Continuing this conceptual reflection, Chapter 3 turns its attention to exploring some of the ways in which the idea of social justice can be understood. Taking Barrington's lead, the chapter intends to support investigation and awareness within public administration of the many complexities of social justice, thereby reducing the level of 'mystery, unpredictability and irrationality' associated with it. It explores ideas about how we might conceive of social justice from a variety of positions; national and international law; historical public policy discussions; political theory as well as religious teaching. It quickly becomes clear from this analysis that social justice is a highly ideological and highly contested concept, as is evidenced in Dáil Debates on the issue in 1940s and 1950s Ireland. In this chapter, presentation of any single prescription of what social justice means is avoided, though the need for a broader dialogue about what justice means in Ireland in the twenty-first century is advocated.

The final conceptual part of the social justice/public administration puzzle is added in Chapter 4 with an extended discussion on the role of civic engagement as a component of social justice. Again, this chapter highlights that a range of opinions and experiences exist on the issue of citizen participation and its importance or otherwise to the operation of democracy. So, for those who endorse a more limited form of representative, elitist or formal democracy, civic engagement may, at best, be a way to stimulate citizen responsibility and self-help, at worst, simply a nuisance. On the other hand, for exponents of participatory democracy civic engagement represents the essence of the original democratic ideal. This chapter introduces a short lexicon of significant civic engagement terms as a means of illustrating some of the values that inform the participatory ideal. It also reflects on international practice in civic engagement, suggesting that much of the practical reality struggles to match the grand rhetoric of citizen participation. The chapter concludes with a discussion of the specific role of public administration in promoting civic engagement and presents a model to highlight the impact on civic engagement of three related factors: attitudes to democratic deepening; the nature public administration responsiveness and the disposition towards social justice. Taken together it suggests that these three variables combine to facilitate or frustrate a deeper and more empowering engagement experience.

Having set this largely conceptual backdrop, Chapters 5–8 address the position of social justice within Irish public administration. To contextualise these discussions, Chapter 5 discusses some of the main elements of Irish public administration, exploring the origins of contemporary administration and the main pillars around which it is built. This discussion locates later analysis of how social justice has been dealt with at different levels in the Irish administrative system. It questions whether the largely undisturbed transfer of administrative capacity from pre-independence Ireland to the newly independent state served to cultivate and embed a culture of conservatism within the public administration system that inhibits a willingness to tackle the complexity of social justice. The chapter goes on to explore the evolution of state agencies and the closely related topics of public sector reform and capacity building and draws on much valuable work undertaken to map the scope of the state sector in Ireland and state agencies in particular. However it adds to these by focusing on the role of agencies in creating both activist and relational capacity for the state, though it suggests that this capacity may well be undermined by the largely technical and instrumental nature of current public sector reform plans.

Building on this, Chapter 6 begins the more detailed examination of the role of public administration system in relation to social justice. It draws on a range of primary and secondary sources to assess the contribution of public administration, focusing on the interrelated themes of knowledge; disposition and capacity, all three being required to enable a stronger social justice orientation. This examination concludes that within Irish public administration, at corporate and individual level, social justice does not enjoy a particularly high level of visibility or status. Instead, evidence drawn from Departmental Strategy Statements, local authority corporate plans, the observations of a range a senior officials, both current and former, as well as civil society leaders, indicates that social justice has been and continues to be largely subservient to other developmental priorities and is seen as something of a luxury at the present moment. The absence of any meaningful plans to encourage a stronger disposition or to extend capacity in this area leaves little prospect that this status quo will change.

Examination of this conclusion extends further through three case studies of national and local level administrative practice in Chapter 7. The first of these looks at the role of state agencies via the experience of the Combat Poverty Agency while the second explores the contribution of the National Anti-Poverty Strategy and the related poverty proofing / poverty impact assessment process. Both of these case studies suggest a less than positive picture of administrative engagement with social justice issues and conclude that while the state may develop a range of policy or structural instruments, there is no guarantee that these will become administratively or politically embedded. By contrast, the final case study captures the experience of a local authority led, urban regeneration programme in Tralee. In this more positive case, a combination of individual initiative amongst local authority and Health Service Executive staff, allied with the support of senior level management, local residents and elected representatives, produces an example of how public administration can operate in constructive, deliberative and problem solving mode.

The final chapter of the book takes on a deliberately normative tone. In setting out an agenda for social justice within public administration it presents ten conclusions and associated avenues of action. These include a reflection of how a broader commitment to social justice might be engendered within Irish society as a means of informing the ethos of public administration as well a consideration of how an ideational shift towards social justice could be generated within public administration. The chapter presents further conclusions on public sector capacity building; on the cultivation of a stronger justice disposition amongst officials; on the renewal of governance and civic engagement; on the relationship between administration and politics; on the development of the relational state and building and on the particular importance of the local level in Irish democratic and administrative life.

These conclusions can of course be accused, with some justification, of proselytising for a more radical, public administration approach to social justice. Perhaps this might be seen by some as going beyond the role of an academic publication. However, taking Dworkin (2011: 351) as a motivation, there seems little point in doing otherwise. 'Poverty' he said, 'makes an odd subject for reflective philosophy: it seems fit only for outrage and struggle.' Perhaps the study of public administration could benefit from a little such outrage.

1

Contemporary challenges for public administration

Introduction

For public administration this is a time of great challenge and opportunity. In the wake of an unprecedented economic collapse the potential exists to renew public administration, creating the conditions for 'reforms to public administration that typically face opposition from advocates of pure private-sector management approaches'. It also provides an opportunity 'for public administration to reassess and reassert itself of the guarantor of law and order in all sectors (including the economic and financial sector), stability, peace and security and a decent standard of living for the majority of people through adequate social protection and equitable public service delivery' (United Nations Economic and Social Council, 2010: 14). To harvest these opportunities however, requires a willingness to name and address some of the many challenges that public administration must confront. More commonly, these tend to focus on reducing public sector numbers and the associated pay bill, enhanced productivity and more efficient government (Boyle and MacCarthaigh, 2011, Deloitte, 2010). Emphasis is variously placed on better co-ordination, reviews of the role of executive agencies, performance measurement, building capacity and addressing inefficiencies in implementation. A number of these more technical elements dominate the approach to public sector reform in Ireland. (Department of Public Expenditure and Reform, 2011). Other not unrelated challenges around leadership, transparency, public service delivery and regulation of the financial sector are also common. Occasionally, deeper challenges concerning the provision of social and financial protection for vulnerable groups or the importance of improving political accountability and engagement with citizens make it onto the agenda (Boyle and MacCarthaigh, 2011, United Nations Economic and Social Council, 2010). It is to these deeper, 'wicked' problems that this chapter draws attention.

Five fundamental challenges to the relevance of Irish public administration are examined:

- The first locates the administrative system in the broader context of the current economic crisis, questions its role as a key shaper of policy during the Celtic Tiger era and speculates about its ability to play a leadership role and chart new directions to avoid repeating the mistakes of the past.
- The second challenge concerns the relationship between public administration and the political system, establishing the role of public administration in agenda setting and policy development, not least in the articulation and preservation of core societal values on issues such as social justice.
- The third challenge turns to the related issue of public confidence in public administration. It presents evidence of an emerging pattern of low public confidence and examines whether the administrative system is willing to or capable of addressing it.
- Beyond the administrative/political dichotomy, the fourth challenge moves on to the look at the rhetorically rich notion of civic engagement and how public administration is challenged to engage with citizens and civil society organisations, not least through the now out-of-favour ideal of governance.
- The chapter concludes with a discussion of a fifth, pivotal challenge, namely how to enhance capacity within the public sector. This questions whether a continued emphasis on technical, instrumental capacities alone is sufficient to enable public administration to shape, guide and deliver a more sustainable and just future.

Challenge 1: public administration in a time of crisis

While the genesis of this book was not in the immediacy of the economic and social crisis that has affected Ireland since 2008, it would be impossible to undertake a discussion on the role of public administration as a social justice actor without some reflection on the on-going crisis. There is no shortage of analysis and argument about the nature and consequences of the contraction in the Irish economy since 2008. The 2013 budget introduced a further €3.5bn adjustment into the public finances through a variety of revenue raising and expenditure reduction measures, coming on top of adjustments of almost €21bn since July 2008. A further €8.5bn in tax increases and further expenditure reductions are expected to be achieved by 2015. By 2015, it is intended that the full scale of the adjustment will be over €33bn, approximately two-thirds of which will come in the form of expenditure reductions (Healy et al., 2012, Department of Finance, 2012). Inevitably, these expenditure reductions impact most heavily on those who are more reliant on public service provision. However, it is noticeable that within the Medium Term Fiscal Statement there is virtually no reference to the equity or justice impacts of the adjustment process (Department of Finance, 2012).

The primary causes of the current crisis are generally agreed: poor fiscal management and a failure to control balance of payments deficits; a property bubble fuelled in no small part by government tax incentives; and failures in banking regulation that ultimately led to the collapse or near collapse of a number of key financial institutions (FitzGerald, 2011). Other analysts, while acknowledging the strength of the development model up to 2000, have pointed to other governmental weaknesses: malpractice within the financial sector, leading to a requirement for massive state investment into the country's main banks; excessive deregulation, which contributed to a failure to understand what was happening in the financial sector; an unsustainable reliance on the tax revenues associated with an overheated construction sector, fuelled by excesses of lending within the financial sectors and an associated and unsustainable increase in exchequer spending, not least to support increases in public-sector wages (Lane, 2011, Dellepiane and Hardiman, 2011). More broadly and with some considerable vision, the National Economic and Social Council (NESC, 2009) has described the crisis as having five interrelated elements: banking, fiscal, economic, social and reputational. As far back as 2009 it called for an integrated response to the crisis to address all five elements, placing social solidarity and fair burden-sharing at the centre of the response.

Beyond the immediacy of the current crisis, broader international analysis points to other, systematic factors that seem to illustrate a predisposition towards income inequality. In particular, the increasing concentration of wealth in a smaller number of hands has been highlighted. According to the OECD (2008a: 17) income inequality and the numbers of people, living in poverty has increased since the 1990s, across two-thirds of countries, mainly 'because rich households have done particularly well in comparison with middle-class families and those at the bottom of the income distribution'. In Ireland, the findings of the 2010 EU Survey on Income and Living Conditions (EU SILC) in Ireland showed that, while income inequality had dropped somewhat between 2005 to 2009, it had again increased considerably between 2009 and 2010, 'the average income of those in the highest income quintile was 5.5 times that of those in the lowest income quintile. The ratio was 4.3 one year earlier' (Central Statistics Office, 2012: 6). This ratio is now higher than any year since 2004. In terms of income inequality amongst OECD countries Ireland is clustered in a group alongside Australia, Canada, New Zealand and the United Kingdom and the Netherlands, within which 'a wide wage dispersion and a high share of part-time employment drive inequality in labour earnings above the OECD average' (Hoeller et al., 2012). More generally since the 1980s, the upward movement in inequality internationally has been attributed to three key factors: increased wealth generation in financial markets as a result of deregulation begun in the 1970s; 'Lower tax rates on top incomes and lower capital gains and property taxation' that have made 'accumulation of wealth easier for the rich' and finally the reduction or abolitions of 'capital income and wealth taxes' (Hoeller et al., 2012: 15). Interestingly, according to an earlier OECD report, concerns about increasing inequality in developed countries is seen as having prompted governments to tax and spend more 'to offset the trend towards more inequality – they now spend more on social policies than at any time in history' (OECD, 2008a: 15). Thus, as a consequence of the actions of the super wealthy, state spending has had to increase in order to lessen inequality. However, with the onset of the economic crisis the somewhat cruel irony is this social spending is now seen as unsustainable, despite general agreement that the failure to address inequality is likely to produce a range of other negative outcomes, not least health and educational disadvantage and associated earnings inequalities. In the process, further income inequality is perpetuated, contributing to on-going intergenerational inequalities (Institute for Public Health, 2011, Nolan, 2009, Layte, 2011). In this regard Layte (2011: 1) claims that: 'There is ample evidence for Ireland that those with less income, education or from a lower social class have a lower life expectancy and poorer health while alive.' This, it is suggested, translates further into consequences for mental health and associated dangers 'because it precipitates feelings of inferiority and shame that are damaging to health and poisonous to social relationships'. Clearly then, addressing inequality is not just a moral imperative; it is a sensible and sustainable approach to ensuring societal cohesion. This is all the more true in the current context, one that presents the public administration system with a particular set of moral and policy challenges.

The role of public administration in the financial and social crisis: complicity or timidity?

While at a surface level the factors discussed above give us some insight into the origins of current crisis they do not delve more deeply to understand why they were allowed to happen. So, why was there a problem with fiscal management; why was a property bubble allowed to develop despite warnings from the Economic and Social Research Institute (ESRI) (FitzGerald, 2011); why was financial regulation so lax; why are high levels of income inequality allowed to persist. A variety of possible explanations have been advanced. Thus, the crisis may be the result of the exercise of undue influence of political lobbying on decision-making, not least a belief that agencies responsible for financial regulation, were 'captured' by vested interest. It may have been induced by public expectation and the need to maintain rising but ultimately unsustainable standards of living that lead to an unwillingness by decision-makers to check excessive behaviour in pursuit of wealth generation. More fundamentally it may have its origins in the recognised dependence of governments on private wealth generation as a means of generating tax revenues, a dependence that ultimately restricts the types of decisions governments believe they can make. Accompanying this explanation is a belief that there is an inherent inability within largely unrestrained, neo-liberal market economies, driven by narrow and self-interested individualism, to accommodate fundamental democratic principles of equality, justice and the common good. Social Justice Ireland has pointed to a series of 'false assumptions' which they say underpinned the eventual collapse of the Celtic Tiger economy. Amongst these were the beliefs that the singular pursuit of high-rate economic growth was automatically good; that benefits from such higher growth would trickle down to all; or that a low tax economy was needed to generate economic growth but that it would still be possible to provide necessary social services and infrastructure within such a taxation regime (Healy et al., 2012).

Intellectual complicity
Confronting all of these macro-explanations is the issue of the belief systems that underpin the choices made by decision-makers, including officials. Exploring the role of public administration in the financial crisis internationally, Ventriss (2010: 411) proceeds from a belief that the natural outcome of unfettered individualism and an increasing surrender to market mechanisms is 'the absence of any viable conceptions of justice and moral norms (and codes) that can provide sufficient solidarity for society. Accompanying this argument, is a concern about the political, administrative and broader societal reluctance to question certain sacred, economic cows and an unwillingness to situate justice considerations as the foundation for economic policy, thereby creating the conditions for the apparently never ending cycle of boom and bust. A key question for consideration therefore is whether public administration acted to constrain the type of 'pathological behaviour' that led to the financial crisis or did it in fact facilitate it, either by simply executing policies handed down by political leaders or by being directly involved in their design? This latter possibility of complicity in the design of policy that led to the financial crisis raises further questions about the ability of or interest in public administration in doing anything other than serving the needs of the market and of the neo-liberal state. This leads Ventriss (2010: 403) to question the extent to which public administration may be 'an integral part of a dominant complex of institutions that legitimizes, knowingly or unknowingly, the present arrangements of societal powers'. He goes on to further question 'whether public administration runs the risk of becoming not only intellectually timid but politically constrained by what the state defines as legitimate considerations and alternatives, thus

undermining any attempt to develop an independent intellectual foundation that would challenge this conceptualization'. The issue of intellectual timidity will be addressed further below.

Meanwhile, on the complicity question, the idea of 'elite integration' has been raised by some commentators, introducing the potential that public administration, particularly at senior levels, may be intellectually and ideo-logically aligned to particular, dominant ideologies and associated policy direc-tions. Elite integration describes the situation where those in decision-making positions, either in public administration, in regulatory bodies or in the private sector, share an ideological outlook on the role of the market and on the rela-tive role of the state, in part because they are drawn from the same social and/ or educational pool, leading to a confluence of outlook and approach. As a result, the capacity for critical or dissenting voices to be heard is stifled and is replaced by a consensual clamour from the 'symbiotic relationship' produced within this 'triumvirate'. This may explain why regulators were largely content for the financial institutions to regulate themselves, the consequences of which are only too obvious (Chari and Bernhagen, 2011). Equally, the closeness of the relationships between developers and some politicians has been well documented, manifest in widespread provision of tax incentives to encourage construction and, at local level, a drive towards excessive rezoning of land for development purposes. The degree to which such elite integration also includes senior officials within the public administration system remains unclear though some have suggested that the current generation of Irish senior civil servants may be more likely to be influenced by neo-liberal thinking than was previously the case (Litton, 2012b). With the more recent emphasis on recruit-ment from the private sector into senior positions in public administration, the potential for elite integration may well increase in Ireland.

Intellectual timidity
Beyond ideological and intellectual complicity, the alternative suggestion that public administration has been intellectually timid is worth considering. The essence of this argument is that officials within public administration should have been more prominent in communicating concerns they might have had about particular policy directions. However, the opaqueness of policy and decision-making processes at national or local level does not facilitate easy exploration of the relative roles of officials and politicians and, as a result, there is a less than complete picture of the degree to which public administra-tion may have tried to provide more measured policy input during the period of the ultimately destructive, property fuelled boom. However, it is worth noting the concern raised by the OECD report (2008b: 266) on the Irish public sector which noted the view of some observers 'that there is grow-ing politicisation of policy advice, and a previously unseen unwillingness of

senior civil servants to provide analysis that runs counter to political wishes'. By contrast, the Independent Review on Strengthening the Capacity of the Department of Finance undertaken in December 2010 concluded that the Department of Finance did in fact warn the government over a number of years 'on the risks of pro-cyclical fiscal action' but that it was not acted upon. Further, it found that this advice was 'more direct and comprehensive than concerns expressed by others in Ireland, or by international agencies' but that it did not seem to impact on the eventual level of spending set out in the budget process (Wright et al., 2010: 21–22). Others however have been less positive in their assessment of the policy advice provided commenting that 'The failure of the Department of Finance to advise strongly about the dangers facing the Irish economy is surprising' and suggesting that at least part of the reason for the weakness in the Department's commentary was 'a culture that discouraged undue emphasis on economics' (FitzGerald, 2011). However, Wright did criticise the Department for not being more forthright in the language used to communicate its concerns. It also accorded some blame for excessive spending on the level of public expectation and on the demands exerted both by programmes for government and the social partnership agreements:

> Over the ten year period of review, the Programme for Government and Social Partnership Processes helped overwhelm the Budget process. Instead of providing an appropriate fiscal framework for prioritisation of competing demands on the Government's overall agenda, the Budget essentially paid the bills for these dominant processes. Relatively clear advice to Cabinet in June on the risks of excessive spending and tax reductions was lost by the time of December Budgets. (Wright et al., 2010: 25)

Such commentary may in part explain the speed with which the current Fine Gael/Labour government have abandoned the long standing social partnership process.

Noticeably though, the Wright report did not provide any evidence of more fundamental questioning by officials of the market oriented economic model, nor does it record how at least some voices within the social partnership process sought to raise such arguments. Equally, the review did not comment on the degree to which other government departments drove budgetary expansion as a means of pursuing their individual departmental and/or ministerial agendas (Connolly, 2007, Hardiman, 2006).

Wright goes on to make a number of significant recommendations proposing that Department of Finance policy advice should be published for wider consumption and for detailed analysis and comment by an independent Fiscal Council, with the exception of policy advice on budgetary matters. The main message however is clear – there needs to be greater transparency on the advice being provided by officials to politicians and there needs to be a high level, independent, external capacity to scrutinise such advice. Without this, confidence in public administration will inevitably suffer.

Challenge 2: managing the relationship between politics and public administration

The issues raised in the last section illustrated the complexity of the relationships that exists between the political system and public administration. Thus, is public administration simply there to implement the will of the political system irrespective of its own assessment of the merit, justice or sustainability of such direction or is there a legitimate expectation of an administrative obligation to assert more independent views. Alongside the representative institutions generated by most democratic systems, public administration has been described as a source of continuity in a system that sees politicians come and go but which sees public administrators in place for many years (Aberbach, 2003). However, the dichotomy between politics and administration is one of the most frequently occurring themes in public administration scholarship, with tensions arising from the need to follow political direction while at the same time maintain professional integrity and being mindful of public interest, legal and Constitutional obligations. This dichotomy has been captured in the distinction between a public choice as opposed to a managerialist model in public administration. In the public choice model the bureaucracy is often presented as the problem to be resolved, where politicians 'must seek to "tame" the bureaucracy via a concentration of power in the hands of elected representatives, aided to the degree necessary by political staff as advisers, political appointees to line management positions, or, at least, greater political attention to the staffing of the career bureaucracy itself' (Aucion, 1990: 126). Public choice undertones are strongly visible in much contemporary popular and academic writing where, according to Box (2008: 5), the preoccupation seems to be on controlling bureaucrats and 'endlessly "reforming" what is portrayed as a permanently dysfunctional public sector'. By contrast, in the managerial model, the excess of control and regulation on line managers is seen as the problem to be remedied by 'an incentive system that promotes the administration of rules and regulations rather than management for results' (Aucion, 1990). This echoes Bryer's (2007) explanation of how public administration operates according to different 'ethical perspectives', as illustrated in Figure 1.1. These different ethical perspectives include:

- a control centred ethic based either on control by elected representatives or control exercised by rigid bureaucratic rules and regulations;
- a discretionary ethic, implying a greater freedom within the administrative realm to act (in line with the managerialist approach); and

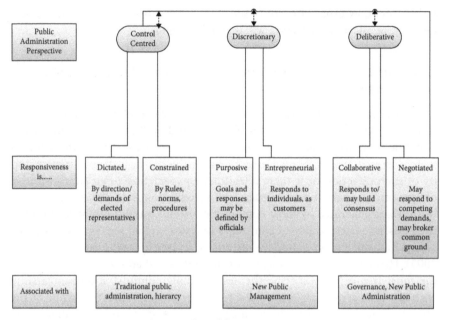

Source: Adapted from Bryer, 2007.

Figure 1.1 The contrasting ethical perspectives of public administration

- a deliberative ethic, in which the potential for a more collective approach to public decisions can be achieved, resonating more closely with Habermas' notions of communicative rationality and power.

The suggestion here is that while more than one perspective may be visible within any given public organisation, it is likely that particular approaches will dominate. Each of the three ethical perspectives is associated with and generates different forms of responsiveness. In the case of a control centred ethic, it is expected that dictated and constrained responsiveness is the order of the day, where dictation/constraint arises either from control by politicians or senior administrative figures or from adhering to the established rules, procedures and regulations of the bureaucracy. Either way, the scope for administrative discretion is considered to be limited, thereby limiting the capacity for responsiveness. A discretionary ethic can produce purposive and entrepreneurial responsiveness, often associated with the advance of New Public Management, where purposive responsiveness is 'the extent to which administrators think and act based upon their own uniquely developed set of professional or public goals' creating the capacity to allow administrators to act 'based on recognition of different needs of groups of people' (Bryer, 2007: 486).

Related to this is the idea of entrepreneurial responsiveness, which focuses more on individual citizens, seeing them as customers whose needs must be met, if necessary by the adoption of more flexible rules and approaches. Finally, a deliberative ethic, moves beyond public choice or managerialism explanations and is seen as having the potential to generate collaborative responsiveness, within which officials can become open to 'new ways of thinking and behaving and which they change their thoughts and behaviours according to the consensus-based decisions of their stakeholders' (Bryer, 2007). Collaboration and deliberation are seen as 'remedies to an uninformed and disinterested public and ethically, they are seen as a means to get members of the public to recognise the consequences of the public decisions they make' (2007). This last perspective operates in a space where the involvement of citizens in the decision-making process is accorded a higher status and often creates much more regular contact between citizens and administrators. However, it may create tension with a control centred ethic, especially where political control resists deliberative process.

It can be imagined that the nature and degree of control exercised by politicians over administrators impacts on their capacity for responsiveness. Svara (2001: 179) believes however, that this dichotomy may be exaggerated, instead suggesting that complementarities and interdependence exists between the elected representative and the executive. Within this the emphasis is placed on creating a harmony between 'the knowledge and values of those who do the on-going work of government' and the 'knowledge and values of those who ultimately set the course for government and ensure that it stays on course' (ibid.: 180). This perspective is strongly endorsed by a range of current and former senior civil servants, virtually all of whom emphasised their place in a democratic system in which the primacy of the elected representative, i.e. the Minister, is respected. According to Dermot McCarthy (2012), former Secretary General at the Department of the Taoiseach: 'I think to characterise the system as passive and inactive would be wrong but equally to say it should not just be proactive but publicly proactive and prescriptive is profoundly anti-democratic and I as a former public servant I would worry profoundly about the day when that happened.' The interplay between ministers and officials is highlighted by another former secretary general, who acknowledged that while in discussions with Ministers 'there would be disagreements alright you know but once the government has decided what its programme is going to be and what its approach is generally speaking you know we'll fall in with that and we try and make sure that that's implemented within the term of the government' (Hynes, 2012). Similarly, another recently retired secretary general commented:

> I believe in the democratic process and I strongly believe in the right of the government of the day to come in and to set out their policy platform and their own policies – provided they are not trying to do something illegal or immoral – I saw

my role as to support the administration of the day in doing that. But inevitably it's not a clean line, it's an iterative process and it's a process where the public servants of the day and the agencies under their auspices have the opportunity to shape policy. (O'Neill, 2012)

Recognising the democratic primacy of the elected representative of course is not seen as prohibiting a role for officials in initiating and advocating policy ideas. Were this to be the case, according to the current secretary general of the Department of Public Expenditure and Reform, it would represent a waste of the potential for innovation that the current civil service offers: 'It is not that the case that politicians from political parties arrive in Government and have all the ideas on all the issues and challenges that are required in order to move the country forward. It is the role of the Civil Service to work with politicians and to have ideas and be innovative in meeting the challenges of the country. Our job is to work with the political system' (Watt, 2012). This contrasts with the local level in Ireland where public administration plays a more prominent role and is 'effectively the driver. I would say of most initiatives in relation to new directions comes from the executive side of the house' (Keyes, 2012), albeit within a policy framework set down by the Department of the Environment, Community and Local Government.

Borrowing from the frequently used governance metaphor, this suggests a relationship between the political process, which has primary responsibility to chart the course or steering the ship and the administrative machinery, which provides the crew to do the rowing, albeit with some input into choosing which way to go. While this metaphor is somewhat simplistic, it does raise a key question. What do the crew of the ship (the administrators) do when those with primary responsibility for plotting the course (the elected representatives) appear more and more to be steering the ship for the rocks? Assuming of course they actually recognise the rocks or have the capacity to look into the distance, do they simply keep rowing as directed; do they stop rowing and insist on changing course; do they become 'proactive' and publicly inform the passengers (the citizens) that the ship is heading to the shore so that they can demand a change of course or do they simply wait until the ship hits the rocks and then hold their hands up say 'we told you this was going to happen'. Of course the crew, the public administration system, may point to their obligation to follow policy as set out by the government of the day. However, grey areas between the purely political and the purely administrative means that increasingly both crew and captain have to accept responsibility for policy failure or success, though of course it's only the captain that runs the risk of sanction at the next election.

I don't think it's credible to say that the Minister is responsible for policy so therefore if the policy goes wrong the Minister is solely accountable. Nor is it straightforward to say that senior civil servants are responsible for administration or implementation and then if that goes wrong they're solely accountable. The reality is that it is very hard to distinguish between the policy and the implementation. For example, the policy could have been wrong or the implementation could have been wrong or a combination of both or maybe the resourcing was not adequate. But ultimately better systems of accountability are required and we are on working on this. (Watt, 2012)

Another reality of course is that the range of policy options pursued by incoming governments is actually very narrow and for the public administration system, any changes are only marginal, as expressed by one current assistant secretary general 'But a government that comes in, is going to make a policy going a bit this way or a bit that way, but it doesn't really matter, because it's not really affecting the infrastructures, not really affecting the state at a fundamental level' (Buckley, 2012).

The potential tensions between the policy-making, policy implementation roles as well as the politically neutral role of civil servants and their willingness to 'speak truth to power' were observed even before the current crisis hit with full force. For example, the OECD (2008b: 266) noted the 'increasing concern, within both the Civil Service and at the political level, over the willingness and capacity of public servants to play this role, as well as the willingness of politicians to listen' while in some cases, decisions by ministers on significant policy departures, such as decentralisation of public administration, were made without any reference to officials. While managing such communications in more 'normal' times has been identified as an issue, the nature of the current crisis justifiably questions whether the public administration system should be given a more formal role, legislatively or Constitutionally defined, to act as a brake on the potential excesses of political decision-making. This could occur in certain named circumstances, particularly when the management both of scarce or abundant resources is in question or when Constitutionally important principles, such as social justice, are at issue. It is likely of course that such a role of course would need to apply in very limited certain circumstances only, though it would place the politics-administrative dichotomy in more sharp relief.

Challenge 3: addressing the quiet crisis of confidence in public administration

The last section discussed the specific role played by public administration in contributing to or addressing the social and economic crisis. In practice, much of the public discourse on the economic crisis has focused more on political decision-making and less on bureaucratic leadership. In the same way, while confidence in politicians is a recurring topic for debate, confidence in the capacity of public administration to respond to contemporary challenges is less commonplace. However, citizens need to have confidence that government and public administration will act in way that is just, fair and equitable,

Table 1.1 Assessment of 'The way inequalities and poverty are addressed' in Ireland (%)

	Very good	Rather good	Rather bad	Very bad	Don't know	Total good	Total bad
SEB315 (May–June 2009)	3	30	38	18	11	33	56
SEB 349 (June 2010)	2	29	41	17	11	31	58
SEB 370 (June 2011)	3	28	38	20	11	31	58
SEB 391 (June 2012)	4	33	38	15	10	37	53

Source: EuroBarometer Social Climate Surveys 2009–2012.

not just in the delivery of services but in its contribution to the determination of policy options. At this point it is not clear that such confidence exists. For example, in Ireland in 2010 a Eurobarometer survey indicated that while 90% of those surveyed believed that poverty needed urgent action by government, only 28% had confidence in the capacity of government to do so, even lower than for private companies. By contrast 69% expressed confidence in the capacity of citizens themselves to address poverty (European Commission, 2010b). Over a sustained period (2009–2012), the conclusions of a series of Special Eurobarometer surveys also suggest that a majority of those surveyed in Ireland considered that issues of poverty and inequality in Ireland are either rather badly or very badly dealt with, as illustrated in Table 1.1.

The low level of confidence in government to address issues of poverty of necessity raises questions about the level of confidence in public administration in Ireland more generally. However, there are different perspectives on this. Historically, MacCarthaigh (2008: 40) suggests that 'The Irish civil service is one of the most trusted public institutions in the state' citing figures from the Irish Social and Political Attitudes Survey (ISPAS) survey of 2002 which indicated that half of those who responded had 'high trust' and 39% 'medium trust' in the civil service. More recently, the Institute of Public Administration has developed a 'Public Administration Quality Indicator' using an aggregate of indicators from sources including the World Bank, the World Economic Forum, as well as data from Eurobarometer on quality of government (Boyle, 2011: 26–27). Amongst the indicators used to determine quality are a number associated with the maintenance of 'traditional public sector values' such as whether:

- government decisions are effectively implemented;
- justice is fairly administered;
- the judiciary is independent from the political influence of members of government, citizens or firms;
- diversion of public funds to companies, individuals or groups due to corruption;

- existence of bribery and corruption;
- when deciding upon policies and contracts, government officials are neutral;
- government policy is transparent;
- the composition of public spending is wasteful;
- police services can be relied upon to enforce law and order.

Other indicators focus on competitiveness and regulation and include indicators that address whether:

- the legal and regulatory framework encourages the competitiveness of enterprises;
- public-sector contracts are sufficiently open to foreign bidders;
- the ease of doing business is supported by regulations;
- intellectual property rights are adequately enforced;
- public- and private-sector ventures are supporting technological developments;
- bureaucracy hinders business activities;
- complying with administrative requirements (permits, regulations, reporting) issued by government is burdensome.

Using these indicators, many of which are business oriented and may not actually capture the concerns of the average citizen, the IPA concludes that 'the quality of Ireland's public administration is seen as slightly above average for the European Union' (Boyle, 2011: 26–27). In terms of traditional public service values, it is proposed that Ireland 'has generally been slightly higher than the EU15 average, and well above the EU27 average' while the ranking on competitiveness and regulation also places Ireland above the European average, in sixth place in 2011 behind Finland, Denmark, Sweden, the Netherlands and Luxembourg. The IPA does note that the data presented needs to be interpreted with great care as it 'comprises small-scale samples of opinion from academics, managers and experts in the business community' and as such is 'limited both in terms of its overall reliability and the fact that it represents the views of limited sections of the community' (2011: 11). The strength of trust in public administration is also highlighted in the IPA report, though the indicators used actually address the much broader issue of trust in government and trust in parliament, not public administration.

However, less positive conclusions emerge over a four-year period from a series of Special Eurobarometer surveys on the social climate within the EU. These more robust surveys, carried out face to face with over 1,000 people in each country, posed questions about the economic and social situation of the country, including the cost of living, affordability of energy and of housing,

Table 1.2 Assessment of 'How public administration is run' in Ireland (%)

	Very good	Rather good	Rather bad	Very bad	Don't know	Total good	Total bad
SEB315 (May–June 2009)	2	20	33	33	12	22	66
SEB 349 (June 2010)	1	18	37	31	13	19	68
SEB 370 (June 2011)	1	21	33	31	14	22	64
SEB 391 (June 2012)	1	19	42	27	11	20	69

Source: EuroBarometer Social Climate Surveys 2009–2012.

the general economic and employment situation *and* the quality of public administration. The first social climate survey was carried out between May and June 2009 and concluded, on public administration, that 'More Europeans are dissatisfied than satisfied with this and the most dissatisfied are the Greeks, Latvians and Irish.' By contrast the countries with the highest satisfaction were Denmark, Sweden, Luxembourg, Estonia, Finland, Austria and Germany (European Commission, 2010c: 11). In Ireland's case, 66% of respondents considered that public administration was badly run (see Table 1.2). The report also concluded that the level of education of respondents is influential in informing perspectives on public administration across Europe with those having higher education levels, i.e. those who continued studying until age 20 or after, have a more favourable view (48%) by comparison with those who left education earlier (40%). Perhaps not surprisingly in the Irish case, the report found that a majority (52%) – considered that the state of public administration had worsened compared with five years earlier, Ireland again being only one of four countries where a majority held such a view (European Commission, 2010d: 129–131). Looking to the future, of those surveyed in Ireland in 2009, 33% anticipated that the quality of public administration would worsen further, the third highest figure amongst the EU27.

Unfortunately, this was not to be a once-off downturn in perceptions on public administration in Ireland and the scorecard from the social climate survey carried out in June 2010 places Ireland fourth from bottom in terms of satisfaction with public administration, albeit that the numbers expecting it to get worse over the coming 12 months had reduced somewhat (European Commission, 2011a). The third social climate survey (Eurobarometer 370) carried out in June 2011 (European Commission, 2011b) again ranks Ireland fourth from bottom in terms of satisfaction with how public administration is run, though again there is some improvement in the score card ranking and a drop in the numbers expecting the situation to worsen in the coming 12 months. Finally, in the recent social climate report produced in September 2012 and based on data gathered in June of 2012, the poor perception of the performance of public administration in Ireland persists, with 69% of respondents considering that it is run rather or very badly (European Commission, 2012).

All in all and contrary to the conclusions of the IPA Public Sector Trends report, the data from this series of reports suggests that satisfaction with the quality for public administration since 2009 has been poor for a majority of survey respondents and has remained poor over a four-year period. While it might be argued that this is an inevitable consequence of the economic crisis, the fact that some increased level of confidence is being reported in government and parliament only serves to highlight the negative perceptions of public administration. For public administration to be in a position to play a strong leadership role, be it around economic recovery or more specifically on social justice, public confidence in its capacity and commitment must be proactively restored, not just at a political level but by officials themselves. However, there is little evidence of public officials taking on a prominent role to bring this about.

Challenge 4: responding to and engaging with citizens and civil society

The challenge to engage with citizens in processes of policy-making and policy delivery is a recurring theme in national and international discussions of public administration and is addressed in more detail in Chapter 4. However, it is important to locate it as one of the on-going challenges facing public administration, not least as a result of the substantial evidence of public discontent with the performance of public administration in Ireland. Writing from the perspective of the Institute of Public Administration, Boyle and MacCarthaigh (2011: 38) suggest that 'Citizen engagement in the design and provision of public services is an issue at the heart of public service reform. Unless the citizen is centre stage in the process, the chances of reform receiving widespread backing are small.' However, there is little in the 2011 Public Sector Reform Plan to indicate that this sentiment is shared by the government, with few suggestions of reform that might lead to enhanced citizen involvement. A little more than ten years earlier, a potentially far reaching political statement offered the prospect of more far reaching progress in this area when the White Paper on Voluntary Activity proposed that 'There is a need to create a more participatory democracy where active citizenship is fostered' where participation was defined as 'an exchange between citizens and government, between those who make policy and people affected by policy choices' (Government of Ireland, 2000b: 63). Unfortunately, the commitment to pursue such a vision of active citizenship was short lived, producing considerable disappointment amongst civil society organisations who had invested time and energy into the White Paper process (Harvey, 2004). More recently, the 2012 White Paper on local government reform 'Putting People First' devoted considerable space to discussing different avenues for civic engagement, but made no decisions that might improve practice (Government of Ireland, 2012a). On the contrary, some of the White Paper proposals to concentrate responsibility for local and community development under the local government sector may well further damage civic engagement potential.

The OECD too has frequently commented on the importance of citizen involvement more generally (OECD, 2009) and specifically addressed the issues in its 2008 report on the Irish public sector. In the latter report it is noteworthy that the main goals of the Irish public sector articulated in a survey of officials were 'open and inclusive policy-making', improving the efficiency of government and the effectiveness of policy; strengthening social cohesion and improving 'citizens' compliance'. By contrast, whereas Irish officials were seeking to improve compliance, the report notes, 'Most other OECD countries responding to the OECD questionnaire put primary emphasis on increasing citizens' trust and improving transparency and accountability as goals' (OECD, 2008b: 224). The OECD report also notes that Irish public sector respondents identified the dangers of consultation fatigue and hijacking by interest groups as on-going risks on the open policy process, defining the former as 'citizens' reduced interest in participating in the future' (ibid.: 225). Interestingly though they do not refer to the definition of consultation fatigue produced a number of years earlier in the 'Guidelines on Consultation for Public Sector Bodies' (Government of Ireland, 2005: 3). According to these guidelines,

> *Certain categories of stakeholders*, although they have an interest in participating in a consultation, *might have weakly developed institutional or analytical capacities*, making it difficult for them to participate in large numbers of consultations. *Where the complexity and volume of consultations on a particular issue prevents a stakeholder from participating* as fully as the stakeholder would wish, *this is known as consultation fatigue*. Consulting bodies, should, in planning and designing consultation processes, have regard for the capacities of organisations and individuals to participate effectively in consultations. (Emphasis added)

In this view, citizens experience consultation fatigue, not because they have put too much effort into it with limited results but because they themselves had a capacity deficit in the first instance that prevents them from dealing with the complexity of the policy-making process. Nowhere is there any notice taken of a requirement on officials to reduce the complexity of consultations. If this type of understanding is typical of public administration attitudes to civic engagement, perhaps it is not surprising then that citizens in Ireland are sometimes a little wary about state sponsored consultation initiatives. Research produced for the government Taskforce on Active Citizenship (2007: 9) noted 'there is cynicism and a lack of confidence in democratic and some other consultative structures, particularly at local level, with individuals and organisations not feeling that they are genuinely listened to'. In order to achieve genuine civic engagement public administration needs to be looked upon as a site for deepening democracy and, consequently, as a site for renewing governance and addressing social justice priorities. However, more traditional understandings of public administration offer only limited capacity to do this, the suggestion being that 'the field has lost touch with the citizen and finds itself distanced from the power of the sovereign embodied in the citizen' (Evans, 2000: 321). What is needed then, to deepen democracy and governance, is a more progressive reconnection between public administration and the citizen and, alongside this, the development of new or renewed systems of local and national governance. Unfortunately, the linkage between a reconceived democratic ideal and the renewed functioning of public administration is not a topic that has been subject of widespread exploration, either within the literature on democratic theory or governance. In saying this of course, the complexity of the challenge is not to be underestimated, nor should it be oversimplified.

Retaining a commitment to governance

A related element of the relationship between the state and its citizens is the ideal of governance. Governance is usefully defined by the United Nations Development Programme (UNDP) as:

> The system of values, policies and institutions by which a society manages its economic and social affairs through interactions within and among the state, civil society and the private sector. It is the way a society organises itself to make and implement decisions – achieving mutual understanding, agreement and action. It comprises the mechanisms and processes for citizens and groups to articulate their interests, mediate their differences and exercise their legal rights and obligations. (Nahem and Sudders, 2004)

In Ireland and elsewhere, the democratic landscape has become much more complicated than a simple relationship between the elected representative and the bureaucrat. Indeed, for much of the period since the 1980s, Ireland has been a leader in the creation of a whole host of governance structures and processes at both national and local level, reflecting an international trend that sought to move beyond a more traditional, narrower understanding of government towards a more engaged and some might say more democratic form of policy-making. More recently however, the commitment to 'governance' as a way of engaging with and solving a host of complex issues has diminished and has been replaced by a retreat to more traditional approaches to decision-making, in the process eschewing the formal input of civil society partners in favour of a politics and bureaucracy led approach to problem solving. This retreat is sometimes justified, both by politicians and bureaucrats, on the grounds that social partnership simply acted as a vehicle for rent seeking behaviour on behalf of the more powerful participants within it, with trade unions using it primarily as a vehicle to enhance the conditions of their members and employer organisations seeing as a means of enhancing the business environment, not least through extensive deregulation. Meanwhile other partners, the farming organisations and the community and voluntary sector, endeavoured to secure some, albeit marginal, influence on policy decisions.

At present it appears that that the idea of governance has been quietly abandoned, portrayed as a failed or failing experiment something to be quietly confined to history, replaced by less formal, more random policy discussions now described as 'social dialogue'. Innovative national partnership structures such as the National Economic and Social Forum (the only one to involve representatives of political parties) and the sustainable development partnership, Comhar, have been collapsed into the National Economic Council. At local level, one of the earliest governance experiments, hailed in their day as an example of 'democratic experimentalism', the area based partnerships, await closer alignment into the local government structure. Meanwhile, other structures established to stimulate local co-operation and co-ordination of effort, City and County Development Boards, are to be abandoned. Ironically, Strategic Policy Committees, which were designed to enhance the policy role of locally elected representatives and to formalise engagement with local civil society interests, are to be maintained despite their limited success in providing a platform for dialogue and deliberation. Does all this mean then that the era of governance is assumed to have failed and that the next stage is a return to the tried and trusted politics-bureaucracy axis? And while it is in some ways understandable that the mechanisms of governance have been associated with policy choices that have brought the country to the edge of economic collapse, might it actually be the case that in reality the true potential of governance was never really explored, understood or embraced. So, rather than the problem being with the notion of governance itself, perhaps the problem was with how it was practised. Within this, the role of public administration is central and presents a challenge to re-imagine governance rather than simply abandon it.

Challenge 5: building public administration capacity

The capacity of public administration at local and national level has been an underlying theme in the challenges already discussed; capacity to respond to the unprecedented economic and social crisis; capacity to support elected government while not losing sight of obligations that transcend government; capacity to build confidence in public administration; capacity to create new and more effective platforms to engage more deeply with citizens. The challenge of enhancing existing and building new capacities is, however, considerable.

In thinking about capacity it is important to recognise that that the role of the state has undergone significant transformations since the 1980s, brought about by a variety of interconnected factors including democratisation; liberalisation; globalisation and the emergence of a new security agenda (Robinson, 2008), echoing earlier analysis by the OECD (Michalski et al.,

2001). These changes have necessitated, in some quarters at least, a renewed focus on the capacity of states to function within, engage with, control and/ or manage the new dynamics arising from the changing nature of economic, social and political decision-making. In many ways the resultant challenges converge to refocus discussions on state capacity away from 'conventional models of public administration' which 'are largely informed by technocratic criteria which emphasise improved bureaucratic skills and incentives through training and pay reforms and modernising the tools and systems of administration (Robinson, 2008: 567). However, it has been argued that much of the focus on state capacity remains fixed on the dominance of a control centred ethic or, on the preservation of a 'command-hierarchy' model (2008: 568) which 'leaves it with a bias towards an understanding of government rather than governance' (Jayasuriya, 2004: 489). This has been done by emphasising particular capacity components, such as, training for individual bureaucrats, improving administrative systems, an emphasis on organisational strengthening, delegating service delivery and reducing the size of the state accountability, reflecting much of the prescriptions of a new public management approach (Pollit, 1995, Savoie, 1995). This type of approach is prominent in much of what is contained in the current public sector reform plan developed by the Department of Public Expenditure and Reform (2011). Whether such an approach to state capacity building is capable of embracing the type of challenges discussed above is less than certain. Instead alternative frameworks of public administration capacity may be required to address the needs of complex administration, in a complex society, in complex and challenging times. One such alternative framework highlights the importance of a suite of capacities, addressing: transformative (social and economic), relational, infrastructural and distributive elements, with particular emphasis on transformative and relational capacities.

Transformative capacity
Transformative capacity, as originally conceived, referred somewhat narrowly to the ability of 'domestic policy elites to pursue domestic policies and economic adjustment strategies in co-operation with organised economic interest groups with a view to upgrading and transforming the industrial economy'(Robinson, 2008: 577). It was initially associated with the Asian Tiger or developmental states, such as South Korea and Taiwan and, some suggest, also applied in Ireland, where the state in different ways, developed partnerships and relationships, both formal and informal, primarily with economic interests to create the conditions for economic growth (O'Riain, 2004). As originally conceived, these developmental states defined 'their mission primarily in terms of long-term national economic enhancement' and saw their role as being to 'actively intervene in economic activities with the goal of improving the international

competitiveness of their domestic economies' (Pempel, 1999: 139). Moreover, in these cases, it was generally considered that, as well as recognising that the role of conscious state action, the evolution of a well-functioning bureaucracy was fundamental to shaping and achieving their development objectives. However, the role of the bureaucracy was not simply to establish 'blind bureaucratic control' but was to 'construct economic rules that advance the long-term technological character of the nation as a whole, rather than simply enhancing the power of government agencies or lining the pockets of predatory rulers' (Pempel, 1999: 142). In the context of this book transformative capacity of course is not seen as being confined to the economic sphere alone; transformative capacity needs to be developed to enable a broader and more sustainable development model, in service of society and the economy, to be imagined and explored. The role of the bureaucracy then transforms into one in which it facilitates the agreement of approaches to social and economic development that advance the long-term economically and socially just character of the nation in a way that benefits the entire society, not just a small number of elites.

Unfortunately, as will be discussed in Chapter 6, much of the literature on Irish public administration and interviews conducted in the writing of this book do not produce a strong sense of confidence that this type of transformative capacity is in ready supply.

Relational capacity

The ability to think and act in a transformative way is of course closely related to the ability to interact and cooperate with a variety of different stakeholders, within the bureaucracy, in the political system and in civil society. Thus, relational capacity is seen as pertaining to the ability of the state to engage with multiple forms and sites of governance (Bache and Flinders, 2004, Jayasuriya, 2004, Jessop, 2004, Robinson, 2008). As such, it too contrasts with the narrow type of technical capacities and attributes often prioritised by public administration systems. Different ideas about how the state relates with citizens and organisations and how it facilitates citizens' relationships with each other have begun to converge into a dialogue about the existence or otherwise of the 'relational state'. Underpinning this for some is a belief that within democratic societies, there has been a transition over the years from the state as: a form of 'paternalistic protector'; through a stage where the primary role of the state is as a provider of welfare 'for a relatively passive public'; and towards a new stage where 'government increasingly acts with the public to achieve common goals, sharing knowledge, resources and power' (Mulgan, 2012: 20). For those who hold with this view the challenge is to envisage how the state can be encouraged to pay greater attention to improving its ability to relate to a variety of actors in a variety of different settings.

Within the debate on the relational state however there are those who suggest that the state is incapable of playing a relational role given its primary concern with 'standardisation', the suggestion being that:

> States work best when a problem has a technical, mechanical solution which can be employed everywhere within a shared geographic space. They are at their worst when they need to respond flexibly to local particularities, when they need to act nimbly or with nuance, and – most importantly of all – when they delve into problems of the nation's spirit or of the human heart. Anything which requires difference, contingency and essential unpredictability is not going to be a skill of the state. (Stears, 2012: 39)

Such a view would appear to resonate with others that reflect on the conservative nature of public administration.

> You will have heard the phrase from I think Whitaker and some others that the Irish Civil Service is inherently conservative. I think that is true in the sense of conservative as being a set of beliefs that are centered on the idea that society should be stable and harmonious. In the Civil Service in my experience; you don't tend to find for example a commitment to social democracy and the ideas of social democracy. Neither do you find a commitment to the other extreme, to neoliberal or very right wing or monetarist thinking, that's extremely rare. What you get instead is this kind of, I suppose, what you call a centre right or centrist's type of view about the way institutions should operate; there is a feeling that there should be equality of opportunity, there should be equal access to the services of the state. (Buckley, 2012)

Thus, if the mainstream bureaucratic instrument of the state is conservative as described and concerned with standardisation, its ability to achieve economic and social transformation and its ability to relate to citizens and their interests is inevitably challenged. In the past, it could be argued, this view of the public sector justified the establishment of commercial or non-commercial state agencies as a means of achieving particular 'non standardised' objectives and supplementing the missing capacity of mainstream public administration. It also offers part of the explanation for the employment of political advisors, designed to extend the range of policy advice beyond that provided by civil servants. Together, these can be seen as adding an activist capacity to the state, enabling it to do things that mainstream public administration would find difficult or challenging, while at the same time ensuring that the core functions of the bureaucracy continue to deliver.

> And you can see that a highly motivated ideological government would need to use that mechanism to a large degree in order to achieve radicalism and this present government is seeking to achieve that through the use of special advisors and to a certain degree by recruiting people directly in from the private sector. And people like myself, career civil servants, can totally understand what's motivating that. And I wouldn't like to give the impression that I view our job as being to frustrate that, it's not. It's simply that any kind of radical 'raiding party' – if you want to use that phrase – can achieve a huge amount, but you need somebody to make sure in the background that the lights stay on. (Buckley, 2012)

Viewed from this point of view the drive towards reducing the number of state agencies, closing them down or integrating them into government departments or local government, may have the attractiveness of returning power to the mainstream system but potentially risks losing or diluting capacity to do things that the mainstream cannot.

Infrastructural and distributive capacity

The final elements of capacity building suggested by Robinson and others are the parallel elements of infrastructural and distributive capacity. In this case infrastructural capacity, concerns the ability of the state to 'penetrate society to extract resources and elicit co-operation from organised interest groups in the pursuit of collective goals'. Effectively, this involves the capacity of the state to design and operationalise an effective system and infrastructure for the collection of taxes. There is little doubt that the technical and operational capacity of the Irish tax collection system is of high quality. However, from a social justice perspective, the key issue is not so much administrative capacity but whether the political will exists to extract resources in an equitable way from all elements of society, including the most wealthy. Despite regular claims from politicians about how much tax the top 10% are paying, the fact that income inequality is high and increasing once again would suggest that it is political as opposed to administrative capacity that needs to be enhanced. This of course brings us into the fourth zone of capacity, distributive capacity. This is seen as 'focusing on the ability of states to distribute the gains of economic development to the wider populace through social welfare measures and transfers funded by general tax revenues' (Robinson, 2008: 575–579). In some cases however, it has been suggested that distributive capacity simply serves to privilege high income earners (Kwon, 2005), a charge that might well be reflected upon in the Irish case. Again though, decisions about income and wealth distribution are inherently political. However, one of the great unknowns within public administration is the extent and nature of the advice (if any) offered by officials on issues of revenue extraction and distribution. Publication of such advice, even historical advice, would provide an important insight into the disposition of the public sector towards wealth distribution and ultimately, its disposition towards social justice.

Conclusions

This chapter has set out a series of challenges for public administration, particularly in the context of the economic and social crisis in Ireland and beyond. It has highlighted the danger that social justice may become relegated to a secondary position, some way behind the single, sacred cow of economic growth. There is considerable irony in this given that it was the blind pursuit of economic growth that ultimately produced possibly the greatest level of social injustice the country has ever seen. Thus, the steroid state lies exposed and the cocktail of artificial stimulants taken to boost tax revenues and falsely inflate the nation's economic muscle are revealed and are rightly condemned for the deep damage they have caused to the fabric of Irish society. Curiously though, even now there remains a reluctance to explore the deeper reasons for the economic crisis and, even more worryingly, there is little willingness to move beyond the type of limited economic philosophy that brought us to the point of crisis in the first place. There is a danger that without some higher order goals, some deeper vision for the future of Irish society, we will simply drift helplessly back in the same direction as before, carried along by the continuing current of neo-liberal inspired economic prescriptions. Instead, the challenge must be to conceive of a state where social justice is the overarching objective, where economic growth is a means to an end, not just an end in itself.

This presents a particular challenge for public administration. As the principal source of advice to government, as a key part of the policy-making process, it has to have to capacity and desire to contribute to the formulation of a new vision for the future and the commitment to drive an agenda that is social justice centred, not social justice avoiding. To do this, there is a pressing need to rebuild confidence in public administration which has been deteriorating in Ireland and other European countries over the past number of years. The constant stream of anti public sector rhetoric, which is often ideologically driven, contributes to this declining confidence. However, public administration institutions seem reluctant or possibly unable to confront these assaults head on. One way to address the apparent decline in public sector confidence is for public administration to become more open to and engage with citizens and their organisations. This can be aided by a visible move towards incorporating a deliberative ethic within public administration, while recognising the need to operate within a democratic context and within a framework of rules and regulations that ensure consistency, transparency and fairness. However, the two are not mutually exclusive. It can also be aided by a more serious engagement with governance processes and civic engagement, not by the apparent retreat from such processes. All of these will require a renewed focus on capacity building, particularly transformative and relational capacity building. Most of all though, there is a need for public administration to engage in a challenging and far reaching discussion of its role in promoting social justice. The discussion of what this might involve is taken up in the next chapter.

2

The role of public administration in promoting and protecting social justice

Introduction

For some, the notion of articulating a more specific and clearly constructed role for public administration in promoting social justice is unnecessary. Arguments about the essentially unbiased and neutral role of public administration are advanced as a means of countering calls for a more activist approach in favour of social justice. Accompanying this are perspectives that locate responsibility for social justice within the realms of the political, implying that administrators simply act on the direction of their political masters and do not have discretion to act on their own initiative. However, as we have already seen in Chapter 1, this notion of an unbiased public administration is highly fallible. The democracy – bureaucracy divide is not a simple linear relationship; administrators are not only involved in the delivery of public policy but are centrally involved in its design. More importantly, public officials, like all other human beings, embody a whole host of beliefs, values, dispositions, prejudices and biases that may cause them to act in a certain way. Moreover, institutions too, not least public administration, develop their own values, personalities and biases. For those outside of such institutions, these values and institutional personalities are not only difficult to recognise, but are even more difficult to change.

This chapter aims to more firmly establish the relationship between public administration and social justice. It argues that any consideration of this relationship must first take a step back and revisit perspectives on the role of the state in contemporary democracies, the suggestion being that advocates of minimalist state intervention inevitably envisage a more limited role for public administration as part of their efforts to reduce the influence of the state on the lives of citizens, usually in favour of greater reliance on market provision. By contrast, those who advocate for a more activist state see the state undertaking a wider range of functions and ceding less space to the market. As such, they anticipate a more comprehensive set of functions, roles and responsibilities for public administration. We then move on to explore some of the arguments as to why public administration should play more of a role in promoting social justice. It is argued that public administration needs be viewed as a democratic institution in its own right and, as a consequence, has a particular role in defending and promoting basic democratic principles such as justice and equality. It then revisits the contested notion of bureaucratic neutrality, suggesting that at best it is a somewhat lazy and naïve assumption, at worst, an excuse to preserve the existing status quo.

Against this backdrop, some of the main elements of the 'war of ideas' in public administration are looked at, particularly the competing ideals expressed in the New Public Administration (NPA) movement as opposed to the more pervasive practice of 'New Public Management' (NPM). Building on this, the chapter concludes with a discussion of some of the conceptual elements involved in advancing a social justice agenda within public administration.

Taking a step back: perspectives on the state

Consideration of the role of public administration in promoting social justice does not exist in isolation from broader philosophical and ideological considerations, not least those provided by perspectives on the role of the state. In reality, it is not possible to explore the more specific terrain of public administration and social justice without first mapping out some of the limitations or opportunities that derive from different state views. Much has been written on the role of the state and inevitably this chapter provides only an introduction to some of the main areas of difference. In the Irish case, as in most developed nations at this point, discussions on the state take place within the confines of a framework of liberal democracy (confined in as much liberal democracy rarely fails to extend its view beyond the boundaries of representative democracy). The liberal conceptualisation of the democratic state has been differentiated in a number of different ways. In one of these, Barber (1984) suggests that liberal democracy can be best understood by looking at three particular alternatives: anarchist; realist and minimalist, all of which seek to protect individual liberties but, in the process, offer quite different views of the extent and scope of influence of state infrastructure.

Within this suite of perspectives, the anarchist tradition is based on a belief that human beings are to be viewed as atomised individuals whose aim is 'not to share in power or to be part of a community but to contain power and community and to judge them by how they affect freedom and private interest' (Barber, 1984: 7). The implication of this is a limited role and scope for government so that it cannot interfere in the pursuit of individual rights and/or liberty. At an institutional level the anarchist perspective, with its emphasis on limiting the impact on individual liberty and restricting collective approaches, sees little need for and, indeed, much danger in excessive development of state institutions. Despite originating from the same well of concern for individual liberty, the realist tradition envisages a significantly stronger state, supported by strong state institutions as a means of preserving individual liberties. It envisages the creation of legislatures and the establishment of institutions that can control the excesses of individual self-interest. The liberal, realist disposition therefore requires strong institutional development as a means of protecting the same principles of individual liberty. Here though, the emphasis is on controlling the actions of those who might impinge on such liberty, the way to do this being through the creation of law making and related enforcement capacity. Finally, the minimalist tradition seeks to achieve some balance between unfettered individualism and the operation of the free market on one side and the dominance of state power exercised in the name of individual liberty on the other. It is concerned with enforcing protection of individual liberty while at the time safeguarding against excessive interference in the enjoyment of that liberty and therefore seeks to create state institutions in order to provide a system of safeguards, checks and balances. Despite the variations within these three perspectives, the unifying element is the primacy of the individual and a limited enthusiasm for collective decision-making or control.

These contrasting views are reflected echoed in the distinction between minimalist, intermediate or activist state functions, as illustrated in Table 2.1.

Table 2.1 Contrasting functions of the state

	Addressing market failure	Improving equity and promoting social justice
Minimalist state	Providing public goods Defence Law and order Protecting property rights Macro economic management Public health	Protecting the poor Anti-poverty programmes Disaster relief
Intermediate state (additional functions)	Addressing externalities Education Environmental protection Regulating monopoly Regulating competition Financial regulation Consumer protection	Providing social insurance Redistributive pension Family allowances Unemployment insurance
Activist state (additional functions)	Co-ordinating private activity Fostering / stimulating markets Cluster initiatives	Redistribution Asset redistribution

Source: Adapted from the World Bank, 1997.

Here, a state that is functionally minimalist, in line with neo-liberal thinking and sometimes associated with a 'negative' liberty orientation, will not play a strong role in promoting and protecting social justice. The minimalist state will concentrate on the protection of individual rights and will focus on the provision of a limited range of public goods. Such a perspective encourages stronger involvement by non-state actors, particularly the private and third sectors, to assume functions that some believe the state should not be involved with. On the other end of the spectrum an activist state, sometimes associated with a positive liberty philosophy, can be expected to assume a stronger role in addressing market failure and the promotion of redistributive and equity agendas. However, whether it does so by direct state provision or through the medium of the market is somewhat unclear. Between the two lies the intermediate function, involving a substantial level of state involvement, particularly in the economic sphere, but still emphasising a strong reliance on the operation of the market. Realistically, Ireland lies some place between the intermediate and the activist level, though it is probably closer to the intermediate due to the somewhat restricted nature of its efforts to pursue equity and social justice priorities.

For some, these distinctions have been equated with ideas of 'positive' and 'negative' perspectives on liberty (Berlin, 2004). In this view, a 'positive' liberties outlook implies that the nature of freedom and liberty involves the state assuming at least some role in looking after the needs and welfare of its citizens, leading to the concept of the social liberal, social democratic or affirmative state in which 'concern with positive liberty will naturally imply a concern with distributive justice, that is to say, with access to that bundle of resources and opportunities which individuals should have in order to realise positive freedoms' (Plant, 2004: 25). By contrast, it is suggested that a 'negative liberties' perspective, envisages the state's role as being to guarantee individual liberties 'by the rule of law enforcing a rule of mutual non coercion … It should not be done by a welfare state securing to individuals resources to enable them to do what they are free to do' (2004: 26).

Why should public administration be concerned with social justice?

While the nature of the state will inevitably shape the degree to which both politicians and administrators may be disposed towards taking a social justice position, even within intermediate or more activist states some may still question whether public administration should be specifically concerned with social justice. Citing the hierarchical, neutral and unbiased characteristics of traditional bureaucracy and its subservience to those who are democratically elected, they may argue that public administration defers to politicians to take the lead on potentially controversial issues of equity and social justice. What is frequently absent from this argument is an appreciation of the purpose of public administration as a component of the democratic infrastructure and its particular role in defending and promoting established democratic ideals of equality and justice. Equally, the strength of the bureaucratic neutrality justification needs to be tested. Each of these arguments will be taken in turn in this section.

The responsibilities of public administration as a democratic institution

For many, Rawls and his articulation of a theory of justice have provided the starting point for discussions on social justice and this book is no exception. However, emphasis is most often placed on Rawls' key principles for fairness, with less attention being paid to his extensive descriptions of the context to which these principles apply. These are particularly important in the context of systems of public administration and provide a basis to justify a more visible and overt role for it in the promotion of social justice. In particular, public administration can be seen as an element of the 'basic structure', described by Rawls (2001: 10) as 'the way in which the main political and social institutions of society fit together into one system of social co-operation and the way they assign basic rights and duties and regulate the division of advantages that arise from social co-operation over time'. Moreover, Rawls sees his theory of justice as applying within the political realm, as distinct from other relationships that exist at the level of associations, the family and the personal. Within the political realm, in order for citizens to be 'free and equal' he considers that 'they must recognise one another as free and equal' and 'basic institutions must educate them to this conception of themselves' (Rawls, 2001: 56). If it is accepted that public administration is one of these basic institutions the argument follows that it should play a role in encouraging a recognition of freedom and equality amongst citizens.

To further consider this idea of encouraging a conception of free and equal citizens, Rawls introduces the notion of society as 'fair system of co-operation'. Here he makes a distinction between social co-ordination and social co-operation. Thus, co-ordination is more about 'activity co-ordinated by orders issued by an absolute central authority' whereas co-operation is based on the idea of 'fair terms' described as 'terms each participant can reasonably accept and sometimes should accept provided that everyone else likewise accepts them'. Within this lies an emphasis on mutuality and reciprocity and an expectation that all are required to embrace their responsibilities as well as vindicating their rights (Rawls, 2001: 5). In practical terms of course arriving at an agreement about the notion of 'fair terms' is complicated by the realities of unequal power, privilege, status and education between groups. To address this, Rawls introduces the notion of 'the original position'. Here, parties involved in the discussion of fair terms would have to hypothesise about the elements of the system of co-operation and operate from behind 'a veil of ignorance'- they would not know 'the social positions or the particular comprehensive doctrines of the persons they represent' (Rawls, 2001: 16). The import of this of course is that all members of a particular society have a legitimate expectation that they can play a part in setting the terms of co-operation and not have these dictated by a central authority or a core elite of decision-makers, within either the public or private sectors. It also potentially implies that the establishment and reestablishment (for each generation) of these terms of co-operation needs to be an on-going process, requiring deeper processes of civic engagement and dialogue. Beyond the hypothetical thought exercise, however, in practice how the input of minority or marginalised groups can be secured in setting the terms of cooperation and the meaning of justice remains a challenge.

A well-ordered society and the basic structure
Another element of Rawls' approach to justice that has an implication for how we think about public administration is his consideration of the 'well-ordered society' (2001: 8). In such a society he suggests that 'everyone accepts and knows that everyone else accepts the very same political conception of justice'. Clearly this is a very ambitious aspiration. However, its potential for realisation occurs in circumstances where 'the basic structure' of society is 'publicly known or with good reason believed to satisfy those principles of justice'. So, just as the establishment of a fair system of co-operation might be expected to give rise to more significant civic engagement, the requirements to create a well ordered society clearly implies a need for deeper and more sustained processes of civic education so that both the basic structure and its associated principles of social justice are more widely known and embraced in society. As Rawls (ibid.: 56) says, 'acquaintance with and participation in [that] political culture is one way citizens learn to conceive of themselves as free and equal, a conception which, if left to their own reflections, they would most likely never form, much less accept and desire to realise'. This idea resonates with the ideas of civic republicanism where 'citizenship should be understood as a common civic identity, shaped by a common public culture' ultimately leading to a strong emphasis on deliberative democracy (Jones and Gaventa, 2002). Lister (1997) too links these different concepts, emphasising the notion of citizenship practice and status, arguing that 'to be a citizen in the legal and sociological sense means to enjoy the rights and citizenship necessary for agency and social and political participation. To act as a citizen involves fulfilling the potential of that status'. However, not realising the potential of this status produces little more that 'latent citizenship' where public representatives are left largely to govern according to their own devices (Barber, 1984). Amongst those who advocate a more engaged and active citizen there is recognition that such a vision will

not be realised without the provision of some degree of external stimulation or facilitation. For many, one of the most important, facilitating conditions is the provision of education for citizenship or civic education, understood not as coming primarily from 'formal pedagogy' but more importantly from the experience of participation (Barber, 1984, Pateman, 2004).

In practical terms, the notions of a fair system of co-operation and the development of a well ordered society have immediate implications for public administration. In the first instance, they challenge public administration to engage less in co-ordination and more in co-operation; suggesting a role in the management of processes to arrive at agreement on the definition of 'fair terms' and acting to balance unequal power, privilege and status, thereby enabling all groups to contribute to defining the terms of co-operation. Moreover, public administration would appear to have an obvious role in fostering a 'well ordered society' through encouraging processes to enable citizens to arrive at a more widespread understanding of what social justice means. It also implies a more conscious process of building a deeper understanding of citizenship, such that people understand both the rights and responsibilities of citizenship.

Debunking the idea of the neutral bureaucracy
Envisaging a different role for public administration as described above inevitably comes up against the idea of the bureaucratic neutrality and contentions that public officials act in an impartial and non-biased fashion. It is not surprising then that challenging the assertion of the neutral, unbiased public administration system has been to the fore in the efforts of scholars in the United States when they began to press for consideration of 'a new public administration', one that would seek to reinvigorate the study and practice of public administration and place social equity at its heart (Marini, 1971). Many of the early arguments and principles proposed by these scholars can equally apply in an Irish context. Frederickson (2010: 7), in an essay originally published in 1971, argued strongly that:

> Pluralistic democratic government systematically discriminates in favour of established stable bureaucracies and their specialised minority clientele and against those minorities who lack political and economic resources ... Continued deprivation amid plenty breeds widespread militancy ... A public administration that fails to work for changes that try to redress the deprivation of minorities will likely be eventually used to repress those minorities.

While this was written at a time of considerable political upheaval in the United States, it is echoed by other global research that contends that, in general, distrust in democratic institutions, including public administration amongst groups experiencing social exclusion is likely to be even higher (Narayan et al., 2000), a feature borne out by the Eurobarometer research referred to in Chapter 1. Within the literature on international development too, the sometimes problematic role of public administration has been highlighted:

> There is an inherent elite bias to the institutions of democracy and to political competition in democracies. Inevitably there is an elite bias in state economic and social policies also, given the political weakness of the poor in demanding responses to their needs. Analysts of public administration have always pointed out that any policy to redistribute existing resources away from privileged groups is bound to attract more bureaucratic and social opposition than either regulatory policies or policies which distribute resources from a new or external source. (Luckham et al., 1999)

As a consequence, as the public administration system develops and implements mainstream policy, it may do so in a way that favours the majority population and may be unwilling to engage in the type of counter majoritarianism that some suggest is necessary to ensure social justice (Devenish, 1993, in Luckham et al., 1999). Indeed, as suggested by Pierre (1999: 375), 'the structure of governance – the inclusion or exclusion of different actors and the selection of instruments – is not value neutral but embedded in and sustains political values'. In fact, far from being neutral it is argued that political institutions, such as those dominated by the state, may promote the inclusion of certain interests while excluding others and as a result, may legitimise some claims and voices and deny others (Immergut, 1992). This may be a function of institutional bias or it may simply result from a lack of awareness of difference and of the uneven impact of policy implementation on different social groups. However it may also derive from a perceived need to minimise threats to institutional stability by excluding interests that might be perceived to be hostile or troublesome (Immergut, 1992).

This theme was subsequently explored by the American Political Science Association which convened a 'TaskForce on Inequality in America', a key element of which addressed disparities in participation and access to decision-makers and resulting influence on policy-making. This TaskForce concluded that:

> The privileged participate more than others and are increasingly well organized to press their demands on government. Public officials, in turn, are much more responsive to the privileged than to average citizens and the least affluent. Citizens with lower or moderate incomes speak with a whisper that is lost on the ears of inattentive government officials, while the advantaged roar with a clarity and consistency that policy-makers readily hear and routinely follow. (American Political Science Association, 2004: 1)

Because of this, some would argue that 'the public administrator is morally obliged to counter this tendency by making decisions in the direction of providing greater equity in service delivery', suggesting that 'variations from

Leabharlanna Poiblí Chathair Bhaile Átha Cliath
Dublin City Public Libraries

equity should always be in the direction of more services to the disadvantaged'
(Pops and Plavak, 1991, as cited in Oldfield, 2003).

This conviction that public administration can and does play a role in
perpetuating inequality and injustice has persisted over time and highlights
'the continuing discrepancy between the ideas and reality of equality' and the
fact that public administration and officials have 'helped to institute inequality
in the past by enforcing discriminatory laws and using their broad discretion
to advance exclusionary social mores' (Johnson and Svara, 2011: 9). The need
to focus on institutions is further reinforced by Barry (2005: 17) in his efforts to
develop a theory of social justice. Here, he suggests, that these basic structures
play such an important part in the allocation of 'rights, opportunities and
resources' that they must be put 'at the centre of the picture' and that they are
'key to the realisation of social justice'. The role of institutions such as public
administration in creating and perpetuating injustice has also been highlighted
in a European context, in particular, the notion of system breakdowns as a
cause of social exclusion (Berghman, 1995). Drawing on the experiences of the
Poverty 3 Programme,[1] this analytical approach proposes that social exclusion
results from breakdowns in one or more systems of society: the democratic
and legal system to promote civic integration; the labour market to promote
economic integration; the welfare system to promote social integration and
the family and community system to promote interpersonal integration
(Berghman, 1995). One immediate benefit of the systems failure approach is
that it isolates state and societal institutions as arenas in which social justice
and social inclusion are to be pursued. As such, it presents the challenge to
articulate a missing discourse on social justice, a public administration discourse, which would enable Sullivan's concerns to be addressed:

> Tackling social exclusion requires action on many fronts simultaneously. However,
> to achieve social inclusion as a result necessitates a programme of reform that
> tackles the institutions of the powerful and the powerless. Unless changes are
> sought in the behaviours, structures and processes of those whose actions exclude,
> there is a danger that all that will result from policies to tackle social exclusion is
> a pathologising of the excluded. (Sullivan, 2002: 507–508)

However, Berghman's focus on system failure is not without criticism. The
principal thrust of this critique is that because key societal institutions, such
as public administration, are themselves are deeply flawed and are 'locked
into processes of discrimination and marginalisation' (O'Brien and Penna,
2007: 6) they cannot act to promote inclusion and need to be replaced. A
similar concern was raised in the United States, the suggestion being that
the institutions of pluralist democracy themselves have presided over the
generation of inequality and therefore have little internal capacity to suddenly
transform themselves and reverse years of bureaucratic bias (Manley, 1983).
Unfortunately, while some of these criticisms may be justified, they do little

to throw light on how inclusion might be advanced and how current systems and institutions will either be changed or replaced. It would appear unrealistic to think that these systems are simply going to disappear. Just as participatory democracy theorists do not see the destruction of the liberal democratic framework as the means to achieving the objective of increased participation, it is equally true that the systems described by Berghman cannot be simply dismantled and replaced.

Adjusting disposition

If it is accepted that institutions of democracy, including public administration, may themselves contribute to injustice and inequality then some action to induce organisational and cultural change becomes necessary. One way to do this, according to Oldfield (2003) is a focus on training and education, though Oldfield also comments on a deeper issue, the use of language within public administration, suggesting that, in itself, it perpetuates prejudice, citing the example of why poor children might be described as underprivileged whereas those from wealthy families are never described as over privileged. Clearly then, bringing about institutional change is not just a simple question of education and training. Shifting attitudes and disposition, institutionally or individually, is far from easy and requires a more detailed engagement with questions of individual and/or institutional dispositions. To this end Mann (1999) argues that three distinct, but interconnected levels of human action need to be explored: intention, meaning and structural ideals. The last of these, structural ideas and how they govern the behaviour of actors within public administration is of particular significance. According to Mann (1999: 168), all three elements must be understood, but crucially, both intention and meaning can be subsumed into a 'multivalent' notion of structure or structural idealism which is concerned with 'penetrating the social meaning of an act or series of acts'. Thus, Mann seeks to understand how a variety of conscious and unconscious influences or 'structural ideas' shape actions and governs behaviour in particular situations. Inevitably individual officials and/or public administration institutions are influenced by a variety of more or less explicit structural ideals. Thus there is a need to look behind 'stated ideological position' towards an appreciation of the 'ideological environment' in which a given actor, individual or institution, operates or has operated and of the structural ideals which derive from it. Mann (1999: 181) borrows from Bourdieu's twin notions of habitus – 'the ingrained dispositions within a given group or class' which are necessary for 'social structures to reproduce themselves among individuals who share the same material conditions of existence' – and doxa – which describes the 'naturalization of the arbitrariness of a given social order in the mind and body of a social agent'. The explanation offered by the notion of 'doxa' is that it allows certain social actors to consciously or otherwise draw on orthodox 'structural ideas' to support their day to day activities. This echoes Lukes' (1974: 21–22) proposition that the 'bias of a system is not sustained simply by a series of individually chosen acts, but also, most importantly, by the socially structured and culturally patterned behaviour of groups and practices of institutions'. It is further proposed that these group behaviours and practices are inevitably influenced by the class origins and experiences of individual public officials (Held, 1987), leading over many years to calls to ensure that bureaucracies would 'resemble the demographic characteristics of the citizenry' – a failure to do so indicating a society that has limited concern for fairness or equality (Oldfield, 2003). In this thinking therefore, the idea of the neutral, unbiased official or institution is replaced by a reality where individuals or institutions are shaped and informed by a variety of more or less explicit dispositions, some of which may be social justice oriented, others which may well reflect prejudice towards certain groups and give rise to overt or more subtle forms of discrimination.

If the impact of structural ideals and ingrained disposition was limited to the possession of particular perspectives and prejudices, it might be less complex to address them. However, the impact of orthodoxy extends not only to individual ideas but also has the capacity to capture the way entire institutions can conceive of issues and problems. Within a public administration context, while there may be some level of effort to address individual attitudes and dispositions, it is rare that any substantial reflection takes places on institutional dispositions or on the way issues and problems are conceived of, understood and solved. This has led to assertion that progress towards equity, equality and justice will only be made if public administration engages in exercises in critical social thinking so as to 'encourage awareness in public administration of societal conditions that tend to shape and constrain scholarship, teaching, practice and social change' (Box, 2005: 3). The impact of such critical social thinking would be to move public administration beyond the limitations of existing systems of thought towards the creation of alternative patterns of understanding for development. Box acknowledges, however, that such critical thinking has been limited largely due to the fact that public administration operates within and/or perpetuates values that are increasingly market oriented and market serving. The crucial question here of course is the degree to which such values are forced upon the public administration system either by political masters or as a result of the spread of a globalised, market-oriented public administration paradigm: New Public Management.

So, in summary, public administration, far from being neutral or unbiased, is in fact shaped by a variety of internal and external influences, responds to some voices more than others, has an underdeveloped capacity or willingness to explore the nature of social and economic problems and, as a result, is challenged to fully embrace and centralise a social justice ethos within its practice.

In the next section, some of the efforts to embed a stronger social justice ethos within public administration scholarship and practice are explored.

Public administration: between conflicting ideals and values

The last section concluded that an assumption of bureaucratic neutrality is misguided and instead argues that the way bureaucracy operates is determined by a range of institutional and individual values, biases and dispositions. To fully contemplate and justify a role for public administration in promoting social justice requires recognition that there are other competing ideas and ideologies that are potentially pulling public administration in other directions. These competing ideas and ideologies can be usefully explored by comparing and contrasting the main tenets of the NPA movement in the United States with the more significant influence of the market oriented NPM.

The concept of NPA became prominent in US discussions on social equity and public administration, following on from the first Minnowbrook Conference in 1967, which was led by a number of emerging academics concerned about the limited nature of discussion on public administration up to then. NPA has been closely associated with social equity and has been defined as 'an academic movement for social equity in the performance and delivery of public service; it called for a proactive administrator with a burning desire for social equity to replace the traditional, impersonal and neutral gun for hire' (Shafritz and Russell, 2002: 466). In keeping with the discussion above, NPA rejected the idea that 'administrators are value neutral' (Wooldridge and Gooden, 2009: 224) and aimed for a more proactive, leadership role for officials in order to achieve social equity and social justice outcomes. Frederickson, a key figure in the NPA movement, advocated that social equity should be accepted as a 'third pillar' for public administration alongside the more standard public administration elements of effectiveness and efficiency. In practice this meant that NPA was 'anxiously engaged in change' and sought 'to change those policies and structures that systematically inhibit social equity', requiring 'organisation and political forms for continued flexibility or routinized change' (Frederickson, 2010: 9).

Some years later, this theme of social equity within public administration was identified as a core concern of the US National Academy of Public Administration which established a Standing Panel on the theme of social equity in governance in 2000. The motivation for the panel lay in a belief that 'public administration, in both its practice and in its theory finds it essential to be forthright about those aspects of our work that turn on issues of fairness, justice and equity'. This led the Panel to set out a Charter to guide its work, the first element of which commits it to 'review and evaluate developments in public administration, including existing and emerging issues and problems, new ideas and current opinions, significant research and research needs, institutional development, and critical matters in social equity and governance in need of attention' (National Academy of Public Administration, 2012). In brief, the central argument being made within NPA is that where inequity and injustice exist, public administration has a role, either in generating that inequity and injustice and/or in addressing it. It may generate inequity either consciously or unconsciously, deliberately or accidently, institutionally or individually. Equally, it may address inequity and injustice in the same ways – consciously or unconsciously, deliberately or accidently, institutionally or individually. However, to do so, NPA effectively requires a strong administrative or executive government, operating within an activist state, implying a stronger recognition of the policy role of public administration.

At the other end of the ideological spectrum NPM, often seen as a child of neo-liberalism (Savoie, 1995), anticipates reduced state involvement in the direct provision of services that might be more effectively delivered by the private sector and others, including civil society. As such, these arrangements 'have enabled the replacement of hierarchical relationships within a unified bureaucracy by "arm's length" relationships between a public purchasing authority and a devolved provider agency' (Pollit, 1995), and have been described as 'the federalisation of central government administrative structures' (Gray and Jenkins, 1995). The extent of its influence can be gauged by its description as the 'guiding intellectual paradigm for the reform and governance of public services over the last three decades ... Under this model of statecraft, attempts to improve the performance of the state have relied on command and control from above and choice and competition from outside' (Cooke and Muir, 2012: 5).

Within NPM, there is a visible attempt to alter the nature of state bureaucracy via mechanisms such as: decentralisation; deconcentration; new budgetary processes; contracting out; various performance related initiatives, including pay and the development of outcome indicators; introducing private sector management techniques; as well as a greater emphasis on monitoring and scrutiny and value for money. The outcome of all of this is intended to be, and in some cases has been, a stronger role for government in scrutiny and oversight and less direct government provision of goods and services (Rhodes, 2000, Pollit, 1995, Gray and Jenkins, 1995). This was initially assumed to represent a weakening of the state but has alternatively been cast as a process whereby the state has simply switched roles and as a result has not been significantly weakened at all (Adshead, 2002, Marinetto, 2003). Governance within an NPM framework suggests considerable institutional adjustment within state institutions, achieved by devolving functions to the private sector or civil society associations or by the state assuming the type of corporate management cultures prevalent within the private sector. Inherent in NPM's insistence on such cultural change is an implication of inefficiency, lethargy and waste in public administration when contrasted with the dynamic and forward looking nature of a managerialist outlook (Savoie, 1995). This impacts both on public sector managers as well as on politicians, the former being given greater autonomy to manage and the latter being expected to concern themselves more with goal setting rather than the minutiae of policy implementation. A further significant institutional evolution is the reduced emphasis placed on input control, mainly through the provision of resources, though in parallel there is a greater concentration on monitoring and evaluations, using performance indicators and related pay processes (Pierre and Peters, 2000, Pollit, 1995).

Advocates of NPA and a social equity focus however are the first to acknowledge their desired progress towards a new way of conceiving of public administration did not achieve the desired traction and has effectively been overtaken by the ideological push towards NPM and the supremacy of market oriented approaches. This has led Box (2008: 14) to conclude that 'public administration is in harmony with its political-economic surroundings when it furthers the goals of people who benefit from minimal public sector interference in the market'. However, he contends that such harmony is disrupted when 'public administration practice or scholarship challenges the status quo by supporting social justice, environmental protection, a quality living environment, or other ends that might conflict with the interests of the powerful'.

Thus it is suggested that there is a 'war of ideas' underway between those who would see public administration as an engine of social justice and others who see it as an inefficient system that can only function effectively with an infusion of market oriented values and practices. Firing a salvo in this war of ideas Weir (cited in Frederickson, 2005: 35) strongly argues 'Ceding the ideological terrain to anti governmental messages like "the era of big government is over" is not good enough in a polity in which simple media messages are not counter balanced by organisational politics. In fact, simple anti-governmentalism amounts to endorsing unchecked inequality'. Others however wonder whether the anti-governmental celebrity of NPM has become somewhat tarnished. Advocating greater consideration of the 'relational state' they suggest that the 'theoretical foundations of NPM have been challenged by a wave of new thinking across the social sciences' (Cooke and Muir, 2012: 6) and question whether we are:

at the emergence point of a new paradigm of public administration in advanced democracies? There are a number of reasons for thinking this might be the case. New public management has now been the dominant policy discourse for some 30 years. In important respects, it has proved its worth; public service management has improved along many dimensions. But its longevity has also exposed its weaknesses and revealed its ideological moorings. Greater efficiency and effectiveness have come at the cost of increased centralisation, reduced trust in government, and an increasing distance between the rhetoric of target regimes and their actuality. (Pearce, 2012: 45)

The relational state, by contrast with the NPM 'delivery' state, emphasises 'the ability to empathise, communicate, listen and mobilise coalitions of citizens and professionals to achieve social goals' (Cooke and Muir, 2012: 10), characteristics that resonate strongly with the principles of NPA and a more democratic ethos to public administration.

Pursuing a social justice agenda within public administration

Thus far, the argument has been made that that social equity is an issue that should concern public administration. The question then arises as to how such a concern can be addressed in practice. While later chapters will look at this issue more specifically in an Irish context, a number of more general principles and approaches have been identified.

Firstly, it is useful to clarify what social justice means in a public administration context. Taking some definitions as a starting point, the US National Academy of Public Administration (NAPA) has defined social equity as 'The fair and equitable management of all institutions serving the public directly or by contract, and the fair and equitable distribution of public services, and implementation of public policy, and the commitment to promote fairness, justice and equity in the formation of public policy' (National Academy of Public Administration). Within this there are clear requirements to focus on social equity, fairness and justice both in policy formation and in policy delivery, delegated or otherwise. To operationalise such an understanding Johnson and Svara (2011: 17–18) have add a further sentence to this definition proposing that 'Public administrators should seek to promote greater equality and to prevent and reduce inequality, unfairness and injustice based on important social characteristics.' In order to do this, they present two parallel requirements of social equity, namely that people are treated the same, in order 'to promote fairness and equality' and are treated differently in order 'to provide justice', essentially laying the basis for a parallel non-discrimination and affirmative action approach. In a similar vein, Shafritz and Russell (2002) advance three key requirements in the promotion of a social equity agenda. The first of these is the obligation to administer the law fairly; the second focuses on human resources and a commitment to recruit a diverse workforce within public organisations while the third, perhaps most challengingly, seeks to foster moral leadership, inspiration and encouragement for others to take on a social equity perspective.

The last of these raises the obligation on the part of institutions and individual officials within them to be aware of and to assume responsibility for the pursuit of social justice. More particularly, the challenge is presented to officials to show moral leadership and to more overtly take up a social justice mantle, raising the sometimes thorny issue of individual and institutional values. Over the years the issue of values and ethics in public sector organisations has been a well-rehearsed theme, in Ireland and elsewhere (Van Wart, 1998, MacCarthaigh, 2008, Goss, 1996, Box, 2008, Meir, 1976). For some, the primary interest has been the origin of values found within public administration and the complexities of resolving competing value sources. For others the main point of interest has been to explore the existence or otherwise of particular public-sector ethics or values that might in some way distinguish public officials either from elected representatives or from the citizens they serve. Others still have endeavoured to establish typologies of potentially competing values as a means of illustrating significant value differences and charting a normative direction of desired change.

Van Wart (1998) in a comprehensive treatment of the changing nature of public sector values has identified five potential sources of values for those working within the public sector, though inevitably they cannot be considered to exist in isolation of each other. The first suggested source is individual values, primarily integrity and, more specifically, civic integrity, seen as meaning 'an appreciation for the Constitution and the laws of the land and a respect for the political-legal system'. More specifically, civic integrity includes a number of sub-values, including: honesty; consistency; coherence; and reciprocity – understood as 'a reasoned attempt to act toward others as you would have them act towards you under similar conditions' (ibid.: 9). Beyond the level of the individual, professional values are highlighted as a 'subtle but important source for administrative decision-making' and are considered by some as having the potential to enhance performance, at least in some areas as a result of the standards set by professional bodies and/or associated education requirements. Organisational values too are influential, in both a positive and potentially negative way, the latter being particularly problematic where forms of 'bureau-pathology' may lead to a situation where 'the convenience of the organisation's members outweighs the convenience of the public it serves' (ibid.: 15). In this case also, leadership style is considered to be particularly important. A further and highly significant source of public administration values is the law. On one hand legal values as a source is somewhat self-evident, describing the role of the Constitution, legislation, rules and regulations. Thus 'the law is a symbol of politically agreed-upon values, which has special significance for those who have dedicated themselves to defining, upholding and implementing the laws through public service'. However, the dangers of excessive legalism as a potential barrier to innovation and productivity have also been highlighted, as illustrated by the impact of the much commented upon *ultra vires* rule on local government in Ireland. Finally, and perhaps most saliently in the current context of economic crisis, is the role of public interest values in informing the activities of the public sector, though arriving at any modicum of agreement on what the public interest might be is far from easy, if indeed there is even consensus that such a thing exists. Public interest has been described either as 'substantive' i.e. the largely undefined concept that is commonly used or as 'aggregative' where the public interest is seen largely as the product of the will of the majority at particular points in time. The latter, it is suggested is the default model but is one that is weak 'since it requires no inquiry, accumulated knowledge or informed thought about the consequences for the larger community' (Box, 2008: 59).

The distinction between these different value sources provides a useful way to think about approaches to deepen a commitment to social justice within public administration, pointing to the need to:

- proactively influence individual values towards a social justice agenda;
- shape professional values, either through professional training routes or through more focused on the job training;
- adjust organisational values, not least through the selection of senior managers with a social justice commitment and requirements to incorporate social justice as a key part of organisational planning processes;
- make greater use of legislative approaches to signal and prompt a change in values or a reinforcement of particular values; and finally,
- engage in collective processes to articulate the concept of public interest and social justice values, in line with Rawls' suggestions for the development of a 'well-ordered society'.

Of these different values sets, it could be argued that the most important is the fostering of stronger organisational values around social justice, on the basis that both individual and professional values will be heavily influenced by the organisational context in which they find themselves. Here again though, it is possible to identify competing sets of public administration values. From an extensive review of the relevant literature Goss (1996) distinguishes between a bureaucratic ethos and a democratic ethos within public administration. With a bureaucratic ethos, the core values include: accountability; competency; economy, impartiality, predictability and trustworthiness. By contrast, in the democratic ethos, closely associated with the NPA movement, values such as advocacy, compassion, confidentiality, individual rights, political awareness and the public interest are considered important leading to the profile of the official in which:

> They have autonomy and professional independence; they are compassionate, caring, and communicative; they keep promises; they encourage the public and agency clientele groups to participate; they are creative and innovative, socially

conscious, and politically aware. They seek justice, fairness, equity, and support for individual rights through bureaucratic representation and affirmative action, and they may serve as advocates in their policy making role. (Goss, 1996: 581)

It would appear obvious then that to foster a more social justice oriented public administration, efforts to deepen a democratic ethos are needed. However, this is not to discount the importance of the values associated with the bureaucratic ethos, particularly when both citizens and officials may have a high regard for values such as competency, accountability and trustworthiness. This was illustrated when Goss compared perspectives on these two distinct sets of values amongst a surveyed group of officials, citizens and elected representatives. From this it emerged that the values associated with a bureaucratic ethos were ranked as the most important for all three groups while there was a lower appreciation for values associated with the democratic ethos.

Moving further, towards a more normative perspective on public administration values, Box (2008) has developed a construct of regressive and progressive societal values, designed to highlight a spectrum or route towards more progressive change in US society. He presents a set of value pairs to illustrate the journey towards what he sees as progressive social change, requiring a transition from: aggressiveness towards co-operation; from judgements based on belief alone towards judgements based on knowledge and evidence; from viewing economics and economic activity as an end in itself towards seeing economics as means to achieving other goals; from an acceptance of 'great inequality' towards a situation of 'limited inequality'; and finally, from a regressive perspective that sees the earth only as a resource to be exploited rather than earth as home, which has to be protected and preserved. The implications of this for public administration and officials within it is the need to become conversant with these progressive values, to recognise the difference between points on the values spectrum and to seek to act in a way that moves towards progressive and away from regressive values. More generally, an argument begins to emerge suggesting that a more social justice oriented public administration system will be distinguishable by particular types of values and, concomitantly, to manage the transition towards a more social justice conscious public administration will require efforts to inculcate a more comprehensive set of democratic as well as bureaucratic values.

Conclusions

This chapter has reviewed some of the conceptual arguments about public administration and social justice and has situated these within a broader set of perspectives on the role of state. It proposed that public administration can play a more effective role within an activist state where the state assumes a more proactive role in improving equity and promoting social justice. From this chapter a number of key conclusions are drawn.

In the first instance, public administration needs to be seen as a key democratic institution, one that has a particular role in creating the basis for a socially just state. Seen in this way, it is challenged to play an important role in facilitating citizens to establish the terms of a 'fair system of co-operation' and in building 'a well ordered society'. While it may not be possible to do this exactly in the way that Rawls might suggest (e.g. behind the 'veil of ignorance') public administration and the education sector can play a key role in approximating processes of dialogue and debate on the meaning of fairness and social justice, that can renew a broader societal commitment to justice, solidarity and fairness.

Alongside this, to become more social justice oriented, public administration will have to face up to the fact that it may not be as neutral as traditional theories of bureaucracy might like us to believe. Recognising and confronting institutional and individual biases and prejudices that hide behind majoritariarn, public administration orthodoxies will no doubt be a difficult challenge but it is one that cannot be avoided. Just where the motivation to name and confront this challenge will come from remains to be seen. It must also be realised that evolving practices of public administration, in Ireland or elsewhere, are not ideologically neutral. Instead, 'reforms' that pass as delivering greater efficiency or effectiveness in public administration represent particular value choices, albeit these values are not necessarily explicit or immediately obvious. These reforms are informed by the values of NPM which operate in harmony with the primacy of the market and private sector management practices but conflict with the values of NPA, an earlier movement in the United States that placed social justice more firmly at its core. Achieving a more prominent position for a social justice ethos within public administration requires debate on these contrasting values and a deeper understanding of the nature of social justice. These issues are addressed in the next chapter.

Note

1 The Poverty 3 Programme was a European Commission funded programme of model actions to address poverty and social exclusion. It operated from July 1989 to June 1994 and in Ireland funded three projects: one rural project, Forum in Connemara; one urban project, PAUL Partnership in Limerick; and one community of interest, the Dublin Traveller Enterprise and Development Group (DTEDG), now known as Pavee Point.

3

Exploring the meaning of social justice

Introduction

What is evident in any discussion on social justice is the lack of agreement on what the concept actually means. Indeed, the notions of justice, equity, equality, rights are contested in many different ways – ideologically, legally, historically, to name but a few. Inevitably this poses problems for those within public administration for whom the challenge of embracing a social justice agenda may appear bewildering and unattractive. In the first two chapters a range of challenges confronting contemporary public administration were set out alongside a specific discussion of the general thinking about the role of public administration as an advocate of social justice. These, however, did not attempt to explore how social justice might actually be defined or understood. This chapter now sets out to explore some of the different understandings of social justice and related concepts. However, it does not seek to arrive at a definitive formula or to present an agenda of social justice priorities that public administration should follow. Instead, the chapter draws on four principal sources to establish the issues and principles that social justice requires us to consider, particularly in a public administration context. In doing so, it looks at legislative sources, including the Irish Constitution and international human rights; at social policy sources that discuss the meanings of social exclusion and social inclusion; at sources in the realm of political philosophy and finally, at ideas of social justice within religious teaching. Inevitably, in a single chapter these are not explored in the detail that specialists of each individual area might undertake. However, the discussion will hopefully highlight some of the main issues and principles involved in each of the four areas and will provide a basis for reflection for those concerned to pursue a stronger social justice agenda within public administration.

Legislative contributions to understanding social justice

When considering the idea of social justice in Ireland in the context of democratic institutions, including public administration, the complexity of the task needs not to be underestimated. At a very basic level, there is neither a clearly nor a definitively articulated understanding of what the concept means which might provide a reference point for those working in the broader public service. When the Irish Constitution, Bunreacht na hÉireann (Government of Ireland, 1937) makes its single reference to the term 'social justice' it does so in the context of restricting the unfettered right to private property. Thus it acknowledges the right to 'the private ownership of external goods' and having guaranteed that the state would not pass laws that would 'abolish the right of private ownership' (ibid.: Articles 43.1 and 43.2) and associated rights, the Constitution does assert, somewhat weakly perhaps, that the exercise of such rights 'ought, in civil society, to be regulated by the principles of social justice' (ibid.: Article 43.3). However, it does not provide a framework that would allow the concept to be more clearly operationalised, politically or administratively.

Subsequently the Constitution does elaborate a series of 'directive principles of social policy', which could possibly be interpreted as a further elaboration of the earlier reference to social justice. However, by contrast with the fundamental rights set out in articles 40–44, the preamble to the article makes it clear that 'The principles of social policy set forth in this Article are intended for the general guidance of the Oireachtas. The application of these principles in the making of laws shall be the care of the Oireachtas exclusively and shall not be cognisable by any Court under any of the provisions of the Constitution' (ibid.: Article 45). Bearing this limitation in mind, the principles do communicate a series of guidelines which mandate the Oireachtas to secure and protect 'as effectively as it may a social order in which justice and charity shall inform all the institutions of the national life' (ibid.: Article 45.1). The Constitution therefore advised that this might be done through:

- upholding the 'right to an adequate means of livelihood' (ibid.: Article 45.2.i);
- the distribution of material resources 'amongst private individuals and the various classes as best to subserve the common good' (ibid.: Article 45.2.ii);
- taking action to prevent 'concentration of the ownership or control of essential commodities in a few individuals to the common detriment' (ibid.: Article 45.2.iii); and
- securing that 'In what pertains to the control of credit the constant and predominant aim shall be the welfare of the people as a whole' (ibid.: Article 45.2.iv).

Article 45.4.1 also contains as specific duty on the state to 'safeguard with especial care the economic interests of the weaker sections of the community, and, where necessary, to contribute to the support of the infirm, the widow, the orphan, and the aged'. Thus, while non-justiciable, it has been suggested that these principles were highly innovative and served as an inspiration to the architects of Constitutions in a number of other countries around the world (Denham, 2012).

While these articles survived into the final version of the Constitution, recent detailed research into the development of the Irish Constitution 1928–1941 illustrates that the Department of Finance was far from enthusiastic about their inclusion (Hogan, 2012). Responding to an early draft of the Constitution circulated to all government departments, senior judges and the Ceann Comhairle, James J McElligott, Secretary of the Department of Finance between 1927 and 1953, commented quite forcefully that the types of principles (initially set out in articles 38–41 of the first draft):

> will not be helpful to Ministers in the future but will provide a breeding ground for discontent, and so create instability and insecurity. They are consequently objectionable and even dangerous. Their provisions are too vague to be of positive assistance to any Government and are yet sufficiently definite to afford grounds for disaffection to sections of the Community, who might claim that the Government were not living up to the Constitution. (McElligott, 1937b)

He went further, suggesting that such principles 'are of an idealistic tendency which, while individually unobjectionable as a statement of social policy, could, if launched into the void in the draft Constitution, recoil like a boomerang on the Government of some future day in circumstances not anticipated by the originators' (McElligott, 1937b). Commenting on a subsequent redrafting of the article McElligott commented with some satisfaction that 'the preamble which now introduces this article deprives it of the character of a declaration of rights enforceable in the courts and to that extent meets the objections urged by the Department of Finance' (McElligott, 1937a). Similarly, referring to provisions dealing with 'social and personal rights' in the draft articles 38–41, Michael McDunphy (1937), in the office of the President commented that 'it is clear that as they stand many of them could be invoked so as to create very difficult situations'. Evidently, even in the early days of the state, the public administration system was reluctant to envisage a strong social justice dimension to the Constitution, presumably fearing its implications for policy and budgetary matters.

Applying the Constitutional provisions

The dilution of the social policy elements of the 1937 Constitution and the lack of any clear articulation of the meaning of social justice inevitably led to difficulties in framing legislation that might be explicitly informed by a social justice ethos. Reference to Dáil debates during the period 1946 to 1959 (after which the term largely drops out of sight) illustrate how the application of the Constitutional references to social justice in legislation proved problematic. For example, in 1946, in a Dáil Debate on the establishment of an industrial court, it was suggested by Patrick McGilligan, TD, that such a court would be enhanced by the presence of additional members with expertise in the area of social justice. However, while citing the Constitutional provision at Article 43, the Deputy acknowledged that he was unsure just what the term 'principles of social justice' meant. Moreover he noted that the:

> phrase has in one case come before an ordinary court in this country for interpretation and evoked the view of one judge that the phrase had no meaning, that it was merely a political shibboleth and that there were no standards by which these principles could be tested, certainly that the principles could not be brought down to any such level as enabled him to find standards which objectively he could apply in particular cases. (McGilligan, 1946)

However McGilligan rejected this judicial opinion and defended the place of the phrase in the Constitution:

> That is not the last word to be said on the principles, and I do not imagine that the phrase was put into the Constitution merely to have a decision of that sort given so that the matter might rest there. I take it that those who framed the Constitution had some idea of social justice and of the principles upon which social justice might be established throughout the country, particularly in relation to the ownership of private property. When the Minister proceeds to set up this court, we suggest that he should add two other people to it, one of whom would be taken from amongst a list of people sent in who have a knowledge of the principles of social justice. I can well imagine to whom I would go if I wanted to get suggestions as to where to find people who might be regarded as having some knowledge of social justice.

Responding to the Deputy's suggestion, the then Tánaiste, Sean Lemass TD, rejected any reference to social justice, contending that:

> If we were to put responsibility on the court to relate wages to economic and social theories, then this court would have to be given powers that we are not proposing to give it. If, on the other hand, we appear to give this court responsibility in relation to social and economic theories we take the risk that people will not use it because it cannot have such responsibility. (Lemass, 1946)

As might be expected, McGilligan rejected the conflation of the Constitutional provision with mere social and economic theory, arguing that 'If principles of social justice are going to be relegated to the category of a social theory, then I part company with the Minister. I believe that I am on a higher level than he is.' Expressing some dismay at the Tánaiste's response, McGilligan concluded: 'There is such a thing as social justice and there are principles relating to social justice which are known to somebody. I do not think we are so devoid of intelligence or information in this country that we will agree to the suggestion that there is nobody in this country competent to adjudicate on matters of social justice.' In a final effort to secure support for his view McGilligan clarified his belief that principles of Catholic Social Teaching might provide some source of wisdom:

> It simply means, in relation to a particular dispute as to conditions of employment or as to wages, there will be one mind on the new court informed by the teaching of the Catholic Church which can interpret the principles of social justice for the other six. I think when we have this pious Constitution we ought to implement it when the opportunity arises.

This exchange provided an early indication of the capacity and/or willingness of the Oireachtas to embrace the concept of social justice. The issue arose again at a later stage in a 1952 committee debate on the Restrictive Trades Practices Bill. Here, Deputy John A. Costello proposed an amendment to more definitively elaborate what the notion of restrictive trading practices would mean (Costello, 1952). This he proposed, amongst other things, should include a specific reference to 'Any practices, measures, rules, agreements or acts' which 'are not in accordance with the principles of social justice.' Deputy Costello acknowledged that these were not easy to define but in the debate reminded the Dáil of the stated willingness of the Supreme Court to arbitrate on 'whether or not those principles have been abrogated by statutory regulations'. Responding, the responsible Minister, again Sean Lemass, while accepting much of the amendment, specifically rejected the inclusion of reference to the principles of social justice saying 'I do not think we can attempt to put into legislation, even as a headline, references to the principles of social justice. As Deputy Costello says, they are not easy to explain or to define' (1952). Again, it would appear, on this occasion the government of the day was unwilling to risk specific reference to social justice as a standard to guide legislative practice.

Some years later in 1959, again in a committee debate, this time on the Third Amendment of the Constitution Bill, the difficulty faced in defining social justice emerged once more. On this occasion T. F. O'Higgins, in opposing the Fianna Fáil proposal to establish a constituency commission to review electoral boundaries, proposed instead that 'there should be inserted in Article 16 of the Constitution a provision that the Oireachtas shall revise constituencies at least once in every 12 years on a fair and equitable basis and in accordance with the principles of social justice'(O'Higgins, 1959). He continued:

> Deputies may ask: 'What do the principles of social justice mean?' I doubt if the Taoiseach will ask that because in the Constitution, as it stands, there are provisions guaranteeing certain rights; rights of property, for instance, are guaranteed in accordance with the principles of social justice. Not so very long ago the Supreme Court of this land, when it was asked to consider whether a particular piece of legislation passed through the Oireachtas at the instance of the Fianna Fáil

Party, affecting certain property rights was or was not Constitutional, because it offended against the principles of social justice, the Supreme Court declared that it reserved to itself the right of deciding what those principles should be; and it declared itself quite competent to do so.

The difficulty of clarifying the meaning of social justice was raised in the same debate by Declan Costello, TD, who, responding to the then Taoiseach, Eamon De Valera's unwillingness to countenance a reference to social justice, emphasised his party's conscious use of the term as a means of guiding constituency revision. However, he avoided defining these principles suggesting that

> I think that would probably be a task for a professional theologian or philosopher, but the fact is that the principles of social justice are referred to in Article 43 of the Constitution. They have, in fact, been interpreted, or applied, in the Supreme Court in a case not so long ago, and it does seem to me that in dealing with constituency boundaries, the principles of social justice are the type of principles of which account should be taken when redistributing constituencies.

Again though, the calls to include a specific reference to social justice in legislation were rejected, illustrating the difficulties in arriving at a workable, operational understanding of the concept of social justice. However, not only has it proved difficult to operationalise, in reality it has rarely been pursued with any great vigour in the Oireachtas.

Social justice as human rights
Beyond the provisions of the 1937 Constitution, the Irish state has committed itself to a whole series of international human rights instruments that go a long way towards articulating the components of a social justice framework. Increasingly, the legislative pursuit of social justice is being augmented by reference to human rights, as articulated in a variety of international and regional frameworks. According to the Irish Human Rights Commission (2010: 10), human rights, which are often divided into civic and political rights and economic, social and cultural rights, are

- universally agreed basic standards which aim to ensure that every person is treated with dignity and respect;
- interdependent and indivisible which means that rights are linked and non-observance of one right may impact on another;
- inherent to all persons without discrimination, and irrespective of the political system of the state. The principle of non-discrimination is at the centre of human rights and features in the major human rights treaties;
- usually set out in law, through international or regional treaties, or national legislation where they form a legal statement of universally accepted principles of how the state should treat its citizens and others within its jurisdiction.

A variety of human rights frameworks make an important contribution to articulating what social justice means, some originating in the United Nations while others, such as the European Convention on Human Rights is a region-specific and legally binding instrument established under the aegis of the Council of Europe and supported by the European Court of Human Rights. This convention was enshrined in Irish Law in 2003. At a European level, member states of the EU agreed in 2000 to the Charter of Fundamental Rights and this entered into force following the passing of the Lisbon Treaty in 2009. This Charter sets out a range of rights in areas such as dignity, freedoms, equality, solidarity, citizens' rights, justice and general provisions. In particular, Chapter V of the Charter (2000: Article 41), on citizens' rights, contains a specific commitment to the right to good administration by EU institutions, stressing that '1. Every person has the right to have his or her affairs handled impartially, fairly and within a reasonable time by the institutions and bodies of the Union.' The Charter further affirms 'the right of every person to be heard, before any individual measure which would affect him or her adversely is taken; the right of every person to have access to his or her file, while respecting the legitimate interests of confidentiality and of professional and business secrecy; the obligation of the administration to give reasons for its decisions'. Finally, Article 41 introduces a right of restitution providing that 'Every person has the right to have the Community make good any damage caused by its institutions or by its servants in the performance of their duties, in accordance with the general principles common to the laws of the Member States.' Crucially though, the Charter of Fundamental Rights applies to the operation of the European Union and to member states when they are implementing EU law.

At the broader international level, there are eight core human rights treaties, the first six of which Ireland has legally ratified. These include:

- the International Covenant on Civil and Political Rights (1966) and its Optional Protocols (1976 and 1989) (ICCPR);
- the International Covenant on Economic, Social and Cultural Rights (1966) and its Optional Protocol (2008) (ICESCR);
- the International Convention on the Elimination of All Forms of Racial Discrimination (1965) (CERD);
- the Convention on the Elimination of All Forms of Discrimination against Women (1979) and its Optional Protocol (1999) (CEDAW);
- the Convention against Torture and Other Cruel, Inhuman or Degrading Treatment or Punishment (1984) and its Optional Protocol (2006) (CAT);
- the Convention on the Rights of the Child (1989) and its two Optional Protocols (2000) (CRC);
- the International Convention on the Protection of the Rights of All Migrant Workers and Members of Their Families (1990);

- the Convention on the Rights of Persons with Disabilities and its Optional Protocol (2006).

Crucially, in the context of this book the IHRC stresses the obligation that falls on states to implement human rights. Clearly, within this, public administration needs to play a key role: 'Government and through it the Civil and Public Service have the primary responsibility to uphold human rights by creating the conditions for them to be effective' (Irish Human Rights Commission, 2010: 12). To support this obligation the Commission provides a dedicated training service for civil and public service bodies to improve knowledge of human rights and has produced a guide to support a deeper understanding of human rights within these organisations.

Human rights and human development: an additional social justice lexicon
Increasingly, the links between human rights and human development are being drawn, further expanding the scope and application of social justice obligations. According to the UN Commission on Human Rights (UNCHR) the right to development is a fundamental human right that is clearly laid out in Article 1 of the Declaration on the Right to Development: 'The right to development is an inalienable human right by virtue of which every human person and all peoples are entitled to participate in, contribute to, and enjoy economic, social, cultural and political development, in which all human rights and fundamental freedoms can be fully realized' (United Nations General Assembly, 1986). Drawing on this common motivation a number of efforts to integrate a human rights approach to achieve human development objectives have been undertaken. Marks (2005: 24) has identified seven such approaches: the holistic approach, such as developed by the UN Development Programme (UNDP) which seeks to 'integrate human rights into a sustainable, human development approach'; a rights based approach, such as taken by other UN agencies; a social justice approach taken by international Non-Governmental Organisations such as Oxfam and focusing directly on the elimination of social inequality; the capabilities approach building on the analysis developed by Amartya Sen and Martha Nussbaum; the right to development approach attributed to the Non-Aligned Movement; the responsibilities approach, emphasising the obligations and duties both of state and citizens; and, finally, the human rights education approach which links the pursuit of human rights with participation and community development approaches, including participatory action research. The human rights education approach also emphasises the importance of facilitating 'human rights education at all levels of schooling, and, in particular, in the training of lawyers, law enforcement officials, members of armed forces, and public officials' (ibid.: 47). While the applicability of human rights based approaches to development have been questioned it

has been suggested that they bring with them a number of distinct advantages (Tsikata, 2004). In particular, it is argued that they help to more clearly identify and nominate rights and duty holders, i.e. they clearly set out the responsibilities of key actors, including public administration. They also focus attention on causes as opposed to symptoms, addressing injustices rather than relieving suffering and, as a result, there is an emphasis on the structural causes of injustice. In rights based approaches, the needs of the oppressed are seen as a starting point, thereby emphasising the needs of the most disadvantaged. Moreover, there is an emphasis on the inalienable, universal, non-negotiable, indivisible and interdependent character of human rights, thereby seeking to make their realisation more of an obligation and less of an option. Finally, rights based approaches incorporate a concentration on institutions and institutional change and moves the focus of attention 'from needs to rights', thereby creating a much more challenging agenda for public administration.

Within discussions on human rights approaches, inevitably a distinction is drawn between civil and political rights on one hand and, on the other, social, economic and cultural rights. While there is a more widespread acceptance of civil and political rights, securing the same treatment for social, economic and cultural rights has proved more challenging. A useful distinction between these two sets of rights has been devised by Marks (2005). This suggests that civil and political rights are seen as absolute; are associated with freedom; demand immediate implementation; can be pursued in court (justiciable); only require the state to adopt a negative liberty perspective and are relatively cost free. Social, economic and cultural rights on the other hand are seen as relative and 'responsive to changing conditions'; seek to promote equality; involve 'progressive implementation'; are not justiciable and instead require political responses; imply a positive liberties perspective and have considerable resource implications.

In short then a human rights perspective on social justice moves the focus much more clearly from a vaguer and somewhat optional approach to one where the achievement of social justice is bounded by a set of defined rights, albeit that some rights are more clearly defined than others. However, attractive as this may be, development or justice strategies that prioritise a rights based approach inevitably encounter charges of impracticality, largely on the grounds that no state could afford the financial cost of delivering the full suite of rights set out in the various human rights framework, particularly social and economic rights. Invariably, the issue of resources is the ground upon which calls for social, economic and cultural rights perish.

Social justice and public policy

As will be shown in subsequent chapters, the term 'social justice' is not one that is commonly used within the ranks of Irish public administration and instead is often associated with external, non-governmental, lobbying groups. This is not to say that public administration is not engaged with matters of social justice, simply that it uses different language. But with this language comes a multitude of different understandings and values, visible in the practical development and application of policy. In recent times in the public policy sphere, the concepts of social exclusion and inclusion have been prominent within this language. However, just as with the broader theme of social justice, ideas about social exclusion and social inclusion are suffused with multiple competing and often contradictory understandings, informed by a miscellany of ideologies, historical analyses and visions for the future of society. Emphasis is variously laid on: income, deriving from economic activity or the provisions of welfare state; on access to services; and, less frequently, on access to decision-making (Silver, 1994, Atkinson and Davoudi, 2000). Despite uncertainty about its meaning the term has become widely used. The European Commission (1992: 8), for example, suggests that: 'The concept of social exclusion is a dynamic one, referring both to processes and consequent situations ... More clearly than the concept of poverty, understood far too often as referring exclusively to income, it also stakes out the multidimensional nature of the mechanisms whereby individuals and groups are excluded from the component practice and rights of social integration and identity.' In a more applied setting the Irish government has continued to make use of the term poverty, though it has done so in a way that embraces a broader definition more akin to the understanding of social exclusion outlined by the European Commission. Thus, the Irish National Anti-Poverty Strategy (NAPS), originally launched in 1997 and developed by the Rainbow coalition government following the 1995 UN Summit on Social Development, defines poverty in the following fashion:

> People are living in poverty if their income and resources (material, cultural and social) are so inadequate as to preclude them from having a standard of living that is regarded as acceptable by Irish society generally. As a result of inadequate income and resources, people may be excluded and marginalised from participating in activities that are considered the norm for other people. (Government of Ireland, 1997b: 3)

Both of these definitions emphasise the multi-disciplinary, dynamic and process-based characteristics associated with the concept of social exclusion. The by now common use of the term, generally acknowledged as deriving from the French concept, describes the situation that results from a breach in the mutual solidarity and obligation that exists between the state and the citizen. Its widening popularity as a term is contrasted with the Anglo Saxon tradition of research on poverty, considered by some to 'patronise or denigrate equal citizens' (Silver, 1994: 3) and which is generally considered to be more narrowly concerned with distributional aspects such as 'the lack of resources at the disposal of an individual household or individual' (Room, 1995: 105).

Table 3.1 A holistic understanding of social exclusion

Income poverty derives from:	*Non-income / human poverty derives from:*
Unemployment / underemployment	Poor access to basic services
Low productivity	Presence of conflict and insecurity
Status of / access to welfare	Disempowerment
	Exclusion from decision-making

Source: Adapted from UNCDF, 2003.

Elsewhere, the UN Capital Development Fund[1] (UNCDF) distinguishes between the income and the non-income or human poverty components of poverty / social exclusion, as shown in Table 3.1 above (UNCDF, 2003). In this approach, unemployment, underemployment, low productivity and access to welfare provision impact on levels of income poverty. However, alongside this, non-income or human poverty derives from poor access to basic services (including the way such services are delivered), from the existence of conflict and insecurity and, crucially, from disempowerment and exclusion from decision-making, all of which have particular implications for public administration.

The UNCDF approach is particularly valuable as it clearly distinguishes disempowerment and the potential to influence decision-making as part of the experience of poverty or social exclusion. In distinguishing between these different dimensions of poverty and social exclusion it therefore presents a challenge to act in a variety of different ways, including a focus on institutions and their values.

Paradigms and discourses of social exclusion

Behind the various definitions of poverty and/or social exclusion lies a diversity of frequently unstated understandings and motivations that inevitably impact on the nature of personal and policy responses. For example Silver (1994) identifies three different paradigms to differentiate between competing understandings of social exclusion. The first, described as the solidarity paradigm, again draws on the original French social solidarity concept. Building on a civic republican ideology it emphasises the importance of social solidarities, a breakdown in which leads not only to economic but also to political exclusion. Within this paradigm the state clearly has a responsibility to restore solidarity with excluded citizens, while at the same time the excluded citizen must also fulfil his/her responsibilities as a citizen. The second paradigm, the specialisation paradigm, is more closely associated with liberalism and neo-classical economics and, as such, is strongly individualistic in nature and arises from the economic division of labour, divisions which, in the liberal perspectives, can be bridged by individuals through their own individual effort and industry. Within this approach, it is largely the responsibility of the individual to overcome his/her exclusion from mainstream society without the possibility of some external support from the state. The third option, the monopoly paradigm, takes a broader, structural perspective. More closely aligned with social democracy, in this instance social exclusion is seen as resulting from the 'formation of group monopoly', maintained by institutional configurations and cultural distinctions in which 'those within delimited social entities enjoy a monopoly over scarce resources. The monopoly creates a bond of common interest between otherwise unequal insiders. The excluded are therefore simultaneously outsiders and dominated' (Silver, 1994: 543). Others too have emphasised the multidimensional nature of exclusion, not only as a product but also as a set of processes that need to be fully understood (Barnes et al., 2002).

Social exclusion / inclusion can also be approached by focusing on the dominant discourses in Europe since the 1980s. Here, it is suggested that a discourse on redistribution dominated the 1980s and 1990s and was joined in the 1990s by two further discourses, one emphasising social integration, principally via paid work and the second described as the moral underclass discourse or MUD, where the 'socially excluded are presented as distinct from the rest of society' and where the main concern is with the behaviour of the poor rather than with processes within wider society (Levitas, 2004: 44). Within these discourses differing conceptual, definitional and ideological variations emerge. However, bridging these differences is a shared and primary focus on those who are excluded, either as the target for action or as the source of the problem. So, while the redistribution discourse may acknowledge some degree of structural causation, its policy prescriptions are likely to be predominantly directed at excluded individuals and concerned about income / welfare related responses, which may be more or less progressive and more or less coercive. There is little emphasis on the behaviour of the wealthy or on more progressive forms of wealth distribution. The social integration discourse on the other hand locates the cause of social exclusion firmly within the realms of the labour market and generates employment and employment-related policy responses, not unlike those that might be anticipated from within the specialisation paradigm. This social integration approach therefore sees paid work as the solution to all ills and has in the past provided the basis for the creation of varying forms of welfare to work programmes, from the voluntary to the mandatory. This employment-related, social integration perspective is seen by some as fundamentally flawed, given that one of the principal requirements of a capitalist system is surplus labour, thereby, necessitating a near permanent situation of un/underemployment. Moreover, it is argued that the approach to social exclusion adopted by the EU, by emphasising the core characteristic of exclusion as exclusion from paid work, has become 'embedded in a more general policy of economic efficiency and job creation' (Moran, 2006: 183). The third dominant discourse, and one that frequently supplements and informs the first two, has been the Moral Underclass Discourse or MUD. This rejects structural or labour market failure as the cause of social exclusion and instead places the responsibility for inclusion not with public policy but firmly on the shoulder of the individual that experiences exclusion, thereby justifying a more individualised distribution and social integration focus. A consequence of this approach, which may represent a more extreme version of Dworkin's responsibilities argument looked at later, may be the labelling of those who experience exclusion into categories of deserving and undeserving poor. It may also feed into the creation of the types of structural ideals that shape institutional and individual disposition, as discussed in Chapter 2. More importantly, it leads to the situation where responsibility for moving from exclusion towards inclusion rests with the individual experiencing exclusion, thereby introducing what Levitas (2004: 48) has called a 'performative notion of inclusion', where it is the performance of the excluded person that dictates whether they are included or not, not that of the social, economic or political systems.

The dominance of these discourses has been usefully captured in Moran's distinction between 'liberalism as is' and 'liberalism as it might be' or narrow and broad conceptions of inclusion. The former is typified by representative democracy, an emphasis on the individual and on some degree of welfare provision. However, structural change is not seen as practical or even desirable. 'Liberalism as it might be', on the other hand, focuses on a vision of society and democracy that is informed by advanced concepts of social justice, that would enable 'a vision of an inclusive society' to be articulated in a way that does not require 'unimaginable transformation of society' but allows for practical but real change (Moran, 2006: 197). The potential for such change is however undermined by an unwillingness to think and act in transformative ways and is instead supplanted by a tendency to become preoccupied only with those elements that can be easily and narrowly measured, as illustrated by the type of 'common indicators' on social inclusion developed by the European Commission (European Commission, 2013). This suggests an unwillingness or inability to develop indicators that might stimulate a focus on systemic factors and institutional change, not least within public administration. As a result it is argued that the dominance of quantitative indicators and 'the way in which poverty is conceptualised over time separates it from the social processes of the accumulation and distribution of wealth, depoliticising it. And depoliticising is a profoundly political act' (Harriss, 2007: 3). Is it the case then that many of those with an active engagement in the design of social inclusion policies have indeed become, or choose to be, depoliticised, in the process excluding concerns about democratic equality and governance from their social inclusion lexicons.

Justice as a philosophical ideal

This book is intended to make a contribution to the applied practice of public administration and its role in developing and delivering a social justice agenda.

However, enhancing public administration practice in this area requires more than an engagement with the mechanics of governing and administration or a reflection on the merit or otherwise of different policies or different forms of service delivery. Instead, it requires us to step back from the world of 'doing' to reflect on the many different concepts, ideologies and philosophies that shape both personal and institutional approaches to social justice. For public administration, if there was ever a time when challenging old thinking and old ways of doing things was needed, it is now. The purpose of this brief conceptual section is to introduce some of the intellectual tools which individuals and institutions in public administration might find useful to reinvigorate their thinking on justice, equality and inclusion.

First though, a word on the merits of engaging, at least at some level, with political philosophy. According to Rawls (2001: 4) the purpose of political philosophy is to enable people to reflect on 'their political and social institutions as a whole and their basic aims and purposes as a society' but also to engage in consideration of issues that are 'realistically utopian' and which can test and probe 'the limits of practicable political possibility'. Thinking about ideas, principles or values offers potential to free us from the limitations of experience and from the binds of cynicism and scepticism that inhibit belief that a different reality is not only worth considering but may well be possible. This is not to deny the danger that political philosophy may be too abstract or may be so ambitious as to make its conclusions seem unattainable. Thus, Dworkin (2011: 352) exhorts political philosophers not to extend the scope of their considerations to a level that is unattainable, reminding them that 'If philosophers build ivory towers they must set some Rapunzel at the top so that we can, slowly, climb higher.' Inevitably in any discussion on the philosophical aspects of social justice we encounter the substantial chasm that exists between the realms of political philosophy and the practice of politics and public administration. In the latter, journeys into the realms of philosophy, theory, concept and definition, particularly on social justice concerns, are often seen as the preserve of academics, holding little relevance to the working public servant or, indeed, the social policy activist. This derives in no small part from the inaccessibility of much political philosophy and perhaps from a belief on the part of political philosophers that engaging with or shaping the world of practice is not their function. Equally, public officials and social policy activists may be reluctant to disengage from their day to day business to involve themselves in more abstract reflection that on the surface may do little to help them achieve their immediate aims and objectives. The absence of an interpretive interface between philosophy and practice leaves both intellectually and instrumentally weaker, producing a reality as suggested by Wolff (2008: 29) where 'political philosophers design theories of social justice, and then social policy activists find them useless for their purposes'.

Approaches to social justice

Any philosophical exploration of social justice is quickly confronted by questions about what we understand justice to be. In this regard, Rawls (2001: 41) asks 'what principles of justice are most appropriate to specify basic rights and liberties and to regulate social and economic inequalities in citizens' prospects over a complete life'. For Rawls, justice requires the pursuit of two main principles. Firstly, he suggests that 'each person has the same indefensible claims to a fully adequate scheme of equal basic liberties, which scheme is compatible with the same scheme of liberties for all' (Rawls, 2001: 43). Here, basic liberties include freedom of thought, of conscience, the right to vote in elections and to participate in associations, physical and psychological rights and the rights 'covered by the rule of law' (2001: 44). Of the principles presented, Rawls emphasises this to be the most important. His second principle has two parts to it, the first dealing with equality of opportunity and the second with the regulation of inequality, the latter better known as the difference principle. Of these, equality of opportunity is considered to be the priority. This second principle proposes that 'social and economic inequalities are to satisfy two conditions: first, they are to be attached to offices and positions open to all under conditions of fair equality opportunity and second, they are to be to the greatest benefit to the least advantaged members of society' (2003: 42–43). Thus, in the first instance offices and positions should be accessible to all but, as importantly 'all should have a fair chance to attain them'. This has implications not least for recruitment into public administration. The second condition, the difference principle, tolerates inequality in society but does so only when any particular inequality is to the benefit of the least advantaged.

To achieve his vision of social justice, Rawls (ibid.: 44) further claims that 'certain requirements must be imposed on the basic structure ... a free market must be set within a framework of political and legal institutions that adjust the long run trend of economic forces so as to prevent excessive concentrations of property and wealth, especially those likely to lead to political domination' (ibid.: 44). Thus, as well as setting out principles of justice, Rawls also pays attention to the landscape within which these principles must be applied. His assertion about the need to locate the activities of the market within a political and legal framework is significant, particularly the need to control 'excessive concentration' of wealth. Thus, he establishes that the scope of social justice is not just limited to a narrow redistributive focus but instead addresses itself to key concerns about democratic institutions, political power and control.

At the level of principle, Dworkin (2011: 2–3) also emphasises two key justice principles, without which he considers that 'no government is legitimate'. Firstly, he proposes, any government 'must show equal concern for the fate of every person over whom it claims dominion' and, secondly, it must 'fully respect the responsibility and right of each person to decide for himself how to make something valuable of his life'. Dworkin sees these principles as placing a boundary around approaches to justice based on redistribution, which might otherwise create impossible demands. However, he appears to recognise that there may be some level of tension between the two 'simultaneous equations' the solution to which 'comprises neither principle but rather finds attractive conceptions of each that fully satisfy both'. In highlighting the importance of personal responsibility, however, Dworkin, like Rawls, stresses that individuals cannot be responsible for inequalities that arise from genetic or 'native' endowments nor for situations that arise from bad luck. As a result, he rejects the arguments of conservatives that the market should be allowed to determine the distribution of resources and argues that to do so would not show equal concern for all citizens (ibid.: 353). However, it has been suggested that the distinction between bad luck circumstances and circumstances that result from personal choice runs the risk of being conflated with the deserving and undeserving poor (Burchardt and Craig, 2008) or the moral underclass discourse discussed previously.

The relationship between rights and responsibilities is an important element of debates on social justice. In the somewhat overlooked Article 29 of the Universal Declaration of Human Rights, an obligation of duty to community which balances rights with a duty to recognise responsibilities to broader society was introduced: 'Everyone has duties to the community in which alone the free and full development of his personality is possible' (United Nations General Assembly, 1948). From this it becomes clear that while there is a legitimate expectation that the state should play a role in promoting and defending the rights of citizens, there is also a duty on all citizens to respect the rights of their fellow citizens and the broader community.

Equality
Within theories of social justice the idea of equality is of course a central preoccupation. As an area of study in its own right, or as a component part of a broader social justice ideal, competing understandings of equality have the capacity to excite a range of responses and argumentation. The comments by the then Minister for Justice, Michael McDowell, TD, on the inevitability of inequality in an interview with the *Irish Catholic* in 2004, generated comment for many years after. In the first instance was the question of equality of what may be considered. Frequently, equality is understood in terms of some type of access to resources, described by Dworkin as including 'personal resources', i.e. 'physical and mental capacities' and impersonal resources, consisting of a person's wealth and 'measured as abstractly as possible' (Dworkin, 2011: 355). This has been contrasted with the more broadly defined idea of equality of functioning, seen as a means of achieving particular capabilities. This particular approach, pioneered by Sen and Nussbaum and which has

influenced the evolution of the UN Human Development Index and the annual Human Development Report aims to expand the focus of equality and justice beyond resources only. While the ideas of Sen and Dworkin are regularly situated in opposition to each other, it could be argued that Sen's capabilities focus need not be radically different from Dworkin's potentially wide description of impersonal and personal resources. Other forms of economic or resource equality are concerned with access to employment or equality of pay for equal work, particularly between women and men. In this regard equality of participation in education and training that might ultimately enable individuals to access better paid employment are significant, albeit that the value of education needs to be seen in more than just economic terms.

Inherently connected with a discussion of resources and/or capabilities equalities is the issue of equality of power and political influence, discussed above and in Chapter 2. At this stage there can be little doubt that inequality of power follows inequality of resources, i.e. the wealthy have greater access to and influence on democratic decision-makers or, in some cases, have capacity for independent decision-making that elected representatives have little option but to follow. Meanwhile, other less tangible but no less important forms of equality are also highlighted, particularly equality of love, care and solidarity as well as in respect and recognition (Baker et al., 2004) echoing at least some of Sen's capabilities approach. In a more specifically Irish context the National Economic and Social Forum (2002: 43) also addressed this issue of how far the idea of equality extends and similarly concluded that equality should be considered in four key spheres: the economy 'concerned with the production, distribution and exchange of goods and services'; the socio-cultural sphere 'concerned with the production, transmission and legitimisation of cultural practices and products'; the political sphere 'covering activities where power is enacted' and the affective domain, relating to 'activities involved in developing bonds of solidarity, care and love between human beings'.

The validity of these arenas of equality are contested in their own right as are expectations about the degree or level of equality which governments can be considered responsible for. These expectations range from:

- *Basic equality*, provides the foundation for thinking about equality and is premised on a belief that 'at some very basic level all human beings have equal worth and importance and are therefore equally worthy of concern and respect' (Baker et al., 2004: 23). Just how much concern is an issue but it is usually associated with the provision of protection against 'inhuman and degrading treatment' and well as providing for some minimum level of basic need. As such it can be associated with the idea of the minimalist state and a perspective of negative liberties.

- *Liberal egalitarianism*, extends the concept of equality within the realms of: respect and recognition; resources; love care and solidarity; power and working and learning' (ibid.: 24). This echoes Rawls (2001: 60) who names five areas or primary goods which, he suggests 'are what free and equal persons (as specified by the political conception) need as citizens'. These primary goods include basic rights and liberties (including liberty of thought and conscience; freedom of movement) 'free choice of occupation against a background of diverse opportunities'; 'powers and prerogatives of offices and positions of authority and responsibility'; 'income and wealth', i.e. that needed to 'achieve a wide range of ends', and finally, 'the social bases of self-respect, understood as those aspects of basic institutions normally essential if citizens are to have a lively sense of their worth as persons and to be able to advance their ends with self-confidence' (ibid.: 58). There is however no universal agreement on just how much equality should be delivered in these areas, with emphasis often being placed on creating equality of opportunity as opposed to equality of outcome.
- *Equality of condition*, demands an even higher level of ambition aimed at ending or significantly reducing inequality. Seen from this perspective, inequality results from deeply rooted structural inequalities in a range of areas, including the economy, democracy, relations between men and women and between different ethnic groups. However, it is stressed that equality of condition does not equate to equality of outcome, but represents a stronger form of equality of opportunity, where individuals get to exercise 'real choices among real options', not simply cosmetic ones (Baker et al., 2004: 34). This is not unlike the position arrived at by Dworkin (2011: 358) in his distinction between ex ante and ex post equality, where ex ante goes beyond a conservative focus on equality of opportunity towards one where governments ensure that citizens have the capacity to face life's 'contingencies' in an equal position.

A concern for equality therefore is a central component of ideas on social justice. It places demands across a range of policy dimensions and generates radically different levels of expectation about the degree of change to be produced in each. Between those who oppose anything more than basic equalities and those who advocate for more far reaching equality of condition the chasm of ideas is wide and some might say unbridgeable. Inevitably there will be those who say that the human condition is unlikely to tolerate little more than some form of liberal egalitarianism, despite the exemplar of the Scandinavian countries highlighted in the much cited book, *The Spirit Level: Why Equality Is Better for Everyone* (Wilkinson and Pickett, 2010) where the positive impact of greater equality on broader societal health and wellbeing was demonstrated.

However, beyond the human condition, there is a danger that the very possibility of believing in more ambitious forms of equality has deserted many of us, including public officials. Whether this is a result of the actions of the self-interested majority or, as suggested by some authors, proof that the majority have been conditioned or 'hoodwinked' to believe that greater equality will in some way damage economic prosperity remains open to question. Concluding that the latter is more likely the case, they question 'whether the economic dislocations resulting from the crisis of 2008 will delegitimate the prevailing mainstream of economics and create room for an economic science friendlier to greater equality' (Wisman and Smith, 2011: 1001). A similar question could be asked of the study and practice of public administration.

Social justice and the right to private property
Few philosophical discussions on the issue of social justice proceed without addressing the core issue of the right to private property. This right is prominently protected in the Irish Constitution as part of a commitment to 'in the case of injustice done vindicate the life, person, good name, and property rights of every citizen' (Government of Ireland, 1937: Article 40.3.2). The degree to which the ownership of private property or wealth is or is not limited, restricted or interfered with by the state has clear implications for the capacity to promote social justice. In reality, in the context of the dominance of the liberal democratic state, it is not the restriction on the right of individuals to own property or to accumulate wealth that is at issue; rather, what is disputed is the degree to which the state has a right to generate the income it needs to create a just society through levying taxes on wealth as property. On one hand, theorists such as Nozick consider any form of taxation on property as theft while on the other a social democratic outlook justifies higher levels of taxation on wealth in order to provide universally available services and produce a more just and equal society. The debate in Ireland in the latter part of 2012 on the introduction of a property tax brought this particular issue into sharp relief. As yet, the broader issue of a targeted wealth tax remains unresolved.

Within liberal democracies, the relationship between the state and the owners of capital and property is governed by a number of fundamental tenets. Firstly, private capital largely provides the basis for the economy, though the state is still clearly a hugely significant economic actor. However, there is a significant dependence on private capital accumulation to provide the basis for taxation which supplies the resources to enable the state to function and, from a political perspective, to enable politicians to be re-elected. As a result, it is suggested that there is an inherent 'self-interest' in safeguarding capital accumulation processes as a means of protecting state revenues (Offe and Roge, 1997). This almost inevitably creates a tension between the rhetoric of citizens as decision-makers at the centre of the democratic system and the influence, real or perceived, exerted by those who exercise significant control over capital resources. Within this structure, it has been argued, with some justification, that the corporation emerges as the first amongst equals and 'wields disproportionate influence over the state and therefore over the nature of democratic outcomes' (Held, 1987: 203). Dahl (1985: 62), not noted as a radical democratic theorist, actually reached the point where he argued that both capitalism and bureaucratic socialism generates 'inequalities in social and economic resources so great as to bring about severe violations of political equality and hence of the democratic process'.

The consequence of the excessive influence by corporations in particular on democratic decision-making is such as to separate political equality from economic equality and renders it unable to take the bold step of linking political equality with the redistribution of resources (Manley, 1983). Thus, a state that depends on capital accumulation to sustain itself finds it difficult to avoid a situation where it has to act to protect capitalist interest and accord them and their priorities an elevated role in decision-making leading to patterns of exclusive or preferential decision-making (Dryzek, 1996, 2000). Where, as in the case of Ireland, the economy relies heavily on foreign owned capital, this dependence appears to be even more debilitating, producing a situation where some policy options, such as higher corporation tax or increased personal taxes for high earners, are automatically ruled out because of their potential impact on corporate profits or on senior employees of foreign firms. This appears to support Held's suggestion that the state will, almost inevitably 'tend to favour a compromise among powerful economic interests, a compromise that is all too often at the political and economic expense of vulnerable groups' (Held, 1987: 212). This produces a situation such as in Ireland where the debate on the loss of sovereignty from the national state to the European level obscures a more fundamental and longer-term loss of economic sovereignty from the state and citizens to the domestic and international owners of capital resources. In considering social justice, particularly in an administrative context, these relationships need to be acknowledged and questioned. Social justice theories must of course be conscious of how governments can generate resources to deliver social justice objectives. However, they cannot be adequately conceived of within boundaries predetermined by the primacy of the interests of private capital alone.

The contribution of religion

Discussions on social justice have long been informed by reference to religious beliefs and principles, as evidenced in the earlier reference to Dáil debates. On one hand religion may be seen as a source of ideas around justice, setting out principles about what it means and how it can be achieved, though there can be no guarantee that all religions, even those drawing from the same source, will arrive at the same conclusion about what these principles are. Religions may also be a source of demands on governments, seeking to ensure that their beliefs and practices are not undermined by public policy or legislation. In situations where a divide between state and religion is narrower, such as in many predominantly Muslim countries, religious teaching often directly informs how the state and its functionaries operate. In more secular states where the division between the spiritual and the temporal have been more firmly established the influence of religious beliefs is more complex and often more camouflaged. However, as well as making pronouncements on social justice, religion has been seen by some as playing a legitimating force for social injustice, perpetuating the view that 'the status quo distribution was appropriate to the cosmic order. Indirectly, it diverted attention away from the material world to a spiritual or moral domain. It reinforced a static view of reality. Everything and everyone had their proper assigned place in this god-given reality' (Wisman and Smith, 2011: 978). In some circumstances too it is suggested that the role of religion and church institutions has been to align itself with and support the state, not least on the issue of violence against the state where 'it has tended to bless the state's use of violence while condemning violent revolution against ruling authorities' (Villa-Vincencio, 1987: 1).

It would be beyond the capacity of this chapter to undertake a detailed analysis of the relative contributions of religion to social justice. Instead, it introduces Catholic Social Teaching (CST) as an example of how adherence to a particular religious belief may shape both a conception of social justice and the way individuals might assume a social justice obligation informed by religion. The decision to explore CST does not reflect any personal preference towards the views on social justice as espoused by the Vatican over many years. Nor does it in any way signal that other religions do not possess equally valid social justice doctrines. However, the reality in Ireland is that until recently, the Catholic Church as an institution has exercised strong influence, both on the formulation of the Constitution and on the shape of a variety of social policy issues. Moreover, beyond this institutional influence, the vast majority of the population of the country continue to describe themselves as Catholic; 84% according to the 2011 Census (Central Statistics Office, 2011). From this it could reasonably be assumed that a significant number of public representatives and officials may be in some way influenced or potentially influenced by the social teachings of the Catholic Church.

Influencing the Constitution
In the earlier part of this chapter, the social justice aspirations of the Irish Constitution were noted, highlighting the concerns of influential civil servants about potentially far reaching commitments to social justice. At the same time

as these civil servants were expressing their views so too an array of figures within the Catholic Church were actively engaged in efforts to secure recognition for religion, for the Catholic Church in particular and, in some cases, directly for Catholic Social Teaching. For example, in advance of the 1937 Constitution, the Jesuits convened a committee, which drew on papal encyclicals, the Polish Constitution of 1921 and the Austrian Constitution of 1934 to produce a preamble and series of articles covering the family and private property (Hogan, 2012). In one communication from a prominent member of this committee, Fr. Edward Cahill, an explicit request was made to incorporate the specific understanding of social justice as elaborated upon within CST into the Constitution though the insertion of a dedicated article:

> Accordingly, the State shall by suitable enactments as occasion demands, bring its system of jurisprudence and its legal code into harmony with the dictates of the natural law as summarised in the social teaching of the Catholic Church, in the sense of which this article (viz Art. 45) as well as Articles 40–4 are to be interpreted. (Cahill, 1937)

The work of this committee was seen as having had significant influence on the final shape of the Constitution. However, Hogan's (2012: 223–224) detailed analysis of the elements of the Constitution most frequently described as having their origins in CST argues that in reality, they are not unique to the Irish Constitution nor are they very far removed from liberal secular values on issues such as property rights, equality before the law and *habeas corpus*. Thus while the Catholic Church was very active in trying to shape the Constitution, Hogan argues that their influence was not as strong as has sometimes been suggested, given the predominantly Catholic character of the country in 1937.

What is Catholic Social Teaching?

Beyond its historical and Constitutional significance, the Catholic Church and, by extension, CST, has continued to exert or attempted to exert an ongoing influence on social policy in Ireland. The purpose of this chapter is not to produce a historical summary of such efforts; rather, it identifies some of those elements of CST that might provide insights into the meaning of social justice, which according to the aforementioned Fr. Cahill, 'has for the student of Catholic social science, a clear and definite meaning ... probably quite unknown in our current jurisprudence' (Cahill, 1937). So, what is Catholic Social Teaching? Perhaps the first thing to say is that despite Fr. Cahill's assertion that CST has a 'clear and definite meaning', this is far from obvious. Having emerged at the end of the nineteenth century in response to 'the injustices of the Industrial Revolution and the threat of Communism' it is suggested that CST offers 'an authoritative Church teaching on social, political and economic issues' that provide 'principles for reflection, criteria for judgement and guidelines for action' (Live Simply Network, 2012). Within CST, drawing from a variety of papal encyclicals, there are a number of core pillars, namely: human dignity; the common good, solidarity and subsidiarity (Jones and Waller, 2010, Roman and Baybado, 2008), with human dignity being seen as the overarching priority, supported by the other three.

The common good may be understood as a 'mutually shared responsibility of all individuals to corporately realise society's full human potential as individuals and as a unified society' (Jones and Waller, 2010: 288) or as a 'duty to share in promoting the welfare of the community and a right to benefit from that welfare. This applies at every level: local, national and international. Public authorities exist mainly to promote the common good and to ensure that no section of the population is excluded' (Live Simply Network, 2012). Indeed, it is argued by the Catholic Bishops of England and Wales that this idea of the common good has to take into account the needs of all sections of the population (Catholic Bishops Conference, 1996). They address this issue directly in relation to the provision of public services, emphasising the importance of a public service ethos:

> Social services in general need other incentives than pure profit, and the introduction of market forces in this area has sometimes demeaned or damaged the sense of vocation and dedication to others that has traditionally been a hallmark of the professions involved. The ethos of public service, in the public sector and especially in local and national government, is an important public asset that must be safeguarded by every possible means. (Catholic Bishops Conference, 1996: 21)

Within CST, solidarity emerges as one of the core principles to be followed. This is described as 'the responsibility of individuals to realize their obligations to fellow members of the human family and the acknowledgement that a bond exists among all members of the community' (Jones and Waller, 2010: 289). Taking this a stage further, solidarity is also seen as being about 'the fundamental bond of unity with our fellow human beings and the resulting interdependence. All are responsible for all; and in particular the rich have responsibilities towards the poor. National and international structures must reflect this' (Live Simply Network, 2012).

The final pillar of CST is the much cited principle of subsidiarity which 'assigns the ownership for an action to the lowest level of social responsibility e.g. individuals, families or intermediate groups' (Jones and Waller, 2010). However, the Live Simply Network citing the papal encyclical, *Quadragesimo Anno*, extends this definition, emphasising that subsidiarity must be considered in relation to the common good such that 'All power and decision-making in society should be at the most local level compatible with the common good. Subsidiarity will mainly mean power passing downwards, but it could also mean passing appropriate powers upwards. The balance between the vertical (subsidiarity) and the horizontal (solidarity) is achieved through reference to the common good' (Live Simply Network, 2012). This distinction is important as the subsidiarity principle for some is seen as justifying arguments in favour of the small state and increased delegation of responsibilities to civil society organisations. Drawing on these principles CST includes amongst its concerns how the state and public administration operates. For example, Pope John Paul II in *Veritatis Splendor*, (John Paul II, 1993) writes that:

> In the political sphere, it must be noted that truthfulness in the relations between those governing and those governed, openness in public administration, impartiality in the service of the body politic, respect for the rights of accused against summary trials and convictions, the just and honest use of public funds, the rejection of equivocal or illicit means in order to gain, preserve or increase power at any cost – all these are principles which are primarily rooted in, and in fact derive their singular urgency from, the transcendental value of the human person and the objective moral demands of the functioning of the State. (John Paul II, 1993: 94)

Of course the CST principles described above offer much space for interpretation and a brief perusal of the relevant literature illustrates quite quickly that they do not always translate into a common understanding of social justice. For example, members of a Catholic Church community in Pennsylvania in the United States discovered that forming a 'social justice group', proved to be more complicated than they might ever have envisaged. The problems for the group, as documented by Kristen Hannum in *US Catholic*, originated in the comments of a chat show host who urged Catholics 'to leave their church if it had anything to do with social justice' which, he suggested, was 'code for socialism'. This comment found wider support, with a former campaign co-ordinator for George W. Bush who claimed that 'social justice and economic justice are code phrases for the religious left who prefer government solutions to human problems funded by the redistribution of wealth' (Hannum, 2012: 14). As a result, the group fractured and only narrowly voted to resist calls to drop the social justice language from its name, albeit causing some members of the group to resign in protest.

This local level example invites a question about the degree to which a less than specific CST in itself becomes a vehicle for competing ideologies that originate in secular political and economic spheres. In this regard, it is suggested by Jones and Waller (2010: 290–292), that the absence of a well-developed and integrated model of CST leads to a situation where more selective championing of certain elements of CST such as solidarity, the common good or a preferential option for the poor takes the place of a holistic approach. However, in making this claim they themselves equally champion a visibly ideological model of CST, skewed in the direction of the subsidiarity principle. This they see as rejecting a strong role for the central state in promoting solidarity and protecting the needs of the poor, instead favouring market or charitable provision. They further suggest that establishing a minimum wage or 'certain subsidy or social welfare programs' violates the principle of subsidiarity and may harm human dignity.

Other more far reaching and complex critiques of CST have also been offered. One such view holds that the purpose of CST is and has been more to do with the Catholic Church's on-going resistance to 'modern ideology (the Enlightenment) and economic liberalism' and to its exclusion from 'temporal affairs' (Laurent 2008: 808) since the end of the eighteenth century. Thus, the growth of the secular, utilitarian state represented a challenge to the long established capacity of the Catholic Church to influence a range of issues formerly under its prevue: 'In the eyes of the Church, the world underwent an overturning of values during the Enlightenment, an overturning that explains the emergence of a field of knowledge supposedly free from moral shackles' (Laurent, 2007: 808). Laurent continues (ibid.: 811):

> The Church's social doctrine should not be read as a declaration of major moral principles designed to help Christians plot the best possible course through modern society, which Vatican II is supposed to have finally accepted, but rather as a demand on the part of various popes that the Church exert a visible, albeit indirect, influence on the temporal world.

Hence, the concern was less about creating a social justice consciousness amongst its membership and more about bolstering the power of the Church vis a vis the state. Such an argument might well explain the gaping contradiction between the considerable efforts of the institutional Catholic Church in Ireland to exert an influence on the creation of the 1937 Constitution and society at large while, at the same time, being apparently much less concerned with the more widespread pursuit of a just and more equal society, in particular through the application of principles of social justice within its own institutions and more broadly in society.

Conclusion

In this chapter some of the elements of what social justice means have been set out. These have demonstrated that understandings of social justice are likely to be informed by a variety of sources including national and international legislative sources, public policy, political theory as well as religious teaching. However, they are also likely to be informed and constrained by dominant economic doctrines that place social justice in a subservient position to the needs of the market and privilege the perspectives of powerful economic actors. What emerges from this analysis is that social justice is not a universally understood concept; it is highly ideological and is highly contested, in a legal sense, philosophically or from a religious point of view. For some social justice implies considerable obligations for government and demands a more interventionist state. For others, the social justice implications for government are narrow and premised on non-interference with the rights and responsibilities of individual citizens. Taken alongside the earlier chapters on the challenges facing public administration and its particular role in promoting social justice, it becomes clear that the task of deepening the acceptance of a social justice approach within public administration is more than a little complex. However, any such approach needs to engage with and be informed by ideas and concepts as a means of exposing the explicit and implicit bases upon which opinions are formed, policies made and services delivered.

Note

1 UNCDF offers a combination of investment capital, capacity building and technical advisory services to promote microfinance and local development in the Least Developed Countries (LDCs), www.uncdf.org/english/about_uncdf/index.php, accessed 26 July 2013.

4

Civic engagement and social justice

Introduction

Public policy in a variety of countries, Ireland included, has recognised the value of some level of deeper citizen participation in democratic and civic life. At the same time, civil society organisations have increasingly asserted the importance of their participation in policy-making processes. It was in this context that the Irish government clearly stated that 'There is a need to create a more participatory democracy where active citizenship is fostered' defining participation 'as an exchange between citizens and government, between those who make policy and people affected by policy choices' (Government of Ireland, 2000b: 63). Reflecting this thinking, since the late 1980s the democratic landscape in Ireland has been populated by an array of governance and civic engagement mechanisms and processes, both formal and informal and at local and national level. Frequently social partnership has been used as a synonym for governance though this descriptor embodies a host of differing characteristics and is one that has clearly fallen out of favour despite for many years having become the 'dominant paradigm of policy-making in Ireland' (Meade and O'Donovan, 2002). Elsewhere, at a populist level, UK Prime Minister David Cameron's Big Society Initiative speaks of 'The idea of communities taking more control, of more volunteerism, more charitable giving, of social enterprises taking on a bigger role, of people establishing public services themselves' (Cameron, 2011). In Austria, the list of benefits deriving from deeper public participation is suggested to include increased trust and democratic interest; higher levels of respect for democratic institutions and more realistic levels of expectation of their capacity; enhanced problem solving capacity and, potentially, a more advanced willingness to accept policy directions (Government of Austria, 2011). In Scotland the production of civic engagement guidelines has been highlighted as an example of good practice (Government of Scotland, 2009) while in Belgium the Flemish Anti-Poverty Network has been 'established by decree' accompanied by a commitment that 'government must consult it on all matters affecting people experiencing poverty' (European Anti Poverty Network, 2009: 27). In developing countries too, notions of good governance and democratic participation have become inextricably linked with democratisation and civil society engagement (Santiso, 2001) and indeed experiences of participatory budgeting in Port Alegre, participatory planning in Kerela and local civic participation in the United States all contributed strongly to the articulation of the powerful concept of Empowered Deliberative Democracy[1] (Fung and Wright, 2001). Likewise, the International Association for Public Participation (IAP[2]) emphasises the need for those who are affected by a decision to have a right to be involved in the decision-making process and, more especially, that they will know the outcome of the decision-making process and how their inputs contributed to it. Even more recently, in March 2012, the theme of the annual conference of the American Society of Public Administration was 'Redefining Public Service through Civic Engagement', signalling a recognition that public participation is an issue that needs to be more deeply considered.

Despite these and other possible exemplars of a drift towards increased citizen engagement there remains a nagging doubt that, in many cases, participatory initiatives are only weakly embedded within the democratic and administrative landscape, rarely moving beyond the local level and, in some cases at least, are simply by-products of a more conscious New Public Management agenda to replace elements of the state's responsibility with less costly and potentially disempowering forms of civil society service provision. This chapter explores the proposition that deeper democratic participation is an essential component of a progressive understanding of social justice. As a consequence, achieving participatory and justice objectives will be inhibited by the absence of more developed understandings and practices of civic engagement, particularly within public administration. The chapter further suggests that civic engagement activities will rarely extend beyond the cosmetic without the conscious cultivation of a more favourable set of dispositions amongst public officials that embrace and legitimise citizen participation as a democratic, administrative and social justice requirement. To investigate these propositions, the chapter firstly revisits some of the commonly used language of participation, highlighting how such language contains multiple and potentially conflicting sets of beliefs, values and understandings and gives rise to a host of competing expectations and tensions. Following this, the relationship between civic engagement and social justice is established, building further on the understandings of social justice established in Chapters 2 and 3. The chapter then proceeds to explore some of the difficulties and dilemmas of civic engagement before going on to discuss in more detail the role of public administration within a civic engagement context.

A lexicon of civic engagement

The language of civic engagement is complex, nuanced, debated, contested, abused and is frequently meaningless. Even commonly used terms such as democracy and citizenship, which most of us would assume to know the meaning of, present an array of possible interpretations and contestations. The idea of citizenship in particular offers new challenges in Ireland to meet the needs of and include those who do not enjoy formal citizenship status.

At times, however, the language of engagement and participation appears to be deployed in deference to the latest trend in public policy or on foot of political or administrative direction. In other circumstances, though, it may well be accompanied by a shift in mindset and a realisation by those who are open to it that civic engagement means more than just having a few bodies on a committee or holding public meetings a little more often. For civic engagement to ever become real and meaningful, engaging with the meaning of words and concepts has to be the starting point. In this regard, particular challenges are posed for public officials to expand their civic engagement lexicon and to understand why civic engagement matters for social justice. Some key concepts – participatory democracy, citizenship and participation, civic engagement and civil society – are introduced below.

Participatory democracy

In general reflections on contemporary democracy it is sometimes suggested that there are two main, competing narratives, those 'which celebrate its ascendancy and those which are concerned about its deficits' (Gaventa, 2006: 3). At this stage, in countries where democracy exists, liberal, representative democracy is generally seen as global democratic orthodoxy and is promoted as such by a host of organisations, including an array of UN agencies and civil society groups. However, those who point to the weaknesses of liberal democracy have introduced phrases such as 'democracy with adjectives, low intensity democracy, neo patrimonial democracy, semi democracy' (Collier and Levitsky, 1997: 431) and point to declining citizen participation in electoral processes and distrust between citizens, politicians and democratic institutions, including public administration (Pateman, 1970, Phillips, 2004, Luckham et al., 1999, Clarke and Stewart, 1998).

Within these different perspectives on the strengths and weaknesses of liberal democracy expectations about the participation of citizens vary considerably. On one hand, in the language of elitist ideas about democracy, participation by the average citizen needs to be limited so as not to displace the primacy of the competitive political process. In this case the role of the majority of citizens is simply to participate, via elections in the choice of leaders and little more. Restrictions on participation in the democratic process were necessary due to an assessment of the limited intellectual abilities of ordinary citizens (Held, 1987) and which sees the 'electoral mass' as 'incapable of action other than a stampede' (Schumpeter, 2003: 283). A common theme running through such elitist theories is the danger to the stability of the democratic system that would arise from any increase in participation from ordinary citizens. Participation is required only from an elite group from which leaders emerge. For those who hold such a view, the potential for civic engagement beyond voting in elections is neither beneficial nor desirable and indeed, is a potential source of political instability.

On the other hand, the language of participatory democracy suggests an alternative potential. The fundamental ambition of these perspectives is to real-ise the ambition of greater participation by citizens and/or citizen's organisa-tions in decision-making. Writers such as Carole Pateman (2004) have argued that in order for a society to be fully democratic, members of that society need to be trained and educated for democracy, a process that happens through the very act of participation. Thus, she suggests, it is wrong to limit citizen partici-pation on the grounds that it might in some way cause instability. Instead, she and others see participation as helping to integrate citizens more deeply into democratic processes (Sorensen, 1997), and as vital to ensure that the 'social and political capacities of each individual' are developed (Pateman, 1970: 43). To build this capacity however, participation opportunities must exist. In the absence of such opportunities, fully democratic systems cannot be said to exist. This is where civic engagement plays such a central role – it is a means of devel-oping the social and political potential of all citizens and deepening democracy. It is not just about making better public policy; the act of participation is in itself an important objective.

Adding further to the participatory lexicon is the idea of deliberative democracy. This is one of the most widely referenced participatory formulas and has been described in a variety of fashions. In general terms it can be seen as 'any one of a family of views, according to which the public deliberation of free and equal citizens is the core of legitimate political decision-making and self-government' (Bohman, 1998). Young (2000: 22) elaborates further describing it as a 'form of practical reason. Participants in the democratic pro-cess offer proposal for how best to solve problems or meet legitimate needs and so the democratic process is primarily a discussion of problems, conflicts and claims of need or interest'. According to Cohen and Fung (2004), deliberative democracy aims to 'shift from bargaining, interest aggregation and power to the common reason of equal citizens as a dominant force in democratic life', a theme echoed by Chappell's understanding of deliberative democracy as 'uncoerced, other regarding, reasoned, inclusive and equal debate' (Chappell, 2012). At the core then of deliberative process are concepts of public reasoning, equality, free and equal citizens, practicality and problem solving.

A further important form of democratic activity is captured in the idea of associative democracy, though here there are significantly different conceptions. Associative democracy is premised on the existence of associations, that is, structures in which citizens organise and come together. On one hand, there is a view of associations as a channel through which functions can be devolved from the state to a variety of citizens associations/organisations (Hirst, 2000). On the other hand, the creation of citizen associations is seen as necessary to create 'a social base', particularly to enable the voices of marginalised communities to be heard (Cohen and Rogers, 1997). In the latter case, it is argued that the state needs to commit resources to ensure such associations are enabled to emerge.

In Ireland, a potentially significant contribution to discussions on participatory democracy was made with the publication of the White Paper on Voluntary Activity – the Relationship between the State and the Community and Voluntary Sector in 2000. This described citizenship as 'A political activity which gives citizens the opportunity to shape the society in which they live. Groups are given the opportunity to become involved in identifying local needs and developing strategies to meet these needs' (Government of Ireland, 2000b: 64). Unfortunately, this potentially influential White Paper was largely ignored by the very government that created it and has been seen as largely ineffective (Harvey, 2004), illustrating how participatory rhetoric can frequently collapse under its own weight.

Citizenship and participation

As is suggested from the discussion above, there are widely diverging expectations about the role of 'the citizen' in a democracy. Those advocating the more active form of citizenship leave little doubt as to its importance and cite Rousseau's view that 'there can be no patriotism without liberty; no liberty without virtue; no virtue without citizens, create citizens and you will have everything you need; without them you will have nothing but debased slaves, from the rulers of the state downwards' (Rousseau, 1758, as cited in Barber, 1984: 213). While much of the thrust of participatory democracy involves the citizen in regular, on-going active democratic activity, the more traditional and limited expectation is of a citizen who participates in the choice of political leadership via the electoral process, but does little else beyond that. Such a narrow liberal concept of the citizen, it is suggested, fails to generate a sense of the 'socially embedded citizen' (Jones and Gaventa, 2002: 4). By contrast, inherent in the notion of a more active citizen is the potential for participation in deliberation on issues of public interest and the common good and some notion of public service. Lister contrasts these different conceptions, emphasising that it is one thing to enjoy the legal status of citizenship, but something entirely different to realise its full potential (Lister, 1997: 35–36).

Some years ago the idea of active citizenship became more prominent in the public arena in Ireland following the recommendations of a government appointed body (Taskforce on Active Citizenship, 2007). The Active Citizenship Taskforce was set up to identify the degree of citizen engagement in community issues and to make recommendations on how it could be enhanced. While it is difficult to pin the Taskforce down on exactly what it meant by the concept of active citizenship, it was variously referred to as being about 'engagement, participation in society and valuing contributions made by individuals, whether they are employed or outside the traditional workforce', implying duties as well as rights (2007: 2) and being ultimately concerned with the 'underlying values which shape behaviour by individuals as members of communities' (2007: 3). Not surprisingly, given its strong focus on the individual, the Taskforce report adopted a narrow concept of democracy and its suggestions to address democratic deficits go little further than recommending the establishment of an independent electoral commission to encourage voting and to undertake related education and publicity activities.

The language of civic engagement

The language and practice of civic engagement builds or should build on foundations of participatory democracy and active citizenship. However, yet again, its many variations contain a myriad of potential meanings, values and implications, some more progressive and inclusive than others. The oft cited Sherry Arnstein (1969: 216) presents a particularly challenging understanding of citizen participation as:

> a categorical term for citizen power. It is the redistribution of power that enables the have-not citizens, presently excluded from the political and economic processes, to be deliberately included in the future. It is the strategy by which the have-nots join in determining how information is shared, goals and policies are set, tax resources are allocated, programs are operated, and benefits like contracts and patronage are parcelled out. In short, it is the means by which they can induce significant social reform which enables them to share in the benefits of the affluent society.

Arnstein's approach clearly identifies a link between civic engagement and the participation of 'have-not citizens'. Building on this definition Arnstein developed a 'ladder of participation' to illustrate different levels of participation. In this she demonstrates how participation (or more correctly, non-participation) moves from involvement that is more about manipulation and being concerned with enabling 'power holders to "educate" or "cure" the participants', through participation which is more tokenistic (including information giving, consultation and various forms of placation), and finally, towards approaches that encourage genuine partnership, delegated power and citizen control. In a similar way, though with less ideological challenge, the Austrian government has distinguished between civic engagement that involves: information provision; consultation and/or co-operative public participation, each with varying levels of involvement in and control over decision-making (Government of Austria, 2011). In a further effort to classify stages of engagement and participation, the International Association on Public Participation (IAP²) proposes five levels at which public participation can take place:

- *level 1* – to inform, requiring little more than one-way provision of information to stakeholders on a specific issue;
- *level 2* – to consult, implying that information is provided to and feedback is obtained from stakeholders in a two-way flow of information;
- *level 3* – to involve, moving towards a process of gathering stakeholders' views and 'ensuring that their concerns and views are understood and considered';
- *level 4* – to collaborate, moving to a higher level of stakeholders' involvement and the designation of stakeholders as partners, 'including in analyses, development and decision-making'; and
- *level 5* – to empower, involving stakeholders having control over final decision.

Finally, Graham Smith (2005) has also categorised citizen participation and engagement as part of his contribution to the Power Enquiry in the UK. In his report, *Beyond the Ballot: 57 Democratic Innovations from Around the World*, he classifies civic engagement innovations under the headings of: electoral innovation; consultation innovation; deliberative innovation; co-governance innovation; direct democracy innovation; and E-Democracy innovation.

Clearly then, civic engagement can take place at a variety of different levels each with its own distinct language. Lower levels of engagement are associated with information provision. Moving beyond this introduces the language of consultation, with or without the possibility of feedback. Higher order engagement introduces the language of collaboration or co-governance, implying some willingness to share power. Finally, the most far reaching but also the rarest form of civic engagement brings us to the language of empowerment, control of decision-making and direct democracy. Clearly, higher order participation presents progressively greater challenges for existing power holders, not least those within the public administration system.

Civil Society

Another important term in the lexicon of civic engagement is civil society. Beyond the direct involvement by the individual citizen, civic engagement is often facilitated by citizen participation in civil society organisations (CSOs). Almost inevitably, the term civil society is also subject to a variety of under-standings, each with particular implications for democratic participation and, more especially, for public administration. Jensen (2006) identifies a number of main approaches: the Lockean concept, the Scottish concept and the more contemporary sphere concept. In the Lockean view a contrast is drawn between a civil society which is characterised by the presence of laws, judge-ment and an enforcement capacity and an uncivil society, which is considered to be devoid of such characteristics. Civil society therefore implies the presence of laws which prevent individual rights being interfered with. The Scottish concept also focuses on individual connections with the state and society and is associated with the perspectives of civic republicanism. Here, civil society is seen 'a public, ethical space regulated by laws, within which citizens pursue their private interests in harmony with the public good'. The final approach to classifying civil society uses spatial imagery and sees civil society as 'a zone of freedom for individuals to associate with others' which is characterised by 'an exclusive set of private norms' (2006: 43). This zone is seen as being distinct from the sphere of government. The importance of civil society in this view is that it provides the opportunity for citizens to learn the principles of modern democracy, much as was suggested earlier by Pateman (1970) and Barber (1984). The preference for one civil society concept over another is inevitably influenced by underlying democratic beliefs. Thus, classical liberal perspec-tives are more likely to see civil society as a means of ensuing protection of individual rights through the Lockean notions of laws and their enforcement potential. By contrast, those with a stronger commitment to participatory democracy are likely to embrace the sphere concept seeing it as principally con-cerned with 'self-organisation for particular purposes of enhancing intrinsic social values' (Young, 2000). For Young, this concept of civil society is uniquely important in addressing political and social inequality, being one of the few ways in which those who are marginalised can come together to seek ways to 'improve their lives through mutual aid and articulation of group conscious-ness' (2000: 165). Building on the sphere concept, a useful working definition for civil society emerges as 'An intermediate realm situated between state and household, populated by organised groups or associations which are separate from the state, enjoy some autonomy in relations with the state and are formed voluntarily by members of society to protect or extend their interests, values or identities' (Manor et al., 1999: 3–4).

One of the notable elements of this definition is that civil society organisa-tions are separate from and enjoy some autonomy from the state. Equally, they are seen as having a role in protecting interests, values and identities, underlin-ing their possible advocacy function. Applying this definition to Ireland, civil society can be seen to include a wide range of groups or associations, large and small, formal and informal, permanent or more transitory and may include trade unions, community and voluntary organisations, farming bodies, business organisations, sporting groups, faith groups etc. However, despite the Lockean undertones, there can be no automatic assumption that all civil society organisations act according to a shared set of values or beliefs or in the pursuit of a common good.

Why is civic engagement an integral element of social justice?

For many advocates of participatory democracy and civic engagement, contemporary liberal democracy is seen as inherently linked to the production and maintenance of social and economic inequality. However, few are foolish enough to think that their participatory approaches will ever replace the mainstay of elections and representation but do consider ways in which liberal democracy can be supplemented by more widespread acceptance of participatory approaches and associated progress towards equality. For Macpherson (1977: 99) a more participatory democratic system is premised on a two-stage approach, which links democratic participation and economic equality. The first involves removing democratic 'roadblocks' which are a prerequisite to greater participation, while the second requires the exploitation of 'loopholes' that may emerge within the dominant model. Taking the roadblocks first, the existence of low levels of democratic consciousness alongside continued social and economic inequality presents, it is suggested, is a significant dilemma or paradox. On the one hand, greater participation and an increased level of democratic consciousness can only be achieved if social and economic inequality is addressed. However, it is considered unlikely that greater social and economic equality will be achieved without an increase in participation and consciousness capable of demanding political change. Hence, social justice requires a higher level of civic engagement. To overcome this paradox, three loopholes or potential spaces for action are identified, namely: the need to generate awareness of the cost of economic growth, particularly in terms of ecological damage; awareness of the potential dangers of 'political apathy' and deeper reflection on the ability of capitalism to 'meet consumer expectations while reproducing inequalities' (Macpherson, 1977: 102–106). While writing in the 1970s, Macpherson's commentary seems even more relevant today.

Macpherson's approach suggests that civic engagement and raising political consciousness is a central element in the realisation of a more just society. More especially, the discussion of roadblocks and loopholes emphasises the need to speak in differentiated terms when considering civic engagement. Participatory democracy or civic engagement, where elites are the only ones who participate will not address the deficits in liberal democracy. It will simply replicate existing power imbalances. While civic engagement has enjoyed a renewed level of interest in recent years, in reality, civic engagement has always taken place within, parallel to or even above, the democratic process and it has most often done so in favour of the economically more powerful, enabling narrowly focused individuals and interest groups to engage in 'rent seeking behaviour to gain rights, privileges and resources from the state' (Plant, 2004). It is worth remembering the conclusion from Chapter 2 where the American Political Science Association (2004: 1) identified how the 'advantaged roar with a clarity and consistency that policy-makers readily hear and routinely follow'. Such sentiments will undoubtedly resonate in the Ireland of today where such engagement and rent seeking behaviours have produced a culture of light regulation, corporate as well as individual greed. More egalitarian forms of civic engagement demand a rebalancing of influence, though it would be naïve to think that civic engagement fora alone will rebalance the influence of private capital within an increasingly market oriented country.

From a social justice perspective, a deeper commitment to civic engagement also has the potential to serve as a vehicle for at least some of Rawls' ambitions for a well ordered society and the basic structure, discussed in Chapter 2. Moreover it can signal a recognition that social justice is not just about income distribution or social integration into the labour market, it is also about having a say in decision-making and as such it addresses the empowerment/exclusion from decision-making elements identified in the UNCDF understanding of social exclusion, discussed in Chapter 3. Thus, civic engagement has the potential to impact on institutional configurations and dispositions by creating new channels of influence, most especially for those excluded from dialogue and deliberation. As a result, the opportunity to shape policy agendas in a different way emerges, though clearly this depends in no small part on the disposition both of elected representatives and officials.

Different ways of listening and hearing

When considering civic engagement as a tool of social justice, some quite fundamental behaviours have to be confronted, not least the capacity to listen and to hear. The essence of democratic participation and civic engagement requires not only the ability to have a voice but to have some chance that that voice will be listened to and heard. Only those who continue to defend an elitist ideal of democracy would at this stage say that periodic voting is anything other than a weak expression of voice. This perhaps is the greatest failing of contemporary liberal democracy. It rarely provides an outlet for citizens' voices, causing them to resort instead to an array of populist radio chat shows and increasingly to social media, to vent their frustrations. Civic engagement offers the potential to remedy this. However, for civic engagement to be real, democratic institutions, especially public administration, must create the conditions for citizens to express their views, be listened to (not least by officials) and listen to the views of others (Young, 2000). It also demands that a balance be struck between the voices of elected representatives and those of citizens and their organisations to ensure that the electoral primacy of the former does not in each and every case drown out the concerns of the latter. This in turn creates a challenge of accountability for civil society organisations, one that it has often found difficult to meet.

More fundamentally, civic engagement as a tool of social justice suggests an openness to hear different voices, particularly the voices of those who express themselves in language, tone and form that is outside the norm for public administration institutions. This is not to say that these voices are always right or that they possess some inherent wisdom, just that they need to be listened to on an equal par with others. Unfortunately, the tendency within public administration (and in democratic practice as a whole) is towards placing greater value on the expert and on his/her technical knowledge and language resulting in a situation where 'the ordinary citizen's voice has been drowned out and her participation in decisions and policies affecting the common good has been reduced to meaningless ritual' (Evans, 2000: 319). In this regard, what passes as 'articulateness' confers privilege on those who have enjoyed the benefits of access to education. An inherent element of such assumed articulateness is a capacity to 'express ourselves according to culturally specific norms of tone, grammar and diction' (Young, 2000). These privileged modes of expression are reinforced by expectations that political communication be free of passion and excess emotion, the presence of either of these indicating a lower level of political maturity or knowhow. In Young's view, this can only be changed by adopting a different view on political communication, where emphasis is placed on including different forms of communication and different arenas for communication. For example going out to where citizens gather, not always expecting citizens to come into formal settings; creating more informal settings for 'conversations' and shifting the balance of power in some cases, using neutral facilitators to do so. Put another way, 'participation means to be able to speak in one's own voice, thereby simultaneously constructing and expressing one's cultural identity through idiom and style' (Fraser, 1990).

Civic engagement dilemmas

Civic engagement has variously been described as complex, messy, difficult, time consuming, rewarding, frustrating and enriching. Within the contradictions embodied in these descriptions two pressing dilemmas are presented: the dilemma of matching rhetoric and reality and the dilemma of maintaining an independent civil society.

The dilemma of matching rhetoric and reality

Taking ownership of the language of participation and engagement and recognising it as an integral part of a more holistic approach to social justice undoubtedly presents challenges as well as opportunities for public administration. Unfortunately, much of the available evidence suggests that the translation of public participation rhetoric into meaningful and mutually satisfying citizen participation outcomes is far from simple (OECD, 2009). Addressing this challenge calls for a commitment to mainstream engagement within democratic institutions; the development of appropriate tools to evaluate engagement; greater use of technology and the design of situation specific participation mechanisms. In practice though, across a range of contexts, the reported experience of public participation has proved to be less than ideal. Recurring weaknesses in public participation include: inadequacy of attention to approach, structures, roles, processes, methods and resources; reliance on formalised structures such as fixed agendas, restricted discussion, speedy decision-making and the use of technical language. In addition, there is often an absence of genuine commitment to community involvement by officials; an excessive and unbalanced burden of expectations placed upon community representatives in terms of representation and accountability, inadequate recognition of diversity within communities; limited effort to monitor and evaluate and inadequate funding for community engagement processes (Burton et al., 2004). A further review of participation in the UK also concluded that participation was frequently used as a tool to achieve largely pre-decided outcomes and suggested that good examples of participation were difficult to find (Beresford and Hoban, 2005). Yet again this was confirmed in the Beyond the Ballot report produced for the UK Power Enquiry which pointed out the 'conflicting policy imperatives for public authorities, where government imposed targets and the need to demonstrate short term performance improvements typically take priority and therefore limit the potential for participation' (Smith, 2005: 106). Thus there are questions as to whether citizen engagement can make an impact on decision-making processes where, as seems to be the case, public bodies are reluctant to establish a stronger link between participation and decision-making.

It is not surprising then that citizens are sometimes a little wary about state sponsored consultation initiatives. As observed in Chapter 1 research produced for the Taskforce on Active Citizenship (2007: 9) noted 'there is cynicism and a lack of confidence in democratic and some other consultative structures, particularly at local level, with individuals and organisations not feeling that they are genuinely listened to'. Ironically, even more high profile national and highly formalised structures of engagement, such as the Irish corporatist social partnership process, may in fact have provided more of an avenue for civil servants negotiating on behalf of their own departmental agendas than it did for civil society actors seeking to influence policy directions (Connolly, 2007, Hardiman, 2006). This has led to suggestions that the anti-poverty agenda of activist civil society organisations has been consigned to a 'residual policy category, shaped primarily by the needs of macroeconomic policy' with the involvement of pro-poor actors in the negotiation process having 'no significant impact' (Connolly, 2007). Ireland is not unique in this however. An examination of participation in two Dutch cities, suggested that despite cosmetic support for the concept of participation, 'citizen participation in policy-making did not lead to a new division of roles between government and citizens in either cities' (Michels and De Graaf, 2010: 488). In the Dutch case also, Edelenbos (2005) concludes that existing political and administrative institutions have been slow to embrace new institutional configurations, observing a noticeable disassociation between the old and newer, 'proto institutions', not least due to resistance and cynicism from civil servants and some political actors. However, while observing this disconnect, there is little reported exploration of the reasons for resistance.

The dilemma of preserving an independent civil society
For civic engagement to take place and for democracy to deepen there is a need for citizens and civil society organisations alike to express their voices without fear of control, domination or recrimination. Civil society which acts as a compliant service delivery extension of the state does little to enhance democratic practice. Moreover, pseudo-engagement spaces, where participants are constrained, either by pre-determined agendas or by fear of losing favour or access to decision-making, do little to deepen democracy and a lot to further damage it. It is worth noting the words of Prionsias de Rossa, former Minister for Social Welfare on this issue. Speaking of the need to develop a more integrated process of social, economic and environmental development he stressed the need to

> re-imagine and reform the democratic process. Democratic reforms should build on the representative democracy which is deeply embedded in Europe, by encouraging the integration of a participative dimension, at local, regional, national and the European/International level. An integrated approach will require not only different policies by government, but different ways of doing government business at all levels in our society both at Dáil and local authority level. This requires deep reforms of our democratic institutions and ways of imagining ourselves as democrats. Such *reforms in my view will only be driven from 'outside' by civil society, not from within, although I am certain there will be many allies 'within' for such deep democratic reforms.* (de Rossa, 2006 emphasis added)

Without a largely independent civil society, due to funding or other institutional restrictions, the type of democratic reform agenda suggested by de Rossa is unlikely to be articulated. This echoes Dryzek (1996) who suggested that the motivation for democratisation has rarely if ever emanated from the state; rather, it is driven by civil society. The state, including public administration, will by default be content with the status quo or at least with some minor tinkering around the edges. Unfortunately, civil society, like public administration, is increasingly caught up in the war of ideas between New Public Administration and New Public Management and finds its autonomy increasingly squeezed. In particular many civil society organisations are now encouraged and/or required to deliver services on behalf of the state. A recent report from the UK concluded that 'Some voluntary organisations are undoubtedly facing a choice between closure and survival with sub-optimal funding or delivery arrangements that can threaten independence of voice, action or purpose' (Panel on the Indendence of the Voluntary Sector, 2012: 6). In this report six main threats to the independence of organisations were identified, all of which are equally applicable to Ireland. These threats were:

- the nature of models of statutory funding, in particular a move from grants to contract based funding;
- a declining ability to influence and shape decisions as a result of less engagement and openness from government;
- blurring of boundaries and perceptions between the voluntary sector, public administration and the private sector;
- self-censorship as a result of fear of losing funding: 'There is always a potential chilling effect when organisations that need to have an advocacy role receive funding from those responsible for policy and decision-making in that area. Fear of losing funding, now or in the future, can be a real threat to independence of voice' (2012: 20);
- threats to the independent management of voluntary sector organisations, not least due to the requirements of state contracts; and finally,
- the absence of strong safeguards to protect voluntary sector organisations.

An earlier report on the independence of the community and voluntary sector in Ireland also identified some of these concerns reporting the 'strong perception that it is difficult to criticise, that criticism is not welcomed or wanted and that there is less tolerance of dissenting voices. From this perspective, the state's interest in listening appears to be fading and indeed a number of participants referenced being "pulled up" by senior civil servants for criticising government policy' (Newman, 2011: 17). Equally, officials are reported as emphasising constraints on public funding and the likely prioritisation of front line services over advocacy activities. While the Irish report did not explicitly name the six challenges identified later in the UK, all six themes are present. How then does this square with the assertion in the Putting People First White Paper that 'at the centre of democracy is the participation of citizens in public life and their right to influence the decisions that affect their lives and communities. Open and inclusive policy-making increases public participation, enhances transparency and accountability, and builds civic capacity' (Government of Ireland, 2012a). It is not clear how open and inclusive policy-making or transparency, or accountability or civic capacity is built by the exercise of stronger state control over civil society organisations.

The experience of the Community Development Programme in Ireland is a case in point. This programme, at its peak in 2005, funded over 180 local and independent Community Development Projects (CDPs) with a specific anti-poverty focus and a local management structure. By 2012, following a series of decisions taken by the responsible parent department, the Department of Community, Rural and Gaeltacht Affairs, all bar a small number of projects were subsumed into the state and EU funded local development companies. The rationale for ending the programme of support for independent community organisations was largely constructed on the grounds of duplication and funding cutbacks. However, there is little indication that the responsible civil servants were aware of, mindful of or even vaguely concerned about the importance of maintaining state support for independent local civil society organisations, nor that they even understood such concepts. Thus, in the case of the Community Development Programme:

- the nature of the funding relationship has changed and has become primarily defined by service delivery;
- the advocacy capacity of the former CDPs has been severely curtailed and projects are restricted on the amount of time allowed for advocacy within new results based planning obligations;
- institutional boundaries have been completely obscured as formerly independent civil society organisations have been brought under the control of local development companies, though at least some of these have made efforts to retain as much independence as possible for the former CDPs. More worryingly, as local development companies are themselves brought more closely under the control of local government, the former CDPs will soon have to operate in an environment of more direct state control;
- self-censorship to protect funding is already anecdotally reported;
- in most cases, independent management companies have been disbanded; and finally,
- community sector organisations had little if any say in the design of their new funding arrangements, indicating that there were virtually no safeguards to protect community or voluntary sector organisations.

This programme is just one example of how the independence of civil society can be undermined by the state and, if it is accepted that a strong civil society is a crucial part of a healthy democracy, its termination is arguably an anti-democratic act. Moreover, from a social justice standpoint it is arguable that the state has a particular obligation to provide resources to ensure that the democratic voice and capacity for engagement by those who are most marginalised is supported to emerge, as per the idea of associative democracy discussed earlier. Whether government and administration is willing to support such a project is, of course, a not insignificant dilemma.

Civic engagement and the implications for public administration

So far in this chapter, the language of participation and engagement has been explored, the relationship between social justice and civic engagement has been discussed and some of the inherent dilemmas and difficulties in civic engagement have been raised. Within this there are specific implications for public administration. While civic engagement is much written about it is less common for the specific role and contribution of public administration to be highlighted. This is not to say that public administration is always the source of success or failure or success of civic engagement, just that its role is pivotal for a number of important reasons.

The different roles of public administration in civic engagement

Public administration plays many different roles in relation to civic engagement and of course how these are delivered varies greatly from institution to institution. The roles include:

1 *Defining the frameworks for civic engagement.* While politicians may determine whether or at what level civic engagement may happen, invariably public officials have a major role in shaping the mechanics of engagement. For example, in the case of the various processes put in place in Ireland following on from the White Paper on Better Local Government (Government of Ireland, 1996), the details of how they were to operate was not determined by politicians but mainly by officials.

2 *Operating the civic engagement machinery.* In most cases public administration provides the on-going, regular interface between the state and civil society and individual citizen participants. Officials are most often on the front line of civic engagement and in some cases contribute time and energy that goes well beyond what could be reasonably expected. However, in other cases civic engagement can be an uncomfortable space to occupy. Where such discomfort occurs, it is often exacerbated by the expectation that officials can simply take on civic engagement responsibil-

ities, usually directed from elsewhere, without any appropriate training or capacity building. Equally though, officials themselves may not recognise their need for such capacity building (Government of Scotland, 2008) and may assume that capacity deficiencies exist only amongst participating citizens and/or their organisations.

3 *Determining who to engage with.* In more formally structured civic engagement processes officials often set the criteria for who should or should not be invited or involved, sometimes in conjunction with politicians, sometimes not. For example, the 2012 'Putting People First' Local Government White Paper continues to emphasise the role of local community and voluntary fora as the channel through which community representatives will be selected to participate on various local structures (Government of Ireland, 2012a). These structures were designed by officials in the wake of the 1996 Better Local Government White Paper as a one size fits all solution to be applied in all parts of the country. The continued reliance on these fora is despite the fact that many of them have limited capacity, are supported with paltry resources and are not always suitable to facilitate the emergence of the voice of more marginalised groups. Past research on the role of community fora as a vehicle for participation raised concerns about their potential to enable elite capture of participation opportunities (Cosgrave and KW Research Associates, 2007). This in turn requires consideration of the need for more distinct organisational spaces to draw representation for marginalised or 'subordinated public groups' (Fraser, 1990).

4 *Deciding who is listened to and who is heard.* Just because an engagement opportunity is afforded, there is no guarantee that the opinions of all participants will be equally valued and listened to, thereby creating a hierarchy of participants, with some 'insiders' realistically remaining as 'outsiders'. For example, within national level social partnership there was a general agreement that the core relationships were between government, employer organisations and trade unions, while relationships with farming organisations and the community and voluntary pillar were seen as less important.

5 *Determining how different groups are listened to.* In some cases, officials may insist on highly formalised and rigid approaches within fixed and inflexible rules; they may react only to inputs they deem to be sufficiently knowledgeable and expert, in the process missing important wisdom and experience and they may discount the value of emotion. More seriously though, as discussed above, they may already have their mind made up and approach listening only as an exercise to seek sources of agreement and validation of predetermined decisions.

6 *Allocation and withdrawal of resources.* Officials have a key role in

determining the allocation of resources to civic engagement processes. Civic engagement is resource intensive, as much in human capital as in financial costs. This may include staff resources to facilitate engagement, support for capacity building, funding for external facilitation or funding for organisations such as the CDPs, which in some cases at least have played a very significant role in enabling direct citizen engagement (McInerney, 2006). As a result, continued reference to civic engagement in policy documents is largely meaningless if not accompanied by appropriate resources and suggest little more than tokenism.

7 *Managing and mediating access to decision-makers in the political and administrative systems.* Officials will often play a role in facilitating access to key decision-makers in the political and administrative systems. Opportunities may be easily provided for some, particularly the more powerful, while denied or delayed for others, often the less organised and articulate.

8 *Enthusiastic engagement or reluctant participants.* Finally, just as some officials may embrace civic engagement processes, others may well oppose their operation, possibly seeing them as anti-democratic (in more traditional elitist terms) or as an intrusion into existing decision-making procedures. If such opposition exists at senior level in an institution it has the potential to send signals to more junior staff that any investment of time and energy into civic engagement is neither necessary nor welcomed. While it is unlikely in the current environment that such opposition will be openly stated, its more passive forms may be even more damaging.

All of these different roles place public administration in a pivotal position when it comes to the level and nature of civic engagement that is undertaken. Despite the fact that its importance to the future of public administration in Ireland has been highlighted on a regular basis (Boyle and Humphreys, 2001, Boyle, 2009, Boyle and MacCarthaigh, 2011) there is little discussion of the barriers towards civic engagement nor of how officials can be supported to play a more meaningful role in deepening democratic participation, in particular, how a deeper disposition towards participation could be engendered.

Towards engagement: deepening disposition
In Chapter 2 the broader question of individual and institutional disposition towards social justice was raised. To get to the point where civic engagement is a natural and recognised part of the democratic context and where all of the above roles can be approached by public administration in a positive and facilitative way, disposition is the key variable. If officials operate from a favourable disposition towards civic engagement, then routes have, can and will be found, even if resources are scarce. The case study on regeneration in

Tralee in Chapter 7 will illustrate this more clearly. Drawing from the discussion in Chapter 1 of variants of responsiveness within public administration; the discussions on the understandings social justice in Chapter 2 and the reflections on participatory democracy and its relationship with social justice above, it is possible to construct a framework to aid an understanding of disposition within civic engagement practice. This framework considers three dispositional variables that are likely to determine the nature of civic engagement outcomes: the disposition towards deepening democracy; a disposition about the nature of public administration (PA) responsiveness; and, finally, the nature of the disposition towards social justice.

The framework speaks, firstly, in terms of disposition towards deeper democracy and the nature of public administration responsiveness, what could be called two-dimensional (2-D) participation and suggests that the interplay between these two variables is likely to produce a number of different but predictable configurations of civic engagement. It then adds the additional element of social justice disposition to produce a three-dimensional (3-D) model of participation, which again produces a number of possible configurations.

Participation in two dimensions (2-D): democratic disposition and public administration responsiveness
Taking democratic disposition and public administration responsiveness first, Figure 4.1 illustrates that a variety of possible participation outcomes may be

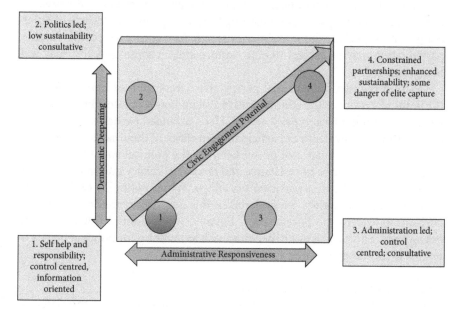

Figure 4.1 Two-D civic engagement

generated depending on the democratic disposition and the level of public administration responsiveness. For example, in circumstances where there is limited openness towards deepening understandings of democracy (from more elitist towards more participatory expressions) and where public administration remains largely control centred, democratic participation is most likely to be restricted to electoral participation, possibly accompanied by an encouragement of individual and community responsibility (type 1). In such circumstances, the notion of active citizenship is likely to be limited to citizens taking responsibility for the delivery of services in their own communities and civic engagement will be limited to information provision with little prospect of feedback. It can be anticipated that there will be little if any systemic change and no shift in the existing balance of decision-making power.

By contrast, where there is a willingness to deepen understandings of democratic participation and where officials are willing to move beyond control centred approaches there is a stronger likelihood of expanded and more collaborative participation opportunities (type 4). In this case, regular and more meaningful citizen participation processes become an integral part of the democratic and administrative experience, requiring systemic change, adjustment in the balance of decision-making power and associated capacity building. However, even with a degree of democratic deepening and openness to more deliberative responsiveness, there is some danger that the depth of such participation may not always extend beyond the purposive, i.e. meeting functional, instrumental objectives. Equally, it may not recognise the need for differentiated participation, i.e. ensuring the participation of a variety of different groups, especially the more marginalised. As a consequence, this form of participation may be subject to elite capture and, in some case, this may well be encouraged.

Within the two-dimensional perspective, circumstances may arise where the political system or the administrative system may separately initiate citizen participation initiatives (types 2 and 3). Here, extended participation may also occur. However, the depth of participation in either of these cases is likely to be constrained by the balance of power between the political and administrative systems and the degree of resistance and territorial rivalry that may overtly or covertly act to undermine participatory efforts. Where politically or democratically motivated initiatives are undertaken this may well represent an effort to curb the power of the bureaucracy. Equally, where administratively driven engagement efforts take place they may seek to make up for political inertia or poor representational delivery.

Three-dimensional participation (3-D)
When the third, social justice dispositional variable is added, the potential for and challenge of deeper and more meaningful participation emerges

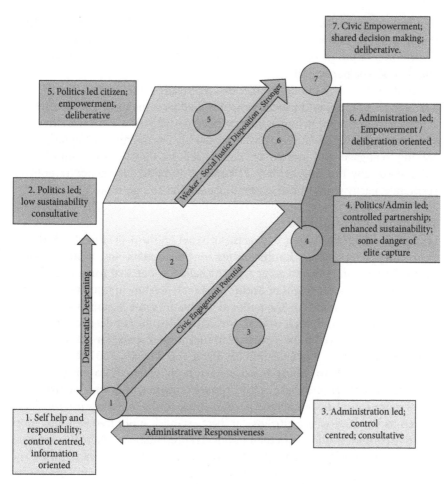

Figure 4.2 Three-D civic engagement

(Figure 4.2). Building on the two-dimensional model, this 3-D experience suggests that a stronger disposition towards social justice, allied with a commitment to deepen democracy and strong public administration responsiveness is likely to produce a model of civic engagement (type 7) that operates from a commitment to civic empowerment, shared decision-making/co-governance and differentiated participation. In this case, a social justice disposition would recognise the role of empowerment in addressing injustice and inequality and would acknowledge the need for system level change alongside measures to address redistribution, unemployment and personal responsibility. Thus, civic engagement is seen to involve significant changes in the level of control of decision-making authority and power. However, this is undoubtedly one of the more complex areas to resolve as there is little likelihood that all actors within the democratic and/or administrative domains will share a common social justice orientation or that they will see the relationship between social justice and democratic participation.

In the same way as in the 2-D model, politically led initiatives (type 5) with a stronger commitment to social justice will address the need to confront elite capture through more strongly differentiated participation. However, they may still encounter administrative resistance, overtly or covertly, particularly when seeking to engage with more marginalised groups. Equally, an administration led and socially just engagement orientation (type 6) may generate political resistance, partly from fear of generating electoral competition.

The significance of the local

Generating progressive civic engagement based on the 3-D variables of democratic deepening, public administration responsiveness and a strong social justice disposition is always going to be a challenge; one that some might say is unachievable. While it might be argued that such pessimism is justifiable within larger democratic units e.g. the national polity, the same arguments cannot be as easily made at local level. Indeed, for many advocates of deeper democracy, the local is considered to be a particularly important space for action (Barber, 1984, Warren, 1996, Parkinson, 2003, Fung and Wright, 2001, Macpherson, 1977, Pateman, 1970). Many reasons have been advanced to emphasise the importance of the local sphere as the primary domain within which citizens can enjoy more complete democratic participation. In the first instance, the 'local' is seen as the level where citizens can best establish more frequent and more effective communication with their political representatives, where the potential for accountability by elected representatives and officials can be maximised and where the complexities-of-scale arguments against citizen participation can be most effectively rebutted. These complexities of scale have been identified as amongst the most difficult to overcome in efforts to build stronger participation in decision-making It should not be surprising then that within the literature on participation emphasis is often placed on the role of the local state as opposed to a more powerful, centralised state. For example, J. S. Mill considered universal suffrage and participation at national level to be of little value 'if the individual has not been prepared for this participation at local level. It is at this level he learns to govern himself' (Mill in Pateman, 1970: 30). Commenting on the challenges posed by the complexity of mass society, Barber suggests that the 'conservatives appreciation of community and the democrats' attachment to participation meet in the strong democrats idea of direct political activity which commences with immediate and local forms of government' (Barber, 1984: 248). Others too suggest that highly centralised systems, such as in the UK, offer little opportunity for citizens to exert influence over politicians. As a result, increased citizen control requires 'the institutionalisation of two way voice channels of influence between political leaders and citizens. For practical reasons it is only possible to establish such two way voice channels at the local level' (Sorenson, 1997: 563). Thus, to begin to make progress on the admittedly difficult challenges of civic engagement, a stronger focus on the local level would appear to be an obvious route. This is necessary, now more than ever, as a result of the introduction of a local property charge. Stronger forms of civic engagement may well be one way of reconnecting local government more strongly with citizens in a way that makes greater sense of a move towards local taxation.

Conclusions

In this chapter the role of public administration in supporting civic engagement was addressed. From this a number of conclusions can be drawn. Firstly, within the increasing emphasis on civic engagement, which is visible in Ireland and internationally, the public administration system has little choice but to play a central role in initiatives to do with citizen participation. Public administration is a core democratic institution and frequently is the designer and operator of civic engagement processes. However, the nature of how it plays such a role continues to be open to question and considerable amounts of research, in Ireland and elsewhere, suggests that it struggles to turn the rhetoric of civic engagement into deep and meaningful participation experiences. Secondly, it is possible that one of the reasons for this may be a failure to more fully understand the language of participation and engagement and to recognise that within this language are a host of implications for behaviour and delivery. This is particularly true if public administration is to operate from a social justice standpoint, requiring it to pay greater attention to who participates, how they participate and how they are listened to. It also challenges officials to resist the loud voices of the powerful and to seek out the perspectives of those who experience exclusion, inequality and injustice. Finally, this chapter has argued that underpinning any role for public administration in civic engagement must be a renewed commitment to explore and adjust both individual and institutional disposition towards participation. This requires reflection on the nature of democracy; on responsiveness within public administration and on the realisation that social justice not only requires the state to provide welfare but also to be conscious of the need for systemic change and individual as well as community empowerment.

Note

1 A more detailed explanation of the main features of Empowered Deliberative Democracy is included in the discussion of the final case study in Chapter 7.

5

The evolution of public administration in Ireland

Introduction

Having explored some of the broader challenges facing public administration in Ireland and having discussed some of the conceptual elements of the relationship between public administration and social justice, attention now turns to practice of public administration in Ireland and its engagement with social justice issues. To set a context for this, this chapter first looks at the evolution and main characteristics of public administration in Ireland, highlighting particular elements that may impact on its willingness or otherwise to embrace a stronger social justice orientation. The intention here is not to present a detailed description of evolution of the Irish system of public administration; this has been more comprehensively done elsewhere (Barrington, 1980, Dooney and O'Toole, 1992, Boyle, 2007, Devlin et al., 1969). Instead, this chapter establishes what is meant by public administration and recaps on the evolution of public administration in Ireland from the inheritance of the extant system in 1922 up to more recent change processes, including the substantial reduction in public sector numbers.

Historical evolution

The general assumption is that Ireland, on achieving independence, inherited its system of public administration largely intact from the pre-existing British system, resulting in only limited administrative disruption. For many years, it is suggested, this system remained largely immune to any significant change (Dooney, 1976). When therefore, in 1922, approximately 21,000 civil servants transferred service to the newly independent state, administrative capacity was largely maintained. As noted by the final report of the Commission of Inquiry into the Civil Service 1932–1935:

> The passing of the State services into the control of a native Government, however revolutionary it may have been as a step in the political development of the nation, entailed, broadly speaking, no immediate disturbance of any fundamental kind in

the daily work of the average Civil Servant. Under changed masters the same main tasks of administration continued to be performed by the same staffs on the same general lines of organisation and procedure. (cited in Chubb, 1970: 232)

It has generally been suggested that this undisturbed transition represented an important 'asset' for the new state though it may also be that case that this undisturbed transition tempered the idealism of the independence movement. Thus, the potentially positive elements of administrative disruption were lost and instead existing systemic weaknesses were maintained. In this regard Barrington (1980) notes how the tendency within the British civil service for short-term planning was one of the weaknesses carried forward into the new state's administrative system, one that has been frequently commented upon since. The new state's departmental system has been well recorded and commented upon since its establishment in the 1924 Ministers and Secretaries Act, in which the Minister was 'declared to be a corporation sole under his style and name as set out in the Act' (Devlin et al., 1969: 12). This laid the foundation for the legal, decision-making primacy of the responsible minister and, it is widely agreed, furthered preoccupation with matters of short term political priority as opposed to longer term strategic thinking at the top levels of the civil service. Effectively, responsibility for government and decision was vested in the different ministers, thereby creating the basis for government departments to become almost as focused on the needs of the Minister as they were on the execution of policy. It is suggested that few ministers and only 'exceptional' civil servants were able to break out of this mode of doing business (Barrington, 1980).

During the first quarter century following independence, described as the 'emergent phase' (1922–1947) of state development (MacCarthaigh, 2012: 7), the largely fixed nature of public administration is generally observed. During this time the main focus of attention was on the operation of the core government departments and the primacy of politics over administration: 'A conservative approach to administration and explicit exclusion of public servants from politics resulted in considerable emphasis on demarcation between political and administrative spheres' (MacCarthaigh, 2012: 8). However it is interesting to note Devlin's observation about a significant policy shift in 1932 towards welfare provision and associated impacts on public administration:

There was a change in the emphasis of national policy following the change of government in 1932. The new Government was committed to increased housing and social welfare programmes and, in the old Sinn Fein tradition, to industrial development aimed at self-sufficiency; it also shared in the world-wide trend towards State action as a remedy for the Great Depression. The new policies involved an expansion in the role and in the personnel of the civil service as the State moved into the fields of industrial promotion and social welfare and, at the same time, the state-sponsored body device came increasingly to be used as an instrument of government executive action. (Devlin et al., 1969: 14)

In the years that followed, protectionism gradually gave way to a new economic outlook, necessitating a change of role of the state and of public administration, not least in its relationship with the political system. This is described by MacCarthaigh as the 'development phase' (1948–1970) during which a stronger policy-making capacity began to emerge. The end of this period also saw the publication of the Devlin Report, the Public Services Organisation Review Group (Devlin et al., 1969) which still provides a starting point for virtually all contemporary discussion on public sector reform in Ireland (Devlin et al., 1969), albeit much of it bemoaning the lack of political commitment to any real, extensive reform process. The subsequent 'modernisation' phase (1971–1990) began a period of considerable change, at least some of it inspired by a move towards coalition governments in which political legacies were created as much by the establishment of new bureaucratic structures as they were by distinct policy proposals and associated policy outcomes (MacCarthaigh, 2012). The other key influence on the public service during this time was of course Ireland's entry into the European Community, a juncture that has not been adequately explored in terms of its impact on the disposition and values of administration in Ireland. This had a number of immediate effects. Irish civil servants were increasingly exposed to the functioning of other approaches to public administration and policy-making, not least those of the European Commission. In addition, the public administration system was required to engage with, transpose and implement a whole range of policy directions, laws and regulations emanating from Europe, not least those advancing an equality agenda. Finally, the very nature of the public sector itself had to change, one obvious area being the increased participation by women as a result of the removal of the archaic marriage bar which had required women to resign from the public sector if they got married.

MacCarthaigh's final phase of development of public administration runs from 1991 to 2008 and is described as the 'management and reform' period. This period is characterised by a sharp rise in the number of new public sector bodies created, again reflecting the priorities of a series of coalition governments. A number of notable initiatives emerged from this period, including the Strategic Management Initiative (1994), Delivering Better Government (1996), the Better Local Government White Paper (1996) and others. However, while this is described as a period of management and reform, in reality there was very little by way of deeper systemic change in the organisation of public administration. This was particularly obvious in the failure to undertake any significant reforms of local government despite the publication of numerous reports and policy statements on the issue during the period. Roughly paralleling the 'management and reform' phase it is worth adding a 'relational phase', to describe the accelerated processes of engagement with civil society organisations formalised in the first instance in the 1987 social partnership process and extended across a range of other national and local level domains over the following 20 years. During this time a variety of relational experiments – collaborations, networks and partnerships – were initiated, some more successful than others, some more deeply embedded, others more transitory. The beginning of the end of this phase can be associated with the early years of the recession in 2008 and with a more full-bodied retreat from partnership pursued following the election of the Fine Gael/Labour government in 2011.

The functions of public administration

According to Barrington (1980: 1) 'Public administration must be one of the oldest professions. It has acted as the handmaid of government as long as government itself has existed, that is for many thousands of years. Despite its age not a great deal is known about the subject.' In clarifying what is meant by public administration, Barrington usefully distinguishes between the term 'the government' – meaning the ministers who are appointed in accordance with the Constitution and who are charged with governing the country – and 'government' which is concerned with 'the processes by which the "the Government" discharges its duties and responsibilities'. In the cases of the latter, the key actors within 'the government' are the elected representatives and of course those who are permanent or otherwise contracted officials (Barrington, 1980). The 'permanent' nature of public administration is frequently a source of comment, with Dooney (1976: 12) suggesting that there is something of a paradox in this, in that the civil service is at one and the same time the permanent servant of the state and also the servant of the administration which is for the time being in power. This potentially raises a conundrum for officials should their service obligations to the state in some way come into conflict with their service obligations to the government, as has been discussed in Chapter 1. Barrington (1980: 3) also emphasises that 'public administration is the system through which politics is transformed into governmental action', though the relationships involved in this process of transformation are not as linear as might be suggested. While there is a tendency in some quarters to include agencies substantially funded by state resources, such as civil society organisations contracted to provide services, such organisations are not considered here as part of the public administration system.

The nature and scope of the role of public administration is to a large extent related to the role and vision of the state in any given jurisdiction. In the type of minimalist state discussed in Chapter 2 the role of public administration is inevitably limited; whereas in an activist state, its range of functions will broaden, as expectations expand about how the state should act to promote the general welfare and liberties of its citizens. Since independence in 1922, the nature of the state's involvement in a variety of areas of social, economic and cultural development has evolved and grown in complexity, in the process requiring a parallel shift in the nature and role of its bureaucratic infrastructure. Thus, public administration has played and/or continues to play a central role in:

- providing advice to government on policy alternatives across a range of policy areas;
- implementing policies agreed by government;
- developing the laws which govern the country's operation and ensuring that these laws are enforced and sanctions are applied against those who breach them;
- supporting the financial management of the state, particularly revenue raising and mobilisation and expenditure elements;
- designing and operating a range of welfare services, such as health, education, housing, social protection etc.;
- facilitating economic development, either through direct involvement in economic activity such as the establishment of a range of commercial and non-commercial state agencies or indirectly though the development of stimulus measures, including incentives, advice and other supports;
- facilitating ministers to carry out their functions, not least acting as 'the eyes and ears' of the Minister (Dooney, 1976) in an effort to avoid political embarrassment;
- designing and overseeing a range of regulatory bodies and functions;
- supporting a variety of interfaces between state infrastructure and its citizens;
- relating to officials within the administrative systems of other countries, particularly at an EU level;
- supporting the maintenance of a range of external relationships.

Public administration therefore is deeply engaged, in one way or another, with virtually every facet of the nation's daily living. As a result it not only exerts considerable influence on both national and local development but also is a potentially powerful platform for change.

Levels of public administration

There are a variety of different levels of public administration in Ireland. In the first instance, a distinction can be drawn between the national civil service and the broader public service. Within this, the civil service itself can be further divided into the civil service of the state and the civil service of the government. This arises from a Supreme Court judgment in 1958 (*McLoughlin v. The Minister for Finance*) which concluded that an official in the Attorney General's Office is a servant of the state and not of the government (Dooney, 1976).

The civil service of the state includes the staff of: the Office of the President, the Houses of the Oireachtas, the Central Statistics Office, the Office of the Comptroller and Auditor General, the Courts Service, the Director of Public Prosecutions (DPP); the Office of the Attorney General, the Office of Public Works (OPW); the Office of the Information Commissioner and the Office of the Ombudsman. In order to preserve the independence of these offices, officials within them are not seen as being under the direction of the elected government of the day, though in some cases at least, the clear spaces between the administrative and political worlds is somewhat blurred, for example in the OPW and the Revenue Commissioners. The civil service of the government includes those employed within national government departments. Currently, Ireland has 16 government departments an increase from the 11 created under the original 1924 Ministers and Secretaries Act. However, there are currently only 15 ministers with the Department of Justice and Equality and the Department of Defence having the same minister. Beyond this, the wider public service includes staff of local government, the Gardai, defence forces and a host of commercial and non-commercial state agencies. Generally speaking, those employed in the broader public service staff are more directly involved in delivering policy and in provision of a variety of services including local government services, health, education and training, security and defence.

As a consequence of the economic crisis, there is considerable pressure to reduce the numbers employed in the public administration system. The current public service reform plan aims to reduce the numbers (i.e. whole time equivalents) employed in the public service to 282,500 by 2015 from a high of over 320,000 in 2008 (Department of Public Expenditure and Reform, 2011). However, the actual number of individual employees in the public service is substantially higher. As shown in Table 5.1 in the first quarter of 2012, the

Table 5.1 Changes in public sector employment, 2008–2012 (CSO)

	2008Q4	2012Q1	Change	% change
Civil service	42,700	39,800	−2,900	−6.8
Defence	11,200	9,100	−2,100	−18.8
Garda Siochana	15,300	13,700	−1,600	−10.5
Education	120,500	111,500	−9,000	−7.5
Regional bodies	40,200	33,500	−6,700	−16.7
Health	139,600	127,200	−12,400	−8.9
Semi-state	57,800	51,500	−6,300	−10.9
Total public sector including semi state bodies	427,300	386,300	−41,000	−9.6
Total public sector excluding semi state bodies	369,500	334,800	−34,700	−9.4

Source: Adapted from CSO (2012a) Earnings Hours and Employment Cost Survey Quarterly.

Table 5.2 Changes in public sector employment using whole time equivalents

	2008	2012	Change	% change
	Qtr 4	Qtr 1		
Civil Service	39,313	36,190	−3,123	−7.9
Defence sector	11,265	9,553	−1,712	−15.2
Education sector	95,024	90,830	−4,194	−4.4
Health sector	111,025	102,811	−8,215	−7.4
Justice sector	15,692	13,622	−2,070	−13.2
Local authorities	35,008	28,576	−6,432	−18.4
Non-commercial state agencies	13,060	10,772	−2,288	−17.5
Total	320,387	292,354	−28,034	−8.7

Source: Department of Public Expenditure and Reform, 2013.

CSO estimated that 386300 people were employed in the public sector, including semi-state bodies (CSO, 2012a). When semi-state bodies are excluded the figure for public sector employment drops to 334,800. This compares to 427,300 and 369,500 respectively in quarter four of 2008, indicating that there has been an overall drop in the numbers employed in the public sector of 9.6% when semi state bodies are included and 9.4% when semi states are excluded. Clearly employment in all sections of the public sector is not declining at the same rate, with defence and regional bodies showing the highest level of decline and education and the core civil service the lowest. Of those employed in 2012, 39,800 are employed in the civil service and the largest cohort of 127,200 is employed in the health sector.[1]

By contrast with the CSO, the Department of Public Expenditure and Reform uses whole time equivalents as the basis for calculation instead of actually employed individuals. According to this method the broader public service, employed 320,387 and 292,354 full time equivalents at the end at the end of 2008 and in the first quarter on 2012 respectively, as illustrated in Table 5.2. However, it includes non-commercial state bodies only, as opposed to the broader semi-state classification used by the CSO. Nevertheless, the trends in employment reduction remain broadly comparable, with smaller changes in the core civil service by comparison with defence, justice and local government.

In terms of the numbers employed in the public service, the OECD has previously commented that the level of employment in the Irish public sector 'is relatively low compared with other OECD countries and significantly less than the level of public employment in Norway, Sweden, France, Finland and Belgium' (OECD, 2008b: 63). The relatively low level of public sector employment noted by the OECD taken in conjunction with subsequent reductions in public sector numbers has clear implications for the capacity of the state to maintain high quality levels of service provision to its citizens. More especially, the significant reduction in the broader public service outside of the civil service, including agencies and local government, will have a particular impact on the state's relational capacity.

Sub-national public administration

As is evident from the figures above there is a substantial public administration presence at regional but more especially at local levels. This is significant as it represents much of the state's day to day interface with the public. At regional level, there are currently eight regional authorities and two regional assemblies, In reality however, these regional level bodies have had a limited range of responsibilities and an even lower level of public visibility. The regional authorities were established in 1994, on foot of 1991 Local Government Act, to play a role in policy co-ordination and monitoring of EU structural funds. In recent times they have been involved in the development of regional planning guidelines and regional economic and social strategies which local authorities are expected to take account of within their planning processes. Membership of the authorities is limited to elected representatives, nominated by constituent local authorities who are also collectively responsible for funding the authority's activities. Regional assemblies, membership of which is drawn from the regional authorities, were subsequently established in 1999, not to fulfil any particular desire to include a regional tier of government in Ireland, but to facilitate and manage on-going access to EU structural funds following Agenda 2000. However, following the publication of the 'Putting People First' White Paper on local government reform, the regional authorities and the regional assemblies will now be rationalised into just three regional assemblies 'to perform a range of strategic functions' in a reconfigured set of regions, namely: Connacht-Ulster; a Southern region, including all Munster counties alongside Carlow, Kilkenny and Wexford; and an Eastern-Midland region, including the remaining Leinster counties (Government of Ireland, 2012a: 89).

The administration of local government

A more significant level of sub-national public administration exists at a county and in some cases, sub-county level. Currently, Ireland is divided into 34 primary local government areas, 29 counties and 5 cities, each of which has its own local authority bureaucracy and representatives elected by the local population. Below these, a further 80 towns elect town councils to perform a more limited range of functions. Significant changes in the configuration of local government have however been proposed in the Putting People First White Paper, merging some local authorities (Waterford City and County) and abolishing town councils. In the case of town councils their representative function will be transferred to a system of municipal district committees, though without a distinct administrative capacity (Government of Ireland, 2012a).

In terms of their functional responsibilities local government in Ireland is generally characterised as limited by comparison with most other European countries (Quin, 2003, O'Broin and Waters, 2007). These responsibilities include housing and building; road transportation and safety; water supply and sewage; development incentives and control (planning); environmental protection; recreation and amenity; agriculture, education, health and welfare; and miscellaneous services. However in the case of education and health and welfare, local authorities have a minor involvement, generally involving the nomination of public representatives onto various committees and/or fora (O'Sullivan, 2003).

In its review of the Irish public sector in 2008, the OECD drew attention to the relatively large share of total government expenditure which is spent at local level, which, at 44% in 2005 was 'comparable with Scandinavian countries and with Japan, Korea, Spain and the Netherlands' (OECD, 2008b: 67). However the OECD did comment on the absence of local taxation and its impact on the scope of local government (OECD, 2008b: 69). Clearly the introduction of the household charge in 2012 and the property tax in 2013 addresses this though their impact remains to be seen. However, the situation remains that local government in Ireland has little power and, what power there is, remains largely concentrated in the executive, i.e. the county/city manager (soon to be retitled Chief Executive Officer) not with elected representatives. There is little disagreement that local government is subject to strong central control from the Department of the Environment, Community and Local Government, the suggestion often being made that the local executive pays a lot more attention to the national department than to local politicians. This leads to assertions that the local government system is, in reality, less of a local government system and more of local administration system.

Legislative frameworks

The operation of public administration in Ireland is governed by a variety legislative instruments, the impact of which is significant, not least because they provide a significant source of values for officials (Van Wart, 1998). In Ireland the Ministers and Secretaries Act, 1924 and its 15 subsequent amendments is one of the most significant pieces of public sector legislation, described by the Devlin Report as:

> a radically new conception of the administration of the public business. Before the Treaty, the main feature of the Irish Administration had been the existence of a large number of independent Boards of Commissioners for the execution of large blocks of executive work. Under the new system these blocks were transferred to the direct control of Ministers ... the Minister is in essence the Department; he is a corporation sole and apart from two limitations a distinct autonomous entity. (Devlin et al., 1969: 21)

It could be argued that the establishment of government departments so powerfully vested in the personality (legal and otherwise) of the minister has laid the basis not only for an administrative structure dedicated to protecting the minister, but for a widely acknowledged weakness for joined up thinking, co-ordination and co-operation. The later amendments of the Act addressed a variety of issues, including the establishment of specific departments,[2] appointments of up to 20 Ministers of State and delegation of functions from Ministers to Ministers of State and defining the meaning of a public service body. In terms of renewing the civil and public sector, the 1973 Ministers and Secretaries (Amendment) Act (Government of Ireland, 1973), took on board the recommendations of the Devlin report and provided for the establishment of a Department of the Public Service and a supporting Public Service Advisory Council, to be appointed by the Minister. However, while the Amendment provided for separate department and a Minister for the Public Service, the enabling legislation stipulated that the Minister of Finance would also be responsible for the Department of the Public Service. Interestingly, at the time of its introduction, the then Minister for Finance presented a clear rationale for its establishment as a distinct department, citing the need to ensure that the needs of public service management would not be 'subordinate' to the 'financial and economic responsibilities of the Department of Finance'. The rationale for the Department was also clearly set out and its role in supporting the 'renewal of the public service' as its first priority was emphasised (Dooney, 1976: 127). The recent establishment of a Department of Public Expenditure and Reform in some way echoes the dedicated focus on the public service, though in the latter case the primacy of public expenditure control clearly drives the public services reform agenda. As a result, the motivation to consider the renewal of the civil and public service as a national resource is somewhat restrained.

Recruitment in the early days of the new Irish republic was governed by the Civil Service Regulations Act. This and subsequent amendments set out how civil servants were to be recruited and managed and sought to ensure the development of a transparent, merit based system through which a non-politicised, public service appointment system would be established. More recently, the Public Services Management Act, 1997 (Government of Ireland, 1997a) has been described by the OECD as 'enhancing the management, effectiveness and transparency of departments and offices and to put in place mechanisms for the increased accountability of public servants'. This Act requires that all departments produce a statement of strategy and requires an annual report on this. Such a strategy statement should be renewed every three years (ibid.: Section 4.1.b.iii). Responsibility for the development of the Strategy rests with 'the Secretary General of a Department or Head of a Scheduled Office, as the case may be'. It is also clearly stated that the preparation of the Strategy shall be 'subject to the determination of matters of policy by the Minister of the

Government'. The role and content of departmental strategy statements are returned to in the next chapter.

Beyond the centre, articulation of the role of local government in Ireland has been significantly enhanced by the passing of Local Government Act in 2001 (Government of Ireland, 2001). This Act addresses a range of issues including local government elections, the functions of local authorities, local authority financial procedures, committee structures to name but a few. From a social justice perspective it is worth noting that the act makes a number of explicit references to the role of local authorities in promoting social inclusion where 'social inclusion or its promotion shall be read as including a reference to any policy, objective, measure or activity designed to counteract poverty or other social deprivation or to facilitate greater participation by marginalised groups in the social, economic and cultural life of the local community' (Government of Ireland, 2001: Section 1.2 (5)). However, while referenced in a number of locations in the Act, there is no particular obligation imposed on the local authority to act to promote social inclusion. Instead the term is accompanied by phrases such as 'shall have regard to' (S.69.1.g.) or 'may undertake' social inclusion measures (S.66.3(a+b)).

The position of the individual public servant

While the evolution of institutional frameworks is clearly important, it is also necessary to focus on the roles and responsibilities of individuals within the civil and public service. Individuals working within public administration carry out a wide and diverse variety of functions. However, what they have in common are a number of basic expectations around how they behave, not least that they should act in a way that serves the public in an impartial and fair manner. In this regard the particular characteristics of those who work in the public sector have been distinguished from private sector employees: 'The administrative system responds to a complex set of demands articulated through the political system which have no parallel in the private sector' (Dooney, 1976: 10). As a result, blanket and sometimes populist suggestions that public sector management processes should mimic those of the private sector or that successful private sector entrepreneurs would automatically enhance the delivery of public services can be seen as somewhat trite. For civil servants in particular the discharge of their duties is complex. On one hand, while they have a duty to serve the public, it is suggested that 'the first duty of the civil servant is to help his minister meet his responsibilities to the Oireachtas' (Dooney, 1976: 10). Part of this requires civil servants to commit to the execution of government policy, irrespective of whether it aligns with their own political preferences (Barrington, 1980). However, the sometimes neat distinction between Ministerial dictate and administrative acquiescence is one that frequently recurs. While many officials declare themselves wedded to the functional divisions between politicians as those who decide policy and civil servants who implement it, this is not always so clear cut as suggested by Barrington (1965: 179):

> One can go so far as to say that, given the nature of the responsibilities of the modern State, it is the duty of public administrators to identify problems, to solve them, to propound the solutions, and so formulate the material for policy-making on which political decisions will be made ... This is not to exclude others from propounding solutions, or to seek to do anything but extend the range and quality of public discussion but it is to pin a clear load of responsibility on administrators to work out and present solutions to problems of national importance.

Governing behaviour

Alongside the overarching legislative provisions that govern public administration, the behaviour of individual officials is further governed by a variety of codes of conduct or behaviour. Civil servants are subject to a Code of Standards and Behaviour which informs and governs how they can act. This Code is drawn up on foot of section 10(3) of the Standards in Public Office Act (2001) and stipulates that civil servants (established and unestablished) should '(a) Maintain high standards in service delivery by: conscientiously, honestly and impartially serving the Government of the day, the other institutions of State and the public; always acting within the law and performing their duties with efficiency, diligence and courtesy.' It also requires all civil servants to 'deal with the public sympathetically, fairly and promptly' (Standards in Public Office Commission, 2008: 7). However, the Code does not explore how civil servants might resolve a hypothetical conflict between serving the government of the day and the public should they feel that the two in some way diverged, for example, on a fundamental social justice issue. Equally it does not explore just what is meant by dealing with the public sympathetically or fairly. The Code also maintains the restriction on the involvement of many civil servants in party political activity stating that 'All civil servants above clerical level are totally debarred from engaging in any form of political activity' (Standards in Public Office Commission, 2008: 10). Previously Dooney had questioned the need for such a restriction, citing examples from other European jurisdictions which not only allowed political activity but in some cases actively encouraged it (Dooney, 1976).

Beyond the core civil service, employees of local authorities are also subject to a code of conduct which arises from the ethical obligations set out in the 2001 Local Government Act. In this case, employees are more specifically required to deal 'with the public courteously, fairly and promptly' to promote equality and avoid bias in their dealings with the public (Department of the Environment Community and Local Government, 2007: 5). Some restrictions on seeking election also apply to some classes of local government employees, though participation in elections to the Dáil is not explicitly prohibited. In the HSE, staff are reminded that 'political opinion should not compromise an Employee's obligations to the HSE nor should they be expressed/disseminated in the workplace' (Health Service Executive, 2011: 14). Again, HSE staff are expected to deal 'with the public sympathetically, fairly and promptly' (Health Service Executive, 2009: 4), though again what exactly this means is not clear nor is there any standard of what fairness might mean. In addition, HSE staff members are expected to 'support and be loyal to the HSE' by, amongst other things, 'ensuring any actions taken maintain public confidence in the HSE and its good name' (ibid.: 5). In terms of elections, a serving HSE staff member cannot be a member of the Dáil or Seanad nor can they be a member of the European Parliament. Should they be elected to any of these levels, they can however be seconded from the HSE and resume their post at a later stage (ibid.: 6). More broadly it is worth noting the HSE has developed a series of social justice related guidelines covering areas such as Equality Legislation; Equal Opportunities and Accommodating Diversity as well as guidelines on the employment of people with disabilities. However, the degree to which these are actively pursued with staff is unclear.

The particular role of state agencies

The existence of agencies outside of the core civil service has been a feature of Irish public administration since before the foundation of the state. While the Ministers and Secretaries Act (1924) did shift the balance of power towards government departments and the person of the Minister, it did not eliminate the role of state agencies and shortly after independence a number of new state agencies were established. According to the Devlin Report (Devlin et al., 1969: 14) the creation of state agencies in the new state represented a 'conceptual change' and an abandonment in particular areas of the concept of the Minister as a 'corporation sole'. He suggests that this development 'brought together in the area of government, persons with public and private sector experience to guide and assess the performance of management of public enterprises' as well as introducing 'new freedoms on the performance of executive functions of government'. State agencies therefore have and continue to address recognised gaps in state capacity through the creation of institutional vehicles to carry out specific functions. Effectively, state agencies contribute substantially to the activist capacity of the state, both in the commercial and non-commercial spheres. In the early years of the new state most of the new agencies had an economic function, either in undertaking and or fostering enterprise and creating essential economic infrastructure, for example the ESB, the ACC, Aer Lingus while in later years non-commercial agencies have become more prominent.

There is no shortage of commentary on the role of state agencies in Ireland, much of it in the mainstream media and much of it questioning the need for and role of state agencies. Even though he was dealing with far fewer agencies in the late 1960s, Devlin anticipated many later critiques of the role of agencies, suggesting that the concept was ad hoc and devoid of any serious attempt 'to rationalise the distribution of executive functions across the public service nor to work out a comprehensive system of communication and control within a unified public service' (ibid.: 14). More recently a considerable level of research on the role and contribution of state agencies has been undertaken (McGauran et al., 2005, MacCarthaigh, 2009, MacCarthaigh, 2010, MacCarthaigh, 2012) and a detailed outline of the changing nature of state agencies is captured in the hugely valuable Irish Administration State Database (Hardiman et al., 2012). In general terms, these analyses divide agencies into commercial and non-commercial state agencies. However, uncertainty remains about the precise definition, characteristics and attributes of state agencies thereby making it more difficult to record and track the exact number of state agencies in existence at any one time (OECD, 2008b). Equally, it has been suggested that the precise rationale for the establishment of state agencies is sometimes unclear, as are arrangements for political accountability (Hardiman and MacCarthaigh, 2008). What is clear however is that from the early 1990s to 2008, a period associated with 'unprecedented economic prosperity and successive ideologically diverse coalition governments' (MacCarthaigh, 2012), the number of agencies created increased noticeably, as illustrated in Figure 5.1.

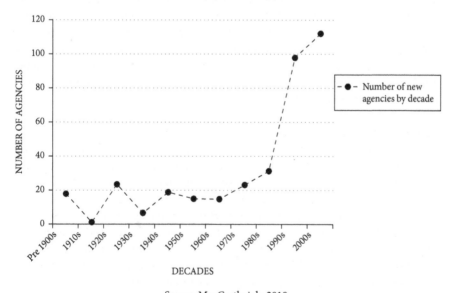

Source: MacCarthaigh, 2010.

Figure 5.1 State agency creation in Ireland

Within the past few years however the overall climate of financial contraction has given rise to a renewed drive to rationalise, abolish or amalgamate a range of state agencies. In November 2011 the government announced its intention to move ahead with the rationalisation of 48 agencies by the end of 2012 and with the identification of a further 46 that would be subject to 'critical review'. However, while the targeted agencies have been identified, there is little by way of public explanation for their selection, for decisions taken nor for the impact of particular decisions on the overall capacity of the public administration system. Nor does there seem to be a clear strategic plan for how rationalisation would proceed. For example, in the November 2011 announcement it was proposed to integrate the Sustainable Development Council, 'Comhar' into the National Economic and Social Council (NESC). Prior to this in March 2010, under the previous government, the National Economic and Social Forum (NESF) had been 'merged' into the NESC. Subsequently, the NESC itself was identified as one of the agencies to be subject to critical review, with a view to considering whether to 'Abolish/disband along with the other bodies in the group (NESDO) having regard to the duplication of functions with the ESRI and the economic advisory role of the new Irish Fiscal Advisory Council' (Department of Public Expenditure and Reform, 2011: Appendix IIb). The basis for and merit of collapsing a number of different partnership based agencies, into one 'super structure' had never been clearly set out – in particular the impact of the loss of a number of significant collaborative, partnership based structures. The subsequent proposals to review the future of the NESC itself however suggest a poorly thought out process as well as a lack of forward planning capacity. Alternatively it may suggest a deliberate strategy to limit the public perception of rationalisation by undertaking a staged process of integration and merger as a precursor to later dissolution. In any case, in October 2012, it was decided that NESC would not be abolished but no public rationale for this decision was provided.

Revisiting the role of state agencies

Given the level of flux in the world of state agencies in Ireland it seems sensible to briefly revisit some of the reasons why agencies were established in the first instance. Generally amongst the reasons suggested for agency establishment are: the provision of additional capacity to deliver particular political priorities; enabling specialist delivery of particular policies, strategies or services; securing additional policy input on strategic issues of social and/or economic importance; and introducing new approaches, work practices and energy that might not be possible within mainstream public administration. These positive rationales point to the potential of agencies to enable the state to function in activist mode, to overcome bureaucratic tendencies towards minimalism and standardisation; as well as adding to the capacity for innovation and invention.

Of course other less positive rationales for agency establishment have also been suggested, such as the relocation of direct political accountability away from the minister, being seen to respond quickly to crisis situations, the efficacy of the response and, finally, enabling the budgetary and recruitment restrictions that apply to mainstream public administration to be overcome in pursuit of a particular policy or political priority.

As an element of the state's activist capacity, agencies frequently have more direct and on-going contact with a range of citizens and civil society organisations. However, the particular role of agencies as a mediator or facilitator of the relational state has received limited consideration. Some commentators have suggested that the core state has little if any capacity to act in relational mode, given its increasing role as an overseer or regulator of service delivery (Stears, 2012). This of course raises dilemmas about whether mainstream public administration can effectively relate to citizens and their organisations. This is particularly challenging in situations where the state acts as a funder and a funding regulator, a role in which it cannot easily enter a relational mode except where relations are defined by domination and control. In such circumstances, trust, mutual respect and reciprocity all struggle for space and there is limited if any room for dissent. So, either the state needs to remove or lessen the potential for regulatory – relational conflicts or it needs to create mechanisms through which its relational ambitions can be realised. In practice, agencies such as the National Economic and Social Council (NESC), the National Economic and Social Forum (NESF) and others have provided an important relational arena in which key civil society actors were enabled to engage directly with senior civil servants, with each other and, in the case of the NESF, with politicians. However, in more recent times, agencies with strong relational capacity and associated with social partnership or having a social justice orientation seem to have been particularly vulnerable. The Combat Poverty Agency, the National Consultative Committee on Racism and Interculturalism, the Equality Authority, the Irish Human Rights Commission, and at local level, area based partnerships, have either been dissolved or have had their remits substantially altered. Some of these are examined in more detail in Chapter 7.

Reform and capacity building

Finally, any discussion on the evolution of public administration would be incomplete without some mention of reform. Since the much cited Devlin Report numerous initiatives to reform national and local level government and agencies have been published. The list of reports and proposals on reform are many – the Devlin Report in 1969; Serving the Country Better in 1985; Local Government Reorganisation and Reform in 1991; the Strategic Management Initiative and Shaping a Healthier Future in 1994;

Delivering Better Government and Better Local Government in 1996; the Quality Customer Service (QCS) in 1997; introduction of the Performance Management and Development (PMDS) system in 2001; Quality and Fairness: A Health System for You in 2001; enhanced financial management systems since 2001 with the introduction of the Management Information Framework; the Health Service Reform Programme in 2003; the Expenditure Review Initiative; A White Paper on Better Regulation, Regulating Better in 2004, including the development of Regulatory Impact Analysis; publication of a Code of Standards and Behaviour in 2004; the OECD report, Toward an Integrated Public Service in 2008; Putting People First, an Action Programme for Effective Local Government in 2012. Alongside these, reform oriented legislation included the Public Service Management Act and the Freedom of Information Act, both in 1997. More recently, a new Department of Public Expenditure and Reform has been established and an associated programme of public sector reform developed, building on many of the initiatives described above. The recent reform programme contains five major commitments to change designed to 'improve the customer experience and address costs' (Department of Public Expenditure and Reform, 2011: 7). These commitments include a renewed focus on 'customer service'; 'identifying innovative means of delivering services; cost reductions; developing new ways of working and strengthening the focus on implementation and delivery'. Progress in these five areas in turn is to be delivered through 14 Public Service Reform Initiatives, which provide a clear indication of the current largely technical direction of reform: Implementation; E-government, ICT, information sharing and customer service; shared services; business process improvement; procurement reform; property asset management; external service delivery; rationalisation and reorganisation; public expenditure reform; government led performance management; organisational performance; leadership/individual performance; public service numbers/workforce planning and redeployment; and legislation and political reform. Along with these 14 public sector wide reforms, it is also proposed that a series of Integrated Reform Delivery Plans will be developed at Departmental and sector level to 'align actions under this Plan' (Department of Public Expenditure and Reform, 2011: Appendix 1).

At local level too there have been repeated calls for more significant local government reform and the real devolution of greater power and responsibility to local government to enable it to more fully realise its potential (Keoghan, 2003, Association of Municipal Authorities of Ireland, 2007). The issue of devolution has surfaced repeatedly in a variety of local government reform debates since the 1970s, although it has not been acted upon in any significant way (Keoghan, 2003). In 1995, the government established the Devolution Commission to make recommendations on possible functions to be devolved to local authorities, on the role of local government in policy-making and, significantly, on the role of local government in the co-ordination of local development efforts (Devolution Commission, 1996). While recommendations were made on all of these areas, those addressing the devolution of functions were not acted upon. Those regarding policy-making and the co-ordination of local development were, however, leading to the 1996 White Paper 'Better Local Government' (Government of Ireland, 1996). This White Paper and the developments arising from it represented a significant watershed in local government/governance in Ireland, encouraging the local government system away from a narrower service oriented outlook into a more central role as a facilitator and co-ordinator of local governance. Just how well different local government units embraced the opportunity varies considerably.

Preceding this local government reform exercise, some of legal restrictions on local government eased, firstly with the Constitutional recognition of local government in 1995 and later with the removal of the *ultra vires* rule which limited local government activities to those specifically legislated for. As a result, in more recent times local government has been enabled to play a broader role by virtue of the introduction of a power of general competence 'to promote the interest of the community' potentially enabling it to promote 'directly or indirectly, social inclusion or the social, economic, environmental, recreational, cultural, community or general development of an administrative area of the authority or of the local community' (Government of Ireland, 2001). In addition, the role of local authorities in providing 'a forum for the democratic representation of the local community' is also recognised (Government of Ireland, 2001). Crucially though, the control of local government by centralised administration not been relaxed. Inevitably in such circumstances the capacity for innovation and local initiative remains inhibited, not least amongst officials reluctant to act beyond the remit set out by national policy. In the current financial context, the potential for local government initiative is likely to remain limited.

There is little doubt that most of the reform initiatives described above and those detailed in the recent public sector reform programme are, in the main, concerned with technical, bureaucratic aspects of public administration, designed to improve on current management functions, enhance delivery of services and cut costs. What is not so prominent are reforms that adopt a more critical, transformative, and longer-term perspective on the role of public administration, particularly its role on promoting social justice. Despite all of these initiatives, on-going doubts about the commitment to and capacity for public-sector reform are expressed: 'Several efforts at public service reform over the decades have failed to adequately achieve more joined-up government. There is now another opportunity to address this, including through the use of strategic priorities to promote shared actions across the public sector, together with a fundamental re-think and rationalisation of the roles of public service bodies at national, regional and local levels' (Boyle and MacCarthaigh, 2011: 5).

Others caution that 'quality of public administration and good governance in general may be escaping our attention by adopting a focus that is confined to concerns with public management measures' (Hardiman and MacCarthaigh, 2008: 16) echoing a similar conclusion in the 2002 PA consulting report (PA Consulting Group, 2002). What emerges here is on one hand a picture of public administration reform that has focused almost entirely on technical aspects of public management contrasted with calls for reform that focus on a broader understanding and functioning of public governance. This latter term has been defined by the OECD (2008b: 236) as 'the formal and informal arrangements that determine how public decisions are made and how public actions are carried out from the perspective of maintaining a country's Constitutional values as problems, actors and times change'. The reforms undertaken within the public sector do focus on how public actions are carried out but there is little evidence of a more detailed consideration or review of how public decisions are made and, in particular, how these reflect Constitutional priorities and are updated to take account of changing circumstances.

Borrowing from a much earlier discussion on democratic reform in the United States it has been said that the cure for all the ills of democracy is more democracy (Adams, 1902). The Irish experience would suggest that a similar maxim has been applied to Irish public administration; the cure for the ills of public sector reform, it would appear, is more public sector reform. Perhaps though a new question needs to be posed: do we simply need more public sector reform or do we need different and better public sector reform? In the current climate, the need to reduce recurring expenditure is preeminent, alongside which, the delivery of more efficient and effective services and the mantra of 'putting the customer' at the centre of service delivery make up a holy trinity of public sector reform priorities. However, given the national shock to the system that has taken place since the beginning of the current economic and social crisis it is far from clear that this is enough. Instead, there is a need to explore the purpose of public sector reform in greater depth and subject it to a more searching analysis, taking into account some of the issues discussed in earlier chapters.

Conclusions

This chapter has reviewed some of the main features of the Irish public administration system. It has observed how the newly independent state's public administration system was inherited largely intact from the British administration and suggested that this may have brought with it an inherent tendency towards conservatism. Early legislative directions also vested huge power and status in the person of the Minister, potentially laying the basis for departmental preoccupation with protecting the image and reputation of the minister, in the process stimulating a low innovation and a risk averse institutional culture. This inherent tendency towards conservatism has been reinforced by a tradition of strong, centralised control, particularly in relation to local government. In more recent years it is possible to identify a number of significant critical junctures for Irish public administration: membership of the European Communities; the creation of the Department of Public Service; the Strategic Management Initiative; social partnership and the increased reliance on state agencies as a mode of policy delivery, especially since the early 1990s. Unfortunately, the abolition of the Department of the Public Service and its more recent reincarnation as the Department of Public Expenditure and Reform could be seen as undermining the potential for public service capacity building by making reform subservient to public expenditure reduction. Ultimately, despite a long and continuing list of more technically oriented reform initiatives, there has been little political drive to undertake meaningful reform of public administration over the years, either because it was not a political priority or because politicians have been reluctant to challenge vested interests in the public sector. Those reform efforts that have taken place have been slow to embed. In the next two chapters a more detailed examination of the role of public administration system in relation to social justice will be undertaken. This will start by looking at its role under the key headings of knowledge; disposition and capacity and will subsequently proceed to reflect in greater detail through a series of case studies.

Notes

1 The CSO notes that its figures are not directly comparable with the estimates produced by the Department of Public Expenditure and Reform (DPER) which bases its estimates on 'full-time equivalents which will change over time based both on changes in working hours and number of persons employed'. By contrast, CSO estimates represent the estimated total number of employees within the public sector.
2 Amendments to the 1934 Acts established a Department of Health and a Department of Social Welfare in 1946, a Department of the Gaeltacht in 1956, a Department of Transport and Power in 1959, a Department of Labour in 1966, a Department of the Public Service in 1973, a Department of Economic Planning and Development in 1977, a Department of Communications in 1983 and a Department of Public Expenditure and Reform in 2011.

6

Assessing the state of social justice in Irish public administration

Introduction

Earlier chapters have presented the various arguments put forward to justify a more active role for public administration in designing and promoting a social justice agenda. Having articulated at least some of ways in which social justice might be conceived, this chapter now turns its attention to exploring the state of social justice in Irish public administration. Inevitably, given the size and scale of the public sector, this does not take the form of a piece by piece examination of the administrative apparatus. Instead this chapter draws on existing secondary sources and a series of interviews with strategically placed public officials and civil society representatives to explore a number of the key social justice themes, emerging from previous chapters. The chapter firstly focuses on knowledge and explores whether there is evidence of any sense of shared understanding of social justice within public administration, either at an institutional or individual level. Building on this it moves on to the issue of disposition and tries to understand whether a disposition towards social justice can be identified, particularly in the types of values present within the administrative system. As a consequence, the role of the individual official and the potential for individual agency are examined. The chapter concludes with an assessment of the level of capacity within public administration to proactively promote a social justice agenda.

Understandings of social justice

In earlier chapters, the complexities involved in delineating the meaning of social justice in a public administration context became readily apparent. Not only are there a variety of legal and moral sources to draw upon but so too there is a range of philosophically and ideologically contested concepts that produce sharply contrasting approaches to economic and social rights, responsibilities and social solidarity. Add to these the competing claims to the soul of public administration made by proponents of the more activist New Public Administration versus the more 'state minimalist' New Public Management (Frederickson, 2007, Goss, 1996, Box, 2005). To these are added the challenges generated by the economic crisis, declining confidence in public administration and the continued complexity of managing the relationship between the realms of the political and the bureaucratic.

Bearing all of these in mind, this section tries to identify if any particular or distinct understandings of social justice exist within public administration in Ireland, that might in some way provide the basis for a more consciously articulated set of principles, values, ethics and approaches that could contribute to tackling the growing sense of social injustice that pervades contemporary, popular commentary in Ireland. It could be said that the search for such principles finds resonance in the argument of former Secretary General of the Department of the Taoiseach, Dermot McCarthy who asserted that 'Successful political communities have a moral base that embodies and supports the values that shape relationships and behaviour. The dedication of the public service to the common good requires that there be some shared understanding of what constitutes that common good.' McCarthy, who was effectively the most senior civil servant in the country for many years and was strongly associated with the era of social partnership and with an expansion of the engagement between government and civil society, further highlights the characteristics of a successful society set out by the National Economic and Social Council (NESC). These include a 'high and sustainable income per head, a good-quality physical environment, access to appropriate services of common interest, a vibrant civil society and civic culture, a concern for human rights and the achievement of greater social inclusion'. Of particular interest though, he emphasises the public sector's role in the realisation of such a successful society, concluding: 'If we are required to be more explicit about the values that define the Irish citizen of today and tomorrow, then the public service must be equally alive to the need to renew and strengthen its own moral and ethical foundations, if it is to be effective in serving the people' (McCarthy, 2009: 98). This final statement leaves little doubt, firstly, that the public service has or should have a clear moral and ethical foundation and, secondly, that these need to be renewed and strengthened on an on-going basis. The argument in this book is that a focus on social justice needs to be seen as the reinforcing mesh in any such moral, values and ethical foundation, underpinned by some level of understanding (shared or otherwise) of the meaning of social justice. However, whether such a normative assertion is supported by the contemporary reality of the Irish public sector is far from certain.

One obvious place to look for the presence of an understanding of social justice within Irish public administration is in the Strategy Statements of each central government department and in the corporate plans of the 34 primary local authorities. The production of the Strategy Statement by Departments is an innovation introduced in the 1997 Public Service Management Act and requires that a Statement 'comprise the key objectives, outputs and related strategies (including use of resources) of the Department of State or Scheduled Office concerned' (Government of Ireland, 1997a: S 5: 1.a). Responsibility for the production of the Strategy Statement is specifically assigned to the Secretary General of each Department. Local authority corporate plans on the other hand are a requirement of the 2001 Local Government Act (Government of Ireland, 2001: S.134.6) and should contain, amongst other things, a statement of the principal activities of the local authority and an outline of the 'objectives and priorities for each of the principal activities and strategies for achieving these objectives'.

So, what do these strategy statements and corporate plans tell us about perspectives on social justice and to what extent is a social justice lexicon to be found within them? It has to be said that the visibility of specific language is not to be underestimated. Language communicates understanding, mindset and disposition. As suggested by Robert Chambers (2004: 3) 'The power of vocabulary to change how we think and what we do is easy to underestimate. It influences the course of development in many ways: through changing the agenda; through modifying mindsets; through legitimating new actions; and through stimulating and focusing research and learning.' To explore this in the context of Irish public administration it is worth seeing if at least the language of social justice features within key official documents. The outcome of a simple key word analysis of the strategy statements of all government departments, using obvious terms such as justice, equity, equality, fairness and inclusion are presented in Table 6.1 below and are quite revealing.

In three departments, Public Expenditure and Reform, Defence and Jobs, Enterprise and Innovation, there are no references to any of these five key terms. While it can be expected that the Department of Defence does not have a direct social justice role, the same cannot be said of the strategies presented by the pivotal departments of Public Expenditure and Reform and Jobs, Enterprise and Innovation. Neither of these makes any explicit reference to social justice, fairness or any of the other related terms. Four other departments make reference of one of the five terms only. In the case of the Department of Arts, Heritage and the Gaeltacht a single reference to social inclusion is made while the Department of Communications, Energy and Natural Resources, makes two references to inclusion, one referring to contributing to social inclusion via the provision of broadband and the other to digital inclusion. Meanwhile, the Department of Transport, Tourism and Sport makes four references to the term 'equality', though all four references are in a single paragraph dealing with accessibility. Somewhat surprisingly, the Strategy Statement of the Department of Social protection makes no reference to justice, equity, equality or fairness,

Table 6.1 Key word analysis of departmental strategy statements, 2011–2014

Department	Keyword				
	Justice	Equity	Equality	Fairness	Inclusion
Agriculture	0	0	4	1	1
Arts, Heritage, Gaeltacht	0	0	0	0	1
Children / Youth Affairs	3	1	1	0	1
Communications, Energy & Natural Resources	0	0	0	0	2
Defence	0	0	0	0	0
Education and Science	1	1	1	0	1
Environment, Community and Local Government	1	2	1	2	2
Finance	0	1	0	1	1
Foreign Affairs and Trade	3	0	1	0	1
Health	0	1	0	2	3
Jobs, Enterprise, Innovation	0	0	0	0	0
Justice and Equality	39	1	35	3	5
Public Expenditure & Reform	0	0	0	0	0
Social Protection	0	0	0	0	5
Taoiseach	1	1	0	2	0
Transport, Tourism & Sport	0	0	4	0	0

though it does make five references to the department's role in promoting social inclusion. This may reflect the narrow role of the department by comparison with the range of community support functions it held between 1997 and 2002 but may also represent a disconnect between social protection and a broader social justice outlook, a point commented upon by Kevin O'Kelly, the final director of the Combat Poverty Agency and himself previously a political advisor to the former Fianna Fáil Minister for Labour, Gene Fitzgerald. On the Department of Social Protection, O'Kelly (2012) comments 'it's a very interesting Department, Social and Family Affairs, it's a massive Department, seven thousand people there you know. But it's not a strategic Department; they don't look at what are the causes of poverty or why you know, what are the problems. They have this attitude that we'll set up a fund and throw money at it'.

Thus, seven government departments make reference to one or fewer of these key terms that should indicate the presence of at least some understanding of, or commitment to, social justice. Without going through each of the other departments in turn, Table 6.1 shows that reference to the key concepts is limited to say the least. Indeed, the relatively high number of references to justice and equality in the strategy statement of the Department of Justice and Equality derives from frequent references to the systems of justice and equality, including the criminal justice system, not to broader understandings and pursuit of equality and social justice. Even the relatively innocuous though much abused term 'fairness' struggles for recognition. In fact, 10 out of 16 government departments make no reference to fairness, despite the fact that 'Fairness' is presented as a distinct section within the current Programme for Government (Government of Ireland, 2011). These include Arts, Heritage and the Gaeltacht; Children and Youth Affairs; Communications, Energy and Natural Resources; Education; Jobs, Enterprise and Innovation; Public Expenditure and Reform; Social Protection and Transport, Tourism and Sport, departments where a concern for fairness might be expected to enjoy greater prominence. It is noticeable however that only the Department of Education and Science makes use of the term 'social justice' in its Strategy Statement, proposing that amongst the values its staff will preserve is a commitment to 'behaving ethically, fairly, and impartially and respecting social justice, equality and inclusion'. Of course the lower visibility of social justice language within the Departmental documents may simply reflect the fact that a political agreement such as the Programme for Government is inevitably going to contain higher levels of political rhetoric that will not be automatically translated into 'real world' of policy delivery. However, even within departments overseen by ministers from the Labour party, which has historically championed social justice within government and public administration, the absence of a language of social justice is noticeable.

One can only speculate as to the possible reasons for the lack of visibility of key social justice related terms in the strategy statements. On one hand it may be argued that officials are largely taking the lead from their minister and, as per their brief under the 1997 Public Services Management Act, follow the policy directions set by ministers. As suggested by Dermot McCarthy (2012) on the issue of social justice, 'I think most public servants would say well yes it is important, it's part of our world but it's about the goals of policy and translating it into some sort of policy relevant context is a matter for the politicians and when they tell us what they want done, we do it.' McCarthy also emphasises the pragmatic orientation of officials and of the public administration system and an explanation for an absence of a more philosophical underpinning in Irish public administration:

> I don't think there's a corporate sense I mean in the way that you'd have a corporate tradition of law in some of the continental systems. I mean we've, we inherited the British tradition of pragmatic, apolitical, non-ideological social and public administration in the more socially engaged dimensions of it. I mean we would be informed by a sort of the blue book sociology: measure it, define it, describe it and then do practical things to improve it. It seems to me that as far as there is a justice take – it is that.

Former Secretary General at the Department of Social Welfare, John Hynes (2012) concludes something similar;

I suppose the term social justice wouldn't be something that would arise very frequently in discussion in my experience but terms like equality, fairness and equality of opportunity and so on, would be common enough. Now I suppose the problem for the public service is there isn't a lot of debate or discussion about these issues as such within the public service I would think you know and we would have depended on the political system or the academic world or you know experts outside the public service to inform us about what these kind of terms meant in practice.

Social justice then has not historically been to the fore in the consciousness of public sector institutions and it doesn't look likely that this will change in the short term. It is important to consider however whether the suggested low visibility of social justice as a priority within public administration is mainly because social justice issues are not prioritised within broader society. As a result, public administration may simply reflect the society within which it exists. According to former director of the Combat Poverty Agency, Hugh Frazer (2012):

It's a hard one. I certainly don't think social justice which is linked to people having rights, especially social rights, is a strong part of the administration, but I wonder if that's more because it's not part of the political and cultural system. I don't think you can really expect your administration to be different from the environment it exists in.

Whether this reflects a type of innate conservatism in Irish society by comparison with other European countries is open to debate. Amongst the arguments in favour of the conservatism thesis is the lack of ideological distinctiveness between the main political parties and a resultant absence of political impetus towards social solidarity. The absence of social solidarity in an Irish setting is commented upon by the current Secretary General of the Irish Congress of Trade Unions, David Begg (2012):

We don't have a great commitment towards social solidarity. In a way we can talk about it in social partnership but social partnership evaporated on the onset of the crisis. Whereas if you look at a lot of the other small open economies social partnership is the default position in every crisis but it just evaporated in our situation because I would say, really, the truth was that people looked at it very superficially, they didn't really see it as a way of achieving social justice. In our case we saw it as perhaps as delivering a good pay increase and employers saw it as something to give us stability and competitiveness and so on. But there wasn't that kind of real, deep sense that we need the type of what the Danes call a negotiated economy and society. We don't have that here, it's not as deep.

In a similar vein it is argued that the Celtic Tiger years perhaps obviated the need to focus on the interplay between values, politics and the economy. In the view of Siobhan O'Donoghue (2012), Director of the Migrant Rights Centre of Ireland (MRCI) and a former participant on behalf of the Community Platform in the social partnership process, 'I think people haven't made the connection between the values that they hold as individuals and the choices they make in the way they live life, and the kind of political system we have. If you think about the Celtic Tiger period, it more or less cushioned everybody from having to make those choices.'

This is not to deny that in the recent and not so recent past, issues of social justice, inclusion and equality have gained some level of prominence within public policy processes, though perhaps without being built upon any deeper, conceptual foundations. A variety of factors have influenced this. On one hand, the presence of the different elements of the now Labour Party within coalition governments have given rise to some notable initiatives to enhance capacity in the field of social justice, including the establishment of the Combat Poverty Agency (proposed by Barry Desmond); the Better Local Government White Paper (developed by Brendan Howlin); the National Economic and Social Forum (overseen by Eithne FitzGerald) the National Anti-Poverty Strategy (NAPS) developed by Prionsias de Rossa; and the Equal Status Act and the associated Equality Authority (initiated by Mervyn Taylor). However, more recent changes in the standing of these initiatives, some discussed in the next chapter, have shown the limited degree to which these efforts have become embedded within the broader public sector infrastructure.

Visibility of social justice at local level

A similar exploration of social justice intent within corporate planning processes was also undertaken at local level. Using local authority corporate plans as the basis for this analysis there is a similar, limited visibility of terms such as justice, equity, equality, fairness or inclusion (see Table 6.2). However, it is noticeable that the language of equality and social inclusion has clearly become much more commonplace, particularly within local authorities. Only in the case of one local authority, Waterford City, is there a complete absence of reference to any of the key terms. And while in some of the corporate plans reference to social inclusion appears to be somewhat cosmetic, others, on paper at any rate, demonstrate a stronger and more integrated approach to the promotion of equality and inclusion. This higher level of visibility of social inclusion and equality may well reflect the role played by agencies such as the Combat Poverty Agency and the Equality Authority in facilitating and encouraging a stronger social inclusion commitment. It also, according to Cavan County Manager, Jack Keyes, reflects a changing reality that 'at political level at local level you definitely have a much stronger sense of social justice now than would have been the case twenty years ago but the economy is now dominating almost everything' (Keyes, 2012). Another factor which might be expected to have influenced the visibility of social justice approaches within local authorities is the presence of a dedicated social inclusion unit. Sixteen such units were established and centrally funded in local authorities between 2001 and 2007.

Table 6.2 Social justice in local authority corporate plans

Local authority	Key Word					Total references per local authority
	Justice	Equity	Equality	Fairness	Inclusion	
Carlow	0	0	3	1	9	13
Cavan[a]	0	0	2	0	6	8
Clare	0	0	0	0	5	5
Cork County	1	1	1	0	4	7
Cork City[a]	0	0	3	0	1	4
Donegal[a]	0	0	2	0	2	4
Dublin City[a]	0	0	4	0	14	18
Dun Laoghaire / Rathdown[a]	0	0	1	0	8	9
Fingal[a]	0	0	1	0	5	6
Galway County[a]	0	0	0	0	13	13
Galway City[a]	0	0	0	0	2	2
Kerry	0	1	1	0	10	12
Kildare	0	0	0	0	3	3
Kilkenny	0	2	9	0	10	21
Laois	0	0	1	0	6	7
Leitrim	0	0	3	0	1	4
Limerick County	0	0	1	0	7	8
Limerick City[a]	0	0	2	0	7	9
Longford	0	0	3	1	8	12
Louth[a]	0	0	1	0	0	1
Mayo	0	0	0	0	2	2
Meath[a]	0	0	2	0	3	5
Monaghan[a]	0	0	10	0	6	16
North Tipperary	0	0	1	0	4	5
Offaly	0	0	3	0	2	5
Roscommon[a]	1	1	3	0	5	10
Sligo	0	0	11	1	11	23
South Dublin[a]	0	0	0	1	3	4
South Tipperary[a]	0	0	0	0	7	7
Waterford County	0	0	0	0	7	7
Waterford City[a]	0	0	0	0	0	0
Westmeath	0	0	0	0	5	5
Wexford	0	2	1	2	7	12
Wicklow[a]	0	0	2	0	19	21
Total	2	7	71	6	202	288

Note: [a]Local authorities in which social inclusion units have been established.

However, there is little direct correlation between the presence of a social inclusion unit within a local authority and the presence of social inclusion, equality and other concepts within corporate plans.

It would appear that in contemporary national level public administration there is a quite limited articulation of a social justice consciousness, as evidenced both in departmental strategy statements and in the assessments of a number of current and former civil servants as well as a number of strategically placed civil society activists, leading one activist to conclude that 'we are being badly served but of course there are a few notable exceptions. There is always some possibility or some opportunity or individual who is in a position of power or influence who can shape things somewhat. But overall if you stand back, the overall picture is appalling' (O'Donoghue, 2012). While the local level presents a somewhat different picture, with some evidence at least of the language of social inclusion and equality being embraced, there is no doubt that significant questions of disposition toward a social justice agenda remain to be answered.

Disposition towards social justice

Given the limited visibility of social justice as a priority within public institutions, it seems logical to question whether there is an issue with disposition. Disposition, attitudes, and values – all of these are central to any discussion of social justice in a public administration context. At an institutional level as well as an individual level, there undoubtedly exists a complex interplay of different dispositions, perspectives, biases and prejudices. On social justice in Irish public administration one leading civil society activist observes 'I would say for a lot of civil servants, they see it as akin to a red rag to a bull. They see it more as code for criticism or as a soft issue and as a way of arguing for more money for the community and voluntary sector. I think they see it as being in conflict with their current priorities' (O'Donoghue, 2012). In this statement lies the potential for creative dialogue, tension and innovation. However, within it also lies the potential for discrimination and injustice, particularly where negative dispositions towards particular issues or groups become institutionalised and lead to the formation of arbitrary behaviours and actions in defence of a given social order, which may in itself reflect the 'ingrained dispositions of a given group or class' Mann (1999: 181). Inculcating a disposition towards social justice does not mean the elimination of a diversity of values and attitudes. However, it does require recognition of the primacy of social justice principles in the exercise of public office and the creation of a culture where dispositions that produce unequal treatment and discrimination are not tolerated. Having suggested that there appears to be limited visibility of and shared understanding of social justice in national government departments and some evidence of a greater penetration within the local government system, this section now goes on to explore disposition towards social justice in greater detail, paying particular attention to values and influences on the nature of public administration.

The war of ideas

In Chapter 2 the relevance of discussions on the nature of the state and its role in society were introduced, the principal conclusion being that a minimalist state has limited capacity to realise a more extensive social justice ambition while those who envisage a more activist state may more effectively countenance such ambition. In practice, it was suggested that these opposing positions are reflected within public administration in the 'war of ideas', more generally between ideas of social solidarity and those of the liberal economy and, more specifically, between the values of the New Public Administration and those of New Public Management (NPM). In an Irish context, this is captured by former director of the Combat Poverty Agency, Hugh Frazer, who suggests that:

> There's this contradiction in our culture because you've had this rhetoric about Catholic Social Justice and statements from Bishops and other opinion formers which seem to be on the face of it quite strong about community and quite strong about looking after everybody in society while at the same time supporting a liberal economic ideology that is the complete contrast to that. So it was almost schizophrenic in its mix. And we definitely have drifted towards to the UK/American models overall and they are certainly not driven very much by rights and justice. (Frazer, 2012)

In the Irish context it is suggested that the Strategic Management Initiative (SMI) is 'the Irish version of NPM' and moreover, 'the ideas that informed NPM are the well entrenched orthodoxy' (Litton, 2012: 32–33). Begg (2012) has no doubt about the degree to which the public sector has embraced NPM ideas: 'they have embraced new public management that's for sure. Funny enough though, they embraced it as an idea, I'm not sure they actually implemented it terribly well but they have embraced it, that's the language they talk'. The exact nature of how NPM manifests itself will inevitably vary. However, in the context of a discussion on social justice, it often emerges as an emphasis on individual initiative and individual responsibility, which draws both on the social integration and the moral underclass discourses discussed in Chapter 3. Here the message is that the state can only do so much and a greater balance between the responsibility of the individual and the responsibility of the state needs to be struck. This view is articulated by McCarthy (2012).

> There is a point of view which is strong enough to be respected not just here again but in other places, which would say well we're not taking a different approach to social policy, it's exactly the same perspective as on economic policy, in other words, that government can only get certain things right, the things for which it is directly responsible and, if it gets those right, good things happen. So you create the conditions, the fundamentals if you like. But that is to a large degree about getting incentive structures right so whether it's in the market or in social behaviour if you get the incentive structure right, if you get government to stick to the things that it knows something about which is a small domain, let the rest of the world get on with it. Now that's a very American sort of position but you

hear it in very much in Britain as well today. It would seem to me that if there is a school of public administration in the Irish public service it would now be close to that view of things.

That such a school of thought exists is supported by Keyes (2012) who argues that whatever focus on social justice had been built in the 1990s is being weakened by the 'conversion to the type of model, for example, that exists in many other countries of public service delivery for example in New Zealand'. He also suggests that the influence of New Public Management is evident in the nature of more recent recruitment into the public sector, contrasting with a previous more socially conscious cohort:

> You got a lot of people born in the forties/fifties when they were promoted they were quite conservative and it was that type of Ireland that they knew. Then there was a period of ten years where the people who experienced the sixties and seventies came through in the civil service and were hugely interested and understood things in the context of social justice. I find now that many senior people in their forties in the civil service, the up and coming stars are not really interested and are quite cynical about social justice, they are increasingly not willing to engage on it and so I think it's a very worrying time.

However, not all would agree that NPM, as it might be understood by comparison with countries such as the UK and New Zealand, has had a significant influence in Ireland, the suggestion being than many of the administrative reforms that have taken place owe their origins more to a concern with administrative efficiency rather than any particular ideological commitment to the ideals of New Public Management (Hardiman and MacCarthaigh, 2008). However the influence of ideology within the public sector more generally, be it NPM or otherwise, is strongly argued by long standing civil society activist Fr. Sean Healy, who suggests that efforts to advance a social justice ideal frequently encounter considerable ideological resistance:

> For the most part there's an ideological resistance within the public sector to social justice. There are honourable, exceptional public servants who did, and continue to do, a very good job. In every generation there are a small number of public servants who have a clear enough understanding of what social justice really is and have a commitment based on that understanding. Within the major departments, particularly in Finance, however, I found a massive, massive resistance to dealing with policy from a social justice perspective. In fact, there was a great deal of emphasis focused in playing it down. (Healy, 2012)

However, such ideological differences may not exist simply between 'insiders' and 'outsiders' and may also exist within the public administration system as suggested by the current Secretary General of the Department of Public Expenditure and Reform, Robert Watt (2012), who wonders whether the use of the term 'social justice' may be contested 'because everybody can claim to be in favour of a concept such as social justice without clearly defining what it means. For example, within the system there are people with different ideas of fairness or justice and completely different views about the size of the State etc.'. However, rather than being an argument against the use of the term social justice, this in fact reinforces the need to articulate a broader systemic understanding of social justice within public administration, in order that such multiple individual constructs of justice and fairness are not allowed to determine policy design and implementation options.

Bounded disposition

While an institutional or individual disposition on social justice may well be guided by an individual or a collective ideology, such dispositions may equally be limited or bounded by prevailing orthodoxies, particularly economic orthodoxies. Whatever the source of these boundaries – ideology, pragmatism, subservience, legalism – the end result is the same: the parameters of the possible narrow and the possible scope for action contracts. As a result, within the social justice arena, options to address poverty, social exclusion and inequality seemed only acceptable if they fit within pre-existing policy boundaries, namely those dictated a more liberal, less regulated, growth oriented, low taxation, free market economy. Thus, the depth of commitment to social justice *per se* is questioned. In the view of one former senior civil servant 'A lot of things in social policy and equality we were forced to do, there was no problem doing it, the money didn't come with the equality, the money came with the labour market, so the equality things that we were forced to do we did' (Private Interview, 2012b). This echoes the experience described by Frazer (2012):

> A message I often heard in Combat Poverty Agency days was there's no point you recommending all those things because they're outside the parameters within which we're operating. So that wasn't saying that they didn't think we shouldn't be saying things about poverty they were saying there's no point advocating a completely different system or a completely different balance because that's no use to us.

Given that these parameters have fairly clearly failed to deliver a sustainable future for the country, it might be expected that a different, wider range of ambitions and options for the future could be now considered. Ironically, one of the first casualties of the economic crisis appears to be a return to the notion of social justice as a luxury item that can only be afforded once economic growth has been restored. Such boundaries once again result in social justice being discussed only in terms of the availability of resources, while considerations of how it could be advanced in other different way, including institutional change, are not considered. In particular, the exploration of concepts and ideas; resource neutral public sector reform; training and capacity building; civic engagement and many other less resource intensive routes remain insufficiently explored:

> The other thing I'd say is that looking at it pragmatically I don't think at the present time or the near future at least there's much prospect of pure social justice goals/instruments or organisations getting much of a hearing, They're just seen, I suspect, in many quarters as a luxury. So the issue for individual public servants and organisations and campaign groups and so on has to be to connect up with these core concerns and redefine them so that achieving social justice is integrated and is integral to a fiscal adjustment that's sustainable – we can spend less and do better because we're doing it this way. (McCarthy, 2012)

This would appear to emphasise the residual nature of social justice in policy terms, as an issue that is secondary to economic development, not as an over-arching framework within which economic development takes place. For social justice activists therefore the implied message is that their policy imperatives must effectively align with the cost cutting and fiscal management agenda of the political and administrative systems – otherwise they will not be taken seriously, justifying Dryzek's (1996) longstanding suspicion of the benefits for civil society organisations of engaging too closely with the state. Equally, the nature of current crisis limits the potential to explore the role of the state more generally or, more specifically, as a social justice actor: 'I suppose at this stage to be frank there needs to be debate about the role of the State, the nature of the State but I don't think there's space at present within the administration system or politically to engage in that. We are exiting a period of crisis which should allow the space for a better debate on these issues' (Watt, 2012).

In circumstances where the capacity to explore, explain or address issues of social justice is constrained one of the first victims is the capacity to innovate – either in terms of innovative interpretation of problems or in terms of the capacity to imagine a range of sustainable solutions. The limited capacity of the Irish administration system to innovate has been much commented upon, in particular the belief of some public servants who feel 'that the system inhibits rather than challenges them, that it does not reward innovation, and is quick to penalise failure' (OECD, 2008b: 28). This conclusion was affirmed in stark terms: 'Because the public sector is a risk averse sector, that's the main problem with it, you can get hung out to dry because it only takes one thing to go wrong and you can get destroyed, improvements require change, change involves risk and risk can go wrong so it is safer to stick with the status quo which involves no risk' (Private Interview, 2012b). From a civil society perspective, a similar assessment emerges: 'The way the civil service is organized and in the way they define success for themselves, is a lot about getting through the system with your nose clean, getting up the ladder. It would seem that the only way you can get up the ladder is by keeping your head down and keeping your nose clean and that means not rocking the boat' (O'Donoghue, 2012). More broadly, the OECD also suggests that nature of central fiscal control may have had a det-rimental impact on local level innovation (2008b: 41). The capacity for longer term planning and visioning is also seen as an on-going weakness and is largely subservient to shorter term actions that do not disturb existing the existing status quo, political or otherwise (Callanan, 2007) leading to situations where 'the urgent is driving out the important' (Boyle, 2009: 20). In the same way MacCarthaigh (2008), in his review of values in the public sector, suggests that innovation and risk-taking 'do not emerge as prominent values informing the work of public servants'. However, whether Litton (2012a: 31) is correct in his observation that 'The anti intellectualism that characterises the overall culture is particularly intense in the civil service' remains a matter of debate.

These cited deficiencies in innovation capacity are not unrelated to the observed conservatism of public administration institutions. Barrington (1980: 11) makes particular reference to the ease with which the Department of Finance was able to oppose 'developmental ideas' on the basis that these require public expenditure and 'in the belief that public spending was necessarily less productive than private spending' and 'could occur only at the expense of private investment'. Given the perception of dominance and the belief that 'everybody is absolutely secondary to the Department of Finance' (Begg, 2012) resistance or perceptions of resistance to different developmental and social perspectives within such a key Department has to be seen as highly significant. This is echoed by Dermot McCarthy (2012) who acknowledged that 'The officialdom tends to be stronger in closing down options than creating them or putting them forward, we can't do this because – you know and sometimes the "because" is a very good reason – it costs too much, it's unconstitutional, you'd never get it through the Dáil, you know the whole gamut of factors.' McCarthy further acknowledges that resistance to ideas may not be unrelated to particular biases that exist within government departments and cites a particular example within the social justice arena:

> I mean government departments like all organisations have their own culture and bias so there are some options that are simply not considered because they're perceived to be either too difficult or giving rise to if you like philosophical or structural problems. I mean refundable tax credits for example they may or may not be a good idea, I'm open to persuasion but the official system is dead set against even considering it in any serious way because it gives rise to too many, one might say subversive ripples, in terms of how things are done. (McCarthy, 2012)

The degree to which such cultures and biases exist and potentially resist a stronger social justice perspective remains an issue for more detailed attitudinal research within public administration.

Values and disposition
Finally, within this discussion on disposition, the issue of values has to be addressed, as the values that guide public officials, whatever their origins, permanence or permeability, are central to the development and maintenance of

individual and institutional disposition towards social justice. In Chapter 2 a number of sources of values within public administration were identified: individual; professional; organisational; legal and public interest (Van Wart, 1998). Alongside these, two contrasting value sets were presented, one described as the bureaucratic ethos, emphasising accountability; competency; economy, impartiality, predictability and trustworthiness; and the other described as the democratic ethos, emphasising, amongst others, advocacy; compassion; confidentiality; individual rights, political awareness and the public interest (Goss, 1996). The importance of values within a public administration context and their contribution to the type of moral foundation described by McCarthy (2012) has been emphasised in one of the few dedicated explorations of the issue within Irish public administration. Thus MacCarthaigh (2008) has emphasised the role of values in providing stability and coherence, while Murray has strongly argued that the 'stewardship of values is at the heart of the strategic management mandate' (Murray, 2007: 125). Such stability and coherence is all the more important at a time when the public sector is subject to a constant barrage of scrutiny and a lot of ill-informed criticism and its attendant potential to undermine morale. In the view of another former Secretary General, Julie O'Neill (2012) with experience across a number of Departments,

> because of all that happened in recent years, along with politicians, the church and bankers, public servants and civil servants have become the kicking toy of a lot of commentators. There is a danger in that because that has a very significant impact on morale. It has a significant impact on why would you want, even if you could get in, to join the civil service. And for those already civil servants, it can have a significant effect on how people value themselves and their contribution. This is potentially dangerous because you actually do want a world where instead of being seen as being in a comfortable post or whatever, people want to join the public and civil service and want to be valued as being part of that because they're doing something unique in society which is different but can be equally valuable to being in the private sector and creating jobs.

The issue of values was explored in a series of workshops undertaken by MacCarthaigh with national civil servants and officials within local authorities. From this he has identified a number of contemporary values that inform how these institutions operate. These are presented in Table 6.3 below and are contrasted with the main elements of the bureaucratic ethos and the democratic ethos. At both national and local level, emphasis is placed on honesty and integrity; fairness and impartiality; loyalty, either the local area or to colleagues; accountability and commitment to the citizen. While both name fairness as a key value, local officials also refer to the importance of equity, though these terms are not defined. Finally, MacCarthaigh (2008) suggests that national civil servants also emphasise values associated with the quality and speed of service delivery and flexibility, which he suggests, may indicate a stronger influence of new public management reform approaches.

Table 6.3 Contemporary values within Irish public administration

Bureaucratic ethos (New Public Management)	National civil servants	Local public servants	Democratic ethos (New Public Administration)
• Accountability • Competency • Economy • Impartiality • Predictability • Trustworthiness	• Honesty and integrity • Fairness • Impartiality and neutrality • Loyalty and collegiality • Commitment o the citizen and accountability • Legality • Flexibility • Quality, including speed, of service delivery • Value for money • Leadership	• Honesty • Impartiality • Integrity • Fairness • Accountability • Legality • Neutrality • Loyalty (to local area) • Equity • Public value • Reputation	• Advocacy • Compassion • Confidentiality • Individual rights • Political awareness • Public interest

Source: Adapted from MacCarthaigh, 2008.

It would seem then that Irish civil and public servants are more likely to identify values that are more closely associated with a bureaucratic ethos, not unlike their US counterparts in Goss's earlier study of bureaucratic values (Goss, 1996). By contrast, the types of values associated with the democratic ethos and aligned with the earlier impetus for a New Public Administration and its closer attachment to social justice, do not appear to be as pronounced. However, there is a somewhat stronger emphasis at local level on fairness, equity and a concern for public value. The idea of fairness as a value is reflected upon in the comments of a number of former senior civil servants, one of whom in particular suggested that 'there would be a general wish and I would think all public servants see themselves as having you know a role in promoting fairness and equity and you know in that sense perhaps there is a view that the role of the public service is to treat everybody fairly, apply the rules and regulations in whatever area they're working in a fair and equitable manner' (Hynes, 2012). In this comment, fairness is clearly seen as something that relates to the manner in which rules and regulations are applied, not necessarily the fairness of their construction in the first instance.

Changing values
Adjusting values and associated individual and organisational cultures is undoubtedly a complex and time consuming goal. Two further elements from

MacCarthaigh's analysis of values are worth highlighting. It is noticeable that the ways in which values are transmitted, as with much capacity building in the public service, are very much dominated by interpersonal exchanges; by absorption of existing corporate culture and codes of conduct; from on-the-job experience and learning, albeit the influence of politicians and legislation is also noted. This is confirmed by Dermot McCarthy, who suggests, regarding the formation or training of civil servants that:

> it's very much on the job in the civil service context because of the generalist system of recruitment. There isn't a very active, structured induction and training system and this training system tends to be skills based rather than formation in the broad sense. So people I think largely pick up what's around them or don't. I mean curiously the public service, even though it's perceived to be you know homogenous and monolithic, arguably it's one of the few employments that tolerates a wide variety of styles and behaviours.

Moreover, where changes in values have taken place, there are a number of particular 'drivers of change' as illustrated in Table 6.4 below. Here the differences between the national and the local level becomes more pronounced, with the social inclusion agenda achieving greater prominence at the local level, reflecting the greater visibility of a social inclusion vocabulary in the local authority corporate plans.

However, what changes are occurring are ascribed to both externally driven, push factors – political expectation, broader society or social change, the influence of the EU, social partnership, public expectation; and, to a lesser extent, internally driven pull factors – public service reform and the influence of new recruits into the system. Most noticeably, however, there is no reference to education or training as driver of values change. This has led some to suggest that there is a need for 'Professional socialisation mechanisms, i.e. processes by which public servants learn and inculcate ethics, standards of

Table 6.4 Factors motivating changes in values at national and local level

National level	Local level
Public service reform	Shift to governance
Less emphasis on precedent	Social inclusion agenda
Greater political expectation	Greater public expectation
Legislative change	Avoidance of risk culture
Social change	Focus on needs of individual public
EU	servants
Social partnership	Import of private-sector management
Expectations of new recruits	practices
Focus on needs of individual public servants	Legislative changes (EU and domestic)
	Legal liability

Source: Adapted from MacCarthaigh, 2008.

conduct and public service values. Training (induction and refreshers) is an essential element (including training in ethics awareness), as are good role models (especially managers)' (Boyle and Humphreys, 2001: 54). However, the Comptroller and Auditor General has previously identified that most of the training provided in government departments is 'technical in nature', leading him to conclude that 'training on the broader front dealing with roles, attitudes and behaviours is less in evidence', suggesting 'an absence of appreciation, at corporate and departmental level, of the value of such training and development as a means of improving performance' (Comptroller and Auditor General, 2000: 38).

A capacity for social justice

The issue of capacity in Irish public administration is a recurring theme. Certainly, advances have been made in some areas, including supplementing the traditional career based system with a position based approach, i.e. allowing some level of recruitment of staff directly into the public sector (OECD, 2008b). Equally, the introduction of performance management systems, particularly within the civil service and local government is designed to enhance performance and effectiveness. In some cases too, individual government departments and or agencies have provided more area specific and intensive training for civil servants, such as that provided for officials in the Revenue Commissioners by the University of Limerick.

While acknowledging these advances, the list of identified capacity weaknesses remains long:

- failure to secure adequate levels of policy co-ordination resulting in a fragmented public policy environment and maintenance of silo mentalities. (Boyle and MacCarthaigh, 2011, Indecon, 2008);
- lack of engagement by many civil servants with real issues or real people and lack of provision of opportunities for such engagement (Callanan, 2007);
- slow pace of change in implementing initiatives under the SMI (Boyle and Humphreys, 2001);
- inadequate levels of leadership, at both senior and middle level management (Boyle and MacCarthaigh, 2011, O'Riordan, 2011);
- delays in undertaking organisational reviews in government departments (O'Riordan, 2011);
- limited capacity to enhance local government staffing through the creation of a graduate level entry programme (OECD 2008b);
- uneven implementation of performance management processes across the public sector and a confusion between measuring real improvements

in the performance of individual staff as opposed simply to conformity with the public sector modernisation process (OECD, 2008b);
- poor internal mobility of staff within the public sector (OECD, 2008b);
- reliance on the creation of state agencies to substitute for the creation of capacity within the core civil service (Hardiman and McCarthaigh, 2008);
- limited capacity to fully embrace civic engagement potential (McInerney and Adshead, 2010).

Of interest in this section is the capacity to deliver on a social justice agenda. In Chapter 1 some of the challenges of capacity building within public administration were highlighted, in particular, the balance to be achieved between technical, expert led approaches to capacity building designed to maintain control and command capabilities as opposed to those that are transformative and relational in nature. From the available evidence it is safe to say that the emphasis on capacity building in Irish public administration, either in terms of what has been done or that which is more recently recommended, remains firmly on traditional, technical up skilling with little focus on relational or transformative elements, thereby producing an imbalance of emphasis between capacity for public-sector management as opposed to broader capacity for public governance (Hardiman and MacCarthaigh, 2008, PA Consulting Group, 2002). To develop a robust social justice perspective transformative and relational capacities are fundamental pillars. Without the ability to conceive of a transformed society and without a willingness to build broader sets of relationships, beyond those who are economically powerful, there is a danger that public administration will continue to act in the service of a development model that has been unable to address injustice and inequality and, some might say, actually contributes to it. Issues of transformative and relational capacity are addressed below.

Transformative capacity
The capacity to envisage, manage and design the transition from one form of economic and social reality to a more sustainable and socially just reality is undoubtedly a complex challenge, not least in the current economic climate. This is especially true in a small open economy such as Ireland where the phrase 'loss of economic sovereignty' has entered into common parlance in a way that could not have been considered at the start of the twenty-first century. However, when sources of inspiration are much needed, the twin influences of T. K. Whitaker and Sean Lemass are still cited many decades later as the touchstones of transformative developmental thinking. Whether this type of potential exists in the current era is questioned by one civil society representative:

> My ideal would be a public service that engaged with government seriously on policy combined with a government that was unafraid of engaging with public servants at a serious policy level. Then decisions could be made that they both

> stood behind and carried forward. I think that's the ideal. I cannot understand why, for the most part, they don't work for that. (Healy, 2012)

Whereas in the case of Whitaker/Lemass the transformation was primarily economic in intent, it could be argued that what is needed now is a transformation towards a society, where social justice is seen as a central, overarching end, served by economic, social, environmental, cultural and other policy instruments. However, at this point in time, a comparable transformative standard bearer is not easily identified:

> We don't have a Whitaker who lines up with a Lemass and begins to pull the country in a certain direction. But that is what we do badly need, we do need leadership within the public service, somebody who can be creative and thinks these things. Because I think the problem with politics very often is it is so short term. Survival is measured in terms of how will I get to the end of the week? But you do need somebody to be doing a little bit of the longer term thinking for government. (Begg, 2012)

Indeed, when asked to identify critical social justice junctures, most of those interviewed for this book, while able to name what they considered to be important events, struggled to name significant junctures that have led to meaningful and sustained transformation towards a more socially just society. The absence of such critical junctures may well point to a lack of sustained leadership within the administration system. The necessity for leadership development within the public sector has been identified previously, particularly 'capacity to work across organisational boundaries' and in particular abilities to 'address the adaptive or 'wicked' problems related to culture and change that require solutions that must come from outside the current repertoire' (Boyle and MacCarthaigh, 2011: 6). This addresses one element of the leadership agenda, institutional and cultural change, but it does not appear to speak to the more deeply rooted need for leadership in the development and promotion of new ideas – the transformation agenda. There is little evidence of confidence that this calibre of leadership will emerge, the suggestion from one observer being that in its place …

> Finance will continue to be its conservative self. It will follow the trend it always has. I wouldn't have seen hugely innovative policies coming from the public service, I mean they're very competent and very honest administrators and so on but there isn't an obvious leader out there to me in the way there might have been with big figures in the past. So, the only leadership at the moment I see is political leadership. (Begg, 2012)

Equally, at local level there is a suggestion that years of centralised decision-making and restricted legal competencies has stifled local leadership capacity (Keyes, 2012) and in a curious way undermined the capacity of local government and local democracy to live up to its potential. This in turn led to a situation in the early 1990s where alternative local development structures were put in place 'to make up for the perceived deficiencies of local authority structures rather than finding ways to embed and give ownership within local authority structures for those kind of initiatives which is what tends to happen in some other jurisdictions' (O'Neill, 2012).

As well as the broader leadership issue, questions about the capacity of the civil service to develop and implement policy have been widely raised over a sustained period of time. More than a decade ago, Boyle and Humphreys (2001: 50) identified a need for a more developed 'policy intelligence/foresight' capacity so as to be better able to 'understand the causal theories which lie behind particular policies'. Callanan (2007: 37) cites concerns that the civil service 'dramatically reduced its analytical skill sets' and records that during the previous era of cutbacks in the late 1980s and early 1990s there was a trend towards closing down units with a policy analysis capacity in order to maintain frontline services. However, these were never replaced subsequently. Even more recently, the willingness of public servants to engage in evidence based policy-making has been questioned by some civil society organisations as well as those within the system. A civil society perspective suggests that 'A great many public servants don't know the stuff they need to know on policy. Often they ignore the evidence or refuse to engage with the evidence on a particular policy issue. An evidence-based approach to policy development is critically important but is very often missing in practice' (Healy, 2012) while a former civil servant is of the view that 'there's too much paper being produced, there's too much stuff produced and not enough high quality stuff. There probably needs to be more opportunities and training of public servants this item needs to be more prominent' (Hynes, 2012). This need to engage more broadly as part of the policy-making process has been acknowledged by existing civil servants: 'We don't talk enough, we don't engage enough, there's a bit of suspicion, on our part there's a suspicion of academics, on the part of the academics there's a sort of an intellectual snobbery towards public servants that they're doing a lesser job or whatever and that needs to be addressed' (Watt, 2012). That at least some of these weaknesses have persisted over time is evidenced in the Third Report of Organisation Review Programme. Reviewing the conclusions on four government departments as part of this overall report, Boyle acknowledged that while a policy and strategy development capacity existed in some cases, problems of 'strategic prioritisation' and deprioritisation remained. However, in case of the Department of Education and Science, he highlights the conclusion that the Department's capacity to 'develop strategic thinking or a holistic approach' is hampered by the depth of its engagement with short-term, operational issues' (Government of Ireland, 2012b: 149).

Just as policy-making capacity has been seen as a weakness, some also suggest that the capacity to assess the impacts of policy decisions needs to be strengthened, not least in the area of social justice. According to Frazer (2012):

'it wasn't that people weren't concerned about having results but they just have no method of actually knowing whether it had any effect'. This was confirmed by another former senior civil servant who commented:

> One of the things I say is I think we're very foolish because we put so much effort into making the money and getting the money and supervising the money and then we make absolutely no effort to look at whether we've spent properly or not other than from a financial perspective. (Private Interview, 2012b)

One possible way to address this weakness is to link career progression with specific capacity building requirements. Again, McCarthy (2012) recalls

> I would have argued strongly for the adoption of the approach that the military take, you know, that at a certain stage you know you get promoted but then if you want to be promoted any further you have to have served in a number of different functions and you have to have undergone successfully you know an appropriate course that shows that you're equipped and then having been promoted you have to do further training and the next stage requires further regulation.

However, beyond formal training there would appear to be a strong argument that policy and strategic capacity is built by exposure to a range of different experiences and perspectives and from direct qualitative experiences. The need to develop more specialist capacity within the public sector has been widely commented upon (Boyle and MacCarthaigh, 2011: 6), though again the specialisms cited as examples– economics and human resources – lean more toward the technical and bureaucratic and less towards the transformational. In order to achieve this specialist capacity, there may be a need to have staff with direct professional experience prominently located within policy units. 'in each policy area, half of them should be professionals from the policy area who actually are carriers of the professional knowledge that belonged to that area and they should have as much power' (Private Interview, 2012b). Such special-ist capacity may be developed within public administration by designing dedi-cated programmes or may be provided by external recruitment into the ranks of the public sector. However, there is little to indicate an interest in recruiting social justice specialists at senior level within the current public sector reform plans, for example, those with expertise in particular social policy areas, social inclusion, democratic participation etc.

Relational capacity
Paralleling the discussion of transformative capacity is the challenge of rela-tional capacity. Relational capacity is largely concerned with the ability to develop interactions with a range of actors in a variety of settings, equally acknowledging the role of those who are economically powerful and those who are not. Of course, this is easier said than done given the intricate sets of relationships that exist between the political and administrative leadership and

those who own or control large sections of the nation's wealth. Some of the challenges involved in developing relational capacity and progressing towards 'the relational state' were set out in Chapter 1. One of these was the ability or otherwise of the state to move beyond its role as an agent of 'standardisation' towards one where it is more willing and able to engage in processes of collaboration and deal with the irregular and the unpredictable.

There is no doubt that public administration has, at different times, developed some level of relational capacity, not least during the era of national social partnership and related processes at the subnational level. However, national and local experiences show that the primary emphasis within these settings has been on building up mutually beneficial relations with more significant economic actors, while at the same time exerting and/or extending dominant relations over those seeking to achieve 'less important' social goals. Where effective relational capacity was built up on social justice issues it has mostly been done via dedicated state agencies, such as the Combat Poverty Agency or the Equality Authority, one of which has been fully integrated in the Social Inclusion Division of the now Department of Social Protection, the other subjected to an almost 50% cut in its budget.

Taking the national social partnership experience as the vehicle to explore relational capacity, the state, in the form of the government and the public administration system, plays a variety of roles, acting as a mediator or conciliator; as a negotiator in its own right; but, most importantly, as the key shaper of policy and ideological direction (Clancy et al., 2005). For those involved in the process there appears to be little doubt that the state was the key driver of the partnership process, a role that was taken on, in particular, by a small core of strategically placed civil servants. Equally, there is general agreement that the core relationships within social partnership were between Government (Taoiseach's Department), employer organisations and trade unions described by one former participant as 'the key inner circle' (Personal communication: Business Sector Representative, 2006, Personal Communication: Farming Organisation Representative, 2006, Personal Communication: Community/ Voluntary Sector Representative, 2006). Despite awareness that these relationships dominated the process, less powerful civil society actors rationalised continued engagement partly in the hope of securing outcomes of importance to their individual constituencies and partly on the basis of needing to be seen to operate in arenas of influence where possible competitors, even within their own sectors, were already in place. For the community/voluntary pillar the opportunity to participate in national social partnership was seen to offer the potential to represent previously unrepresented voices, to place perspectives on key issues such as long term unemployment on the agenda and to mitigate the effects of the 'dominant effects of economic liberalism' (Murphy, 2002). However, for some, the presence of the disparate and less structured community and voluntary sector created something of a 'governance mire' that had the potential to strangle the overall process (Personal communication: Trade Union Representative, 2006).

Of course it is not simply the relative economic strength of the different partners that determines the nature of negotiating relationships. For at least some in the community and voluntary sector, participation in social partnership negotiations required them to negotiate those who were funding their organisations. It has been suggested that this has led to a significant reduction in the autonomy of community and voluntary sector and inevitably shapes the nature of their capacity to relate to the state (Hughes et al., 2007). Given the significance of state funding, it is also important to note that the mechanism though which such funding was provided had also changed in a quite dramatic way, from a pattern of more dispersed funding through different departments and statutory bodies to one where one government department, namely the now extinct Department of Community, Rural and Gaeltacht Affairs, exerted significant funding control (Harvey, 2008). Hence, the potential emerged for relations with a large number of civil society groups to be dictated by the ethos, understanding and perspectives of one Minister and a small group of civil servants. It could therefore be argued that the social partnership era, despite introducing the community and voluntary sector into national governance arenas, in parallel neutralised its possible impact through the exercise of an increased level of funding related, central government control on many of the participating organisations. Thus, while encouraging a form of associative democracy through the facilitation of associations to represent marginalised groups, government subsequently undermined the potential for relationship building and democratic deepening through the exercise of increased control and domination. If social partnership is symptomatic of broader experiences (and there is reason to believe that this is the case) it could be concluded that in Ireland, the state has been more concerned to engage with civil society in the pursuit of its own policy priorities, rather than to engage in a genuine process of dialogue and deliberation. In saying this, however, while the mainstream institutions of the public administration, the civil service and local government in particular, may been less than capable of building more progressive and sustained relational capacities, other parts of the state's administrative infrastructure have been more successful. In the past, elements of public policy and relational capacity, both economic and social, have been provided by a variety of external agencies. One immediate example is the National Economic and Social Council, seen by many as highly influential, particularly in setting the framework for social partnership agreements (McCarthy, 2012; O'Neill, 2012). Within the social justice sphere specifically, agencies such as the Combat Poverty Agency (looked at in more detail in the next chapter), the National Economic and Social Forum, the Equality Authority, the National Consultative

Committee on Racism and Interculturalism and others have played a significant role. Few of these have survived unscathed from the drive towards agency rationalisation, which appear to have paid little if any attention to their relational strengths. Moreover, the degree to which their relational capacity was valued or their policy outputs were welcomed by the mainstream public administration system is, at best, suspect.

Conclusion

This chapter has begun the process of looking more closely at how the public administration system in Ireland addresses the issue of social justice. It has done so by trying to gauge the level of commitment to social justice in terms of understanding and visibility, disposition and capacity using both secondary and primary sources. From this, the inescapable fact seems to be that at a corporate level within public administration institutions, social justice has a very low level of visibility. There are few, if any, examples of a 'whole of institution' approach to social justice or related concepts such as equality, equity, fairness or inclusion. This is despite the fact that fairness as an ideal occupies such a prominent place within the Programme for Government. More broadly, the public sector as a whole does not operate upon a clearly articulated foundation of social justice values or ethics that might inform subsequent corporate planning processes. In some ways however, this is not surprising as Irish society as a whole does not have a clearly defined sense of social justice, despite the present environment being replete with commentary on the relative fairness or justice of one or other policy or budgetary initiative. The absence of a social justice disposition and associated values is in some ways not surprising given the competition for the hearts and minds of public institutions and their staff. As has been the case in many other countries this competition has been dominated by the neo-liberal, market oriented ideas of New Public Management, transposed into Ireland through the Strategic Management Initiative and related reform initiatives. By contrast, a more active pursuit of social justice necessitates a shift in disposition, towards a New Public Administration perspective, where democratic values of inclusion, equity and participation provide the mandate, vision and inspiration for public officials. In the next chapter, these issues and the potential for a different approach will be looked at more closely through the experiences of a number of national and local case studies.

7

Social justice and public administration in practice

Introduction

Having explored some of the broader issues of social justice understanding, disposition and capacity in the last chapter, this chapter now moves on to look at a number of more specific cases, which provide some indications of how social justice is viewed within public administration. Each case study addresses a particular theme as well as exploring a specific empirical experience. Firstly, an instance of the use of agencies as a vehicle to achieve social justice objectives is examined through the experience of the Combat Poverty Agency. The second case involves the relationship between politics and public administration, looking in particular how the National Anti Poverty Strategy was received by the public administration system and, how the potentially valuable Poverty Impact Assessment process was dealt with. The third case moves into the area of individual agency and seeks to understand how an individual or group of individuals can act in apparently small ways to produce different outcomes for communities. To highlight this, the particular case of a local, urban regeneration programme in Tralee will be looked at. These cases are not exhaustive nor can they be presented in the level of detail that would do them full justice. However, they will help to illustrate some of the issues and challenges faced in seeking to embed social justice approaches within the public administration system.

State agencies and social justice

In Chapter 5 the rapid expansion in the number of state agencies created since the mid-1980s/early 1990s was observed. While this occurred across a range of policy arenas, a number of significant agencies with what could be called a social justice remit were also established. These included: the Combat Poverty Agency, established in 1986 and subsequently 'integrated' into the Office for Social Inclusion in 2009; Area Development Management Ltd, set up in 1992 and renamed as Pobal in 2005 and which was responsible for the establishment of different forms of local area based development partnerships; the National Consultative Committee on Racism and Interculturalism (NCCRI) established in 1998 and closed in 2008 due to funding cuts; the Equality Authority, established in 1999 but substantially retrenched in 2008 and soon to be merged with the Irish Human Rights Commission, itself set up in 2000 following the Good Friday Agreement; the National Disability Authority, established in 2000 and the Family Support Agency, established in 2003 and soon to be incorporated into a new Child and Family Support Agency. A more comprehensive list of agency type and structure is recorded in the Irish State Administration Database (Hardiman et al., 2012). Over time these agencies have taken on a variety of functions: providing advice to government departments and politicians; providing information to the public; carrying out assigned advocacy roles; and, in some cases, taking on regulatory responsibilities, with the public administration system itself being in some situations the subject of such regulation. Unfortunately, not all of these functions sit easily with the mainstream public service, with the advocacy role in particular proving to be somewhat controversial. To explore the broader disposition of the public administration system towards the role of agencies and their involvement in promoting social justice, one agency, the Combat Poverty Agency, is looked at more closely.

Case study 1: the Combat Poverty Agency
The Combat Poverty Agency (CPA) was formally established in 1986 during the period of the 1982–1987 Fine Gael-Labour Coalition, under the remit of Barry Desmond, the then Labour Party Minister for Social Welfare. It was established by statute under the Combat Poverty Agency Act (Government of Ireland, 2006a: S4.1) to carry out four principal functions:

1 provision of advice and recommendations to the minister on 'all aspects of economic and social planning in relation to poverty in the State';
2 initiating and evaluating measures to overcome poverty;
3 research into 'the nature, causes and extent of poverty in the State'; and
4 provision of public information, with a view to promoting 'greater public understanding of the nature, causes and extent of poverty in the state and measures necessary to overcome such poverty'.

In addition to these functions the CPA was also mandated to evaluate and comment on different programmes designed to address poverty, whether it be in relation to government departments, statutory agencies or community/ voluntary sector organisations. It was also empowered to identify and test new policies or programmes designed to overcome poverty and to collect information on poverty and community development. The 1986 Act further provided for the CPA to have a strong role in the promotion of community development, including the provision of financial support. Finally, the CPA was to establish and maintain 'contact with such Departments of State, statutory and other bodies and voluntary agencies as seem appropriate to the Agency to enable it to perform its other functions'. Speaking in the Dáil in December 1986 the then Taoiseach, Garret FitzGerald, commented:

> A new agency was established or, to be more precise, an earlier agency abolished by Fianna Fáil was put on a firm statutory basis, safe from their depredation should they ever return to office, to advise the Minister on all aspects of economic and social planning relating to poverty in the State, to initiate measures aimed at overcoming poverty, to examine the nature, cause and extent of poverty and to promote a greater understanding of those causes. Up to now no institutional mechanisms existed which were charged with these functions. The Combat Poverty Agency fills this gap. (FitzGerald, 1986)

In practice, this mandate enabled the CPA to engage in a range of different activities during its lifetime. It undertook significant amounts of research and information gathering and produced a variety of submissions into national policy-making processes. It directly managed funding programmes, particularly the Community Development Programme and the programme of funding for National Anti-Poverty Networks. It also provided a high level of support to local anti-poverty initiatives, including direct support for local government through the Local Government Anti-Poverty Learning Network. In terms of public information provision it generated a wealth of highly accessible public information material on poverty and social exclusion and established a variety of platforms to engage with civil society groups working on issues of poverty and social exclusion. Thus, at its height the CPA contributed an evidence based, policy perspective; managed and supported funding programmes designed to build local and national civil society capacity; produced public information and provided an accessible point of contact between the state and civil society organisations on issues of poverty.

In more recent years the role of the CPA changed and its range of activities were gradually narrowed, for example:

- in 2002, responsibility for the Community Development Programme[1] transferred to the newly established Department of Community Rural and Gaeltacht Affairs (DCRGA);
- in 2003 proposals were made to decentralise the CPA to Monaghan;
- in 2004, responsibility for the National Anti-Poverty Networks Programme[2] transferred to DCRGA;
- in 2005, training on poverty and social inclusion for local authorities was moved from CPA to the Institute of Public Administration to allow for its

incorporation into the Institute's mainstream training provision for local authorities'; and

- in 2006, responsibility for the Local Government Anti-Poverty Learning Network was also transferred to the IPA.

Most significantly, in 2007 a review of the role of the Combat Poverty Agency was initiated and undertaken by a steering committee drawn from an interdepartmental group with membership from eight government departments and including the then acting director of the CPA. The decision to undertake the review was prompted by the Office for Social Inclusion and is thereby suggested as having been an administrative rather than a political priority 'One could assume that a review of a state agency was not high on the agenda of an incoming government (though this may not have been the case) so the intervention by OSI to a new government was a significant step towards closure' (Doyle, 2009: 103). The conclusions of this group were informed by a narrow consultation exercise with the board of the CPA, the chairs and directors of the NESC and the NESF and with a number of the government departments represented on the review steering committee. At least part of the justification for the review, it is claimed, was 'the emergence of comprehensive strategies to promote social inclusion' and 'extensive new institutional developments in support of social inclusion'. The steering committee was tasked to identify possible overlaps and duplication between CPA and these institutional developments and to 'report on the on-going validity of the CPA remit' (Department of Social and Family Affairs, 2008: 2).

In its review the Committee noted that a variety of other reviews had previously been carried out, one finding of which was that 'CPA's role and traction is better established with the non-government than the governmental sector' (ibid.: 4). It pointed to the changing institutional landscape within which the CPA operated, including an increased role for social partnership and 'the relatively successful mainstreaming of the anti-poverty/social inclusion agenda within the Irish governmental system' though it noted 'that CPA's connections with this policy centre are at present relatively weak' (ibid.: 11–12). In the same vein it noted that the uptake of the significant volume of CPA policy submissions was limited commenting that these 'do not appear to have had formative or other major effect on policy development by Government departments' and 'show insufficient appreciation of implementation constraints and competing societal interest'.

In relation to its information and public awareness function the Steering Committee report observed 'The inherent tension for CPA (or for any similar organisation) between the policy advice and promotional functions.' It continued 'The more an organisation becomes associated with active campaigning for particular propositions, the less it may be regarded as having sufficient objectivity and impartiality properly to perform the policy advice function. We regard this difficulty as requiring good practical judgment from an organisation and not as ruling out the combined roles of policy advice and promoting public understanding' (ibid.: 17). The clear implication of this was that CPA had in the minds of some officials become to be seen as an advocate or as a campaigning organisation for particular issues.

Having considered these various factors and having explored the possibility of alternative institutional merger with the National Economic and Social Development Office (NESDO) which includes the NESC and NESF, the Steering Committee eventually concluded in its final report in September 2008 that an integration of the CPA with the Office for Social Inclusion was its preferred route. However, the CPA nominee dissented from the Committee's conclusion. This recommendation was speedily accepted by the government in October 2008 and incorporated into legislation in December 2008 (Government of Ireland, 2008). Formal integration took place in July 2009. This decision did produce some short lived political reaction, focusing mainly on the abolition of a statutory agency with capacity to provide an independent critique of government policy. For example, the Labour Party commented:

> The Labour Party strongly believes that undermining the independence of the Combat Poverty Agency would be a retrograde step. It would completely destroy the objectivity of the only statutory organisation with a specific and all-encompassing role in the eradication of poverty. It would represent nothing less than the silencing of criticism of the Government, however objective and constructive that criticism may be. (Shorthall, 2008)

This perspective was echoed by Sinn Fein TD, Arthur Morgan (2009), who suggested that 'The Minister's decision to strip the Combat Poverty Agency of its independent statutory status and to integrate it with the Office for Social Inclusion is nothing short of censorship.' Whatever about censorship, there is little doubt that the relationship between the mainstream departments and the Combat Poverty Agency had become less than constructive.

Understanding the demise of the Combat Poverty Agency

Like many other state agencies, the Combat Poverty Agency was established, to fill a gap that was not being addressed by the mainstream public administration system. In this case, the function involved the provision of policy advice, experimentation, promoting understanding and supporting civil society organisations and community development, albeit in the controversial sphere of poverty and social inclusion. It follows then that should such a capacity gap no longer exist then the need for an agency such as the CPA no longer existed either. This clearly was the conclusion of the majority of the steering committee that conducted the CPA review and hence their recommendation to merge the agency back into its parent department. However, the evidence base for this conclusion is far from obvious.

In some ways it is questionable that the review process was ever going to come up with any other answer and in view of the then Director of the CPA, the outcome of the review was a foregone conclusion 'Oh yeah there was no doubt, I mean that was fairly obvious from the very beginning that it was, it was a set up you know' (O'Kelly, 2012). For example, the Review's terms of reference sought to explore how CPA's role might be duplicated by newer institutional developments but when it concluded that there was some overlap, it did not ask the obvious question, which was whether the 'newer developments' did or could carry out the role more effectively than the CPA. Indeed there was no visible analysis or description of how or how well these 'newer developments' were dispensing their functions. The references to the comprehensive social inclusion mechanisms are questionable at best. While it is true that some structures and mechanisms had been set up, by the time of the review a number of these had been shown to be paper thin, as the example of Poverty Impact Assessment below will illustrate. Equally, the frequent references to social partnership as an arena that duplicated the work of the CPA is most curious, given the limited social inclusion benefits that accrued from it (Connolly, 2007). However, for some reason there was no consideration of the possibility that the need for rationalisation was not solely an issue for the CPA but was also relevant to some of these so called newer developments also. Neither was it considered that the issue for exploration should have been a broader one of how policy advice can best be developed and supplied to the government on poverty, inclusion and justice issues and then to construct the appropriate institutional arrangements accordingly. The nature of the review process has also been questioned by Doyle (2009: 105) who undertook a detailed analysis of the closure. She concluded that 'The Department of Finance review guidelines were not fully complied with and a value for money review was not done, so these did not cause the closure. An independent external reviewer might have produced different conclusions and recommendations, so the way the review was structured was significant.'

However, at the nub of this issue appears to be the CPA contribution to policy-making. The somewhat bland conclusion that the CPA policy outputs had not influenced policy-making pales somewhat under closer interrogation. While this was simply presented as a failing of the CPA; little if any time was given to consider whether, in fact, it might be the mainstream public administration system which was simply unwilling or unable to absorb the types of policy proposals being presented. Even if an agency such as the CPA wished to be connected to the policy centre(s), it seem obvious that it is powerless if the policy centre(s) do not wish to be similarly connected. In reality, no matter how good the policy outputs were from the CPA, judging it on the basis of how others absorbed its advice seems somewhat bizarre.

Moreover, the suggestions that the CPA recommendations were partisan and subjective seem to simply ignore that the Agency was set up to provide advice on how to tackle poverty. Thus, in many ways it had little option but to be partisan and subjective around issues of poverty and inclusion. The perception from one civil society leader is that civil servants may in some way have assumed that the evidence underpinning the Agency's advice was in some way tainted: 'the system, for the most part, was convinced that what was actually happening was Combat Poverty was deciding what was required in policy and was then producing data to support that policy approach. Their understanding of advocacy research was that it produced the required results no matter what the data might imply' (Healy, 2012). Whatever the understanding of advocacy research amongst officials, it does seem to be the case the CPA had become too closely identified with the agendas of social justice oriented civil society organisations, in the process placing it outside the state 'family' and more in the grey zone between state and civil society.

What is not in doubt however is that the majority of members of the review steering committee concluded that the continued existence of the CPA was no longer necessary or desirable, a conclusion that was perhaps inevitable given the nature and the narrowness of its consultation process. Thus, while there is only limited value in sifting through the ashes of the CPA, there is a value trying to understand if the rationale for its demise was simply a function of institutional duplication and limited policy impact or whether instead the mainstream political and public administration system simply did not want to hear what it had to say:

> That ended up being kind of an issue largely because, I would say, of the way the Agency used the media to criticise and put pressure on the political system to promote what it saw as the appropriate way to go. It was in the position of, I won't say conflict, but disagreement with the government a lot of the time, producing stuff that was very directly critical of the government. It was part of the system but at the same time not part of the system – there was a bit of confusion there. (Hynes, 2012)

Speaking of the Combat Poverty Agency also, former secretary general, Julie O'Neill (2012) considered that:

> There was almost an inevitability that a government would begin to get uncomfortable about funding a body to 'beat it up' for want of a better word. There is a natural desire while in opposition to press certain issues and to create the institutional structures or support the entities who will lobby for those. And then there is a growing discomfort once in government at the pressure coming from those very entities, particularly in a situation where resources are constrained.

Thus, it may be that a combination of political and administrative disquiet with the CPA was the more significant reason for its demise as an independent structure, rather than its supposed policy weaknesses and functional redundancy. However, the impact of the closure goes beyond the closure of one amongst many state agencies. Instead it weakens an independent agenda setting and future planning capacity (Doyle, 2009: 114). Taken in light of the discussions on capacity in the previous chapter, this further weakening of social justice capacity within public administration, where it was already weak, seems to indicate a somewhat limited disposition towards a more comprehensive approach to social justice.

Addressing the politics/bureaucracy dichotomy

The complex set of relationships between elected representatives and officials has been raised in earlier chapters. From this, any assumption of a neat demarcation of policy-making roles between the two is quickly dispelled. Both clearly have an input into policy-making though it is suggested that once a political decision has been made on policy, then officials will seek to implement it, even if it something that they may not personally agree with. The policy-making process has been described as 'incremental' by Dermot McCarthy (2012): 'officials do I think take a very active role in trying to make sure that the incrementalism is in the right direction and that you know the facts are known and so on. But they engage with the language that is shared with the political system you know and they take very much the objectives from the political system'. Of course, this process is more straightforward when the political objective is to be delivered through a single department. It unfortunately becomes more complicated when a whole of government approach, even one sanctioned by the Cabinet is required. One such example, the National Anti-Poverty Strategy, is now examined.

Case study 2: the National Anti-Poverty Strategy
The final declaration of the UN Summit on Social Development affirmed and acknowledged that

> the people of the world have shown in different ways an urgent need to address profound social problems, especially poverty, unemployment and social exclusion that affect every country. It is our task to address both their underlying and structural causes and their distressing consequences in order to reduce uncertainty and insecurity in the life of people. (United Nations, 1995: 5)

Having been announced by Prionsias de Rossa,[3] in Copenhagen as part of Ireland's contribution to the summit, the content of the National Anti-Poverty Strategy (NAPS) was finalised two years later in 1997, after a process of national public consultation and engagement with social partners and other interests. The original NAPS set out a comprehensive definition of poverty and sought to address it by setting a global target for poverty reduction as well setting specific targets in relation to educational disadvantage, unemployment and income adequacy. Other more general aspirations around rural and urban poverty were also set out. Shortly after its launch the NAPS was described by as 'a critical landmark in the development of economic and social policy in Ireland and a potentially historic development. If it is implemented with real energy and commitment over the next decade, the strategy has the potential to contribute to a radical transformation of Irish society and to build a fairer and more inclusive society' (Fraser, 1997: 4).

The main interest of this case study is not in evaluating the success of the NAPS or its various successors in meeting their targets, though clearly this is of importance. Instead, the case study focuses on trying to understand how the strategy was viewed by public administration institutions. In this regard, as well as setting a series of targets, the NAPS introduced a number of specific institutional mechanisms which have been gradually added to over subsequent years. Initially, political and administrative oversight mechanisms were identified to support the strategy, including a cabinet subcommittee and a NAPS interdepartmental committee, while day to day responsibility was placed under the remit of a Strategy Management Initiative team in the Department of Social Welfare. At local level, the creation of new structures under the Better Local Government initiative (Government of Ireland, 1996) was seen as a route towards local level implementation, though this was not elaborated upon in any detail in the original strategy. The National Action Plan on Inclusion (2001–2003) expanded these institutional arrangements further. It established a senior officials group, promised the appointment of liaison officers in each government department to act as the first point of contact on the NAPS, though, as it turned out, liaison officers were appointed in a limited number of departments only, generally those with a direct social inclusion responsibility. A NAPS unit was also established in the Department of Social, Community and Family Affairs, eventually evolving into the Office for Social Inclusion and more recently into the Social Inclusion Division following the incorporation of the Combat Poverty Agency. To capture and monitor impacts arising from expenditure under the National Development Plan, a new Equal Opportunities and Social Inclusion Co-ordinating Committee was also established. Various references are also made over the years to the operation of different thematic working groups, often through the mechanisms of social partnership. By 2007 upwards of 12 different structures had a named responsibility in relation to the NAPS and its various succeeding incarnations. There was a cabinet committee on social inclusion, chaired by the Taoiseach; various Oireachtas committees; a Senior Officials Group on Social Inclusion; The Towards 2016 Partnership Steering Group on Social Inclusion; the Office for Social Inclusion; the National Economic and Social Development Office (including the NESC and the NESF); the National Development Plan Monitoring Committee; the Combat Poverty Agency; the Local Government Social Inclusion Steering Committee; County/City

Development Boards; Social Inclusion Units in government departments and 'in half of all city/county local authorities by the end of 2008' and the Social Inclusion Forum, operated under the auspices of the NESF (Government of Ireland, 2007). Whatever reasons may explain the success or failure of the NAPS, there was clearly no shortage of institutional arenas within which it was to be a priority.

The rise and fall of the NAPS

In seeking to understand the role and relevance of the NAPS and its place within public administration understanding its genesis is especially important. In this case the interaction between the Combat Poverty Agency and the Minister for Social Welfare, Prionsias de Rossa, was significant with the general idea being initially proposed by the CPA and further developed by the Minister:

> I mean the Poverty Strategy was in a sense our idea. I remember when De Rossa was going to the UN World Summit on Social Development in Copenhagen in 1995 he asked for suggestions as to what he could talk about. I suggested that, given the emphasis the UN was putting on a comprehensive and integrated approach to tackling poverty, it would be a good opportunity to announce the development of such an approach in Ireland, something we had been arguing for some time … And somehow he got the Cabinet to agree to announcing such a strategy even though, at that stage, nobody knew exactly what it was and still didn't when he came home, but still he went ahead and announced it. (Frazer, 2012)

Prionsias de Rossa too has identified the role of the Combat Poverty Agency in the process highlighting, in particular, its capacity to link into European level research on poverty and responses to it. This relationship between the CPA and the Minister of the day was accompanied by a willingness by the Minister to act on substantial ideas, even if they hadn't been fully agreed by Cabinet 'I was bold and I announced it … I thought it best to do it before … before I tried to get approval for it, you know' (de Rossa, 2012).[4] This description of the origin of the NAPS becomes quite central to understanding its later implementation path. Effectively, in advance of its announcement, only a limited number of senior level politicians or officials were involved in discussions on its creation. It was perhaps inevitable that it would subsequently struggle to find deeper acceptance within either within the political or administrative systems. In the absence of substantial political motivation, administrative commitment is unlikely to follow:

> a lot depends as well on, it depends to some extent on the Minister, obviously … if they are engaged with it. And then that will drive it because when they sit down on a weekly basis or whatever with their secretary general and say, well what's happening on that … then the secretary generally feels he has to or she has to make sure there is progress on that. But if there is not that kind of pressure, if it is not part of the culture of that organization already … it won't happen. (de Rossa, 2012)

This suggestion of administrative disinterest appears convincing and is echoed elsewhere. In the opinion of one former secretary general, who had previously worked in the Department of Social Welfare: 'The elaborate mechanisms around it never kind of quite worked from my perspective – you know you felt they were a sledge hammer to crack a nut … It was seen as an irritant I think' (O'Neill, 2012). The resistance to setting targets proved to be a particular problem as recalled by de Rossa (2012): 'There was a lot of resistance to the targeting in particular setting the targets and really having to designate anybody within their departments to deal with them.' The limited engagement with the NAPS contrasts with the impetus put behind later initiatives such as Regulatory Impact Assessment, to ensure that policy was not encumbered by excessive regulation, the suggestion being that the latter was heavily pushed across the wider civil service. According to a current assistant secretary in the Revenue Commissioners:

> I have never read the National Anti-Poverty Strategy, I never had to, and I was never asked to. And I think that that kind of summarizes the difference in emphasis, it wasn't really promoted by senior government ministers to the degree that it impinged on the consciousness of somebody like myself, because I mean the National Anti-Poverty Strategy has as much relevance to me as the regulatory review requirement, it's something of which I need to be aware and what have you. But it didn't … no it simply wasn't sold with that single mindedness of purpose. (Buckley, 2012)

This suggests that on an issue that had to be addressed on a whole of government basis there was an absence of champions to drive and proselytise for an ambitious initiative. While the identification of the NAPS with a socialist minister may have further marginalised it within the administration system, there is no doubt that when de Rossa left office, it struggled even more. In his absence, it is suggested that 'the Department of Social Welfare couldn't drive a cross-governmental initiative on social justice' (Frazer, 2012). This seems all the more curious given the array of structures put in place to support the NAPS though perhaps it proves that the establishment of a battery of policy structures is no substitute for a real commitment to and capacity for policy implementation. In terms of institutions at the present time in 2013, the Cabinet Sub Committee on Social Inclusion no longer exists and instead there is a broader committee on social policy. Similarly the senior officials group now deals with the broader remit of social policy. The Towards 2016 agreement is no longer functional and in its place is a less structured 'social dialogue' process (Department of the Taoiseach, 2012). The National Economic and Social Forum has been integrated in the National Economic and Social Council, which itself narrowly escaped closure during 2012. The Combat Poverty Agency has ceased to function as an independent agency and now operates as part of the Social Inclusion Division in the Department of Social Protection. Meanwhile the City/County Development Boards are to be abolished under the reform of local government process to be replaced by Socio Economic Committees which centralises greater control in the local government system. The Social Inclusion Units in local authorities have in many cases been downgraded due to funding restrictions and were never established, as intended, in central government departments.

It is important to note that others have a more nuanced analysis of the influence of the NAPS, suggesting that it did influence the social partnership process. 'It didn't embed in the sense that people didn't reach for it you know at the start of every meeting or whatever but I would argue it did have a bearing on how policy advanced at a number of fronts and some of the heavy lifting if you like of that transferred into the partnership agreements' (McCarthy, 2012). Its role as a lever to force progress on key issues is also suggested by Sean Healy (2012) while others still argue that it has had an influence on consciousness of poverty and the very ability to even use the term: 'There's no doubt the consciousness of poverty and of the dimensions of poverty has improved. I can remember when there was a great reluctance to discuss poverty or to use the term widely in policy discussion but that is certainly not the case now' (Hynes, 2012). Overall though, while marginal impacts may have been achieved the key point remains that the NAPS was not warmly embraced by the public administration system. This is perhaps most evident in the case of poverty proofing and poverty impact assessment discussed in the next section.

Poverty Proofing and the NAPS
Alongside the raft of institutional arrangements described above, the NAPS did make an effort to develop operational tools to support the public administration system to more effectively design policies to address poverty and social exclusion. One of the most significant of these was the introduction of poverty proofing, subsequently rechristened, Poverty Impact Assessment (Office for Social Inclusion, 2006b). The concept of poverty proofing, originally introduced in 1998, was defined as: 'The process by which government departments, local authorities and State Agencies assess policies and programmes at design, implementation and review stages in relation to the likely impact that they will have or have had on poverty and on inequalities which are likely to lead to poverty with a view to poverty reduction' (Office for Social Inclusion, 2006b). Subsequently the Minister for Social Welfare, Dermot Ahern described poverty proofing as 'a major tool in ensuring that Departments are kept aware of the possible implications of policy on those most in need and it is a system this Government is committed to as part of its social inclusion strategy' (Ahern, 2001).

While poverty proofing was to be originally applied at national level, the Programme for Prosperity and Fairness (2000–2002) expanded this to emphasise the strong linkage between the NAPS and local authorities, commenting that poverty proofing would be extended on a phased basis to a local level through the local authorities and Health Boards (Government of Ireland, 2000a). There is little doubt as to the importance ascribed to the process in its subsequent description as 'the principal instrument for mainstreaming social inclusion at central government level' (Government of Ireland, 2003). It was intended that poverty proofing would assist in monitoring the achievement of targets; enable government departments to assess anti-poverty impact; ensure that policies did not exacerbate poverty but, on the contrary would benefit people living in poverty and would subsequently aid in the overall monitoring and evaluation of the NAPS (O'Connor, 2001). Following two reviews of poverty proofing experiences, one by the National Economic and Social Council (O'Connor, 2001) and a subsequent review carried out by the Office for Social Inclusion (Office for Social Inclusion, 2006b), it was decided to rename the process, Poverty Impact Assessment (PIA). The rationale for this was to communicate its role at the early stages of policy development not at the end. The recommended publication of PIAs was also designed to increase transparency and reinforce a commitment that it should be undertaken in consultation with relevant actors (Office for Social Inclusion, 2006b).

However, while the concept of poverty proofing did offer the prospect of innovation, implementation has lagged a considerable way behind. In reviewing different aspects of the application of poverty proofing, the Office for Social Inclusion (2006b) noted that in respect of departmental statements of strategy and annual business plans 'while most made reference to the NAPS or NAP/inclusion, only a very small number even mentioned poverty proofing and none contained any evidence that they had been poverty proofed'. More noticeably the same review, in respect of government memoranda, commented that:

> The impact on poverty is generally given just a cursory mention, stating that the policy measure under consideration will have either a positive, negative or neutral impact on people experiencing poverty and in some cases giving a generalised reasoning for this view. The rationales behind these statements or the data on which they are based are generally not mentioned. This approach is mirrored in the case of other proofing requirements and does not indicate that the process contributes to a greater understanding of the issues involved. (Office for Social Inclusion, 2006b: 26)

To compound this sense of lost potential the OSI review concluded that because of an absence of capacity to monitor poverty proofing it was difficult to know whether the impacts of different policy options on poverty were being captured. Equally, it was difficult to ascertain the success in 'sensitising policymakers to social inclusion issues generally' (2006b: 28). Despite this the Poverty Impact Assessment process continued to be cited as a model of good practice in social inclusion (Office for Social Inclusion, 2006a). However, the reality of how it was perceived within public administration and beyond is quite different, as described by Dermot McCarthy (2012):

> Our system is not very rigorous in its approach to policy-making and you know, particularly quantitative assessments are not as deeply embedded as they might be. So poverty proofing was light, it wasn't deeply influential I suppose as a process. I know it is/should be an important instrument in animating strategy but it's not the only one. Arguably a more profound influence is what impact it's had on people's understanding of what they're about and are they pointed in the right direction and whether having adapted the appropriate orientation whether they follow that through rigorously.

Unfortunately, it does not appear as if the NAPS has had much of an impact on understanding and attitudes within the civil service, though some positive impact has been reported at local level: 'I do believe NAPS had a real impact at local level. In some instances unfortunately it is treated as a "tick box" exercise. But the general level of awareness and skills has been dramatically improved' (Keyes, 2012). Inevitably given that poverty proofing has had such limited practical application, it is hard to see how it could have contributed to formulating deeper understandings. One senior official has contrasted the approach taken to promoting Regulatory Impact Assessment (RIA). In this case, he recalls:

> The Department of Enterprise and Employment I think it was at the time, actually sent people at principal officer level around every department to attend meetings of any committees that had to do with regulation of law, to remind them of the government commitment to reducing the level of regulation. There was no such initiative of which I'm aware around poverty. (Buckley, 2012)

Clearly, the RIA, which was designed, amongst other things, to minimise the impact of regulation on the functioning of the economy was seen by the public administration system as something to be prioritised whereas poverty proofing/ PIA was not. For example, the Department of Enterprise and Innovation website provides no less than 25 documented RIA exercises (Department of Jobs Enterprise and Innovation, 2012). By contrast, the website of the former Office for Social Inclusion (now the Social Inclusion Division) can only furnish three worked PIA examples, all from 2006. Taken at face value, this in itself speaks to the disposition of public administration towards social justice. It is not surprising then that some civil society commentators concluded that 'Poverty-proofing was a total failure; it wasn't properly pursued nor policed. It became nothing more than a box-ticking exercise which always concluded that the government was succeeding 100% in its efforts to poverty proof its decisions despite ample evidence to the contrary being available' (Healy, 2012). Equally, it has been suggested by one current assistant secretary that the absence of capacity building and support to enable poverty proofing to take place has been problematic:

Probably what was missing was again the capacity building around just how to use that tool, how to look at that, how to consider what the impact of your policy might be, from a poverty or a gender or an equality perspective. People wouldn't have felt very confident trying to figure out how to do that. And they were more comfortable saying, well somebody knows about that, we'll give it to them to do and then tell us, write that paragraph for us. So it was kind of like the aspiration paragraph then got written in, as opposed to any kind of real analysis of oh God do we need to be doing things differently now because we have analysed how poverty dynamics work in our area. (Private Interview, 2012a)

By 2012, it had become clear that the potential value of the PIA process, already a marginal activity, had become even more diluted by references to its 'integration' within the Regulatory Impact Assessment process. According to Minister Joan Burton (2012), 'Poverty Impact Assessments are integrated within the Regulatory Impact Assessment process, which includes a specific requirement to examine the impacts of regulatory proposals on the socially excluded and vulnerable groups.' This understanding was further confirmed by Minister Pat Rabbitte (2012) who seemed to have taken this interpretation a stage further, saying that 'In all cases where a RIA is undertaken a Poverty Impact Assessment is integrated within the RIA process.' However, the 2009 Revised Guidelines on undertaking a RIA, makes no detailed reference to the integration of the PIA into the RIA, though it does emphasise that the RIA 'should examine and identify potential impacts on socially excluded or vulnerable groups'. It goes on to state that 'Where significant impacts under any of these headings are identified, a higher level of analysis will be required for the RIA' (Department of the Taoiseach, 2009: 29). It does not, however, state that the requirement to carry out a PIA has been removed and indeed stresses in a subsequent appendix the importance of carrying out a RIA in line with provisions already in place for poverty impact assessment (Department of the Taoiseach, 2009: 94). What is not clear from public documentation is on what rationale or on whose advice have ministers dispensed with the stand alone process of poverty impact assessment.

In reality, within the RIA process the focus on poverty is almost non-existent and seems to be confined to a lone heading on the 'impacts on the socially excluded or vulnerable group' within a section on 'other impacts'. A random look through some of the partial and full RIA examples available on the Irish Government website (www.gov.ie) provides little evidence of attention being paid to the formal requirements of a Poverty Impact Assessment. For example, in a RIA screening exercise on the 'Proposal for legislation regarding septic tanks and other on-site wastewater treatment systems' the assessed impact on the socially excluded or vulnerable groups is reported as follows: 'The resultant improvement in the environment generally, on surface and groundwater and therefore on drinking water quality will be to the particular benefit of vulnerable groups such as infants, elderly or immuno-compromised persons whose health might otherwise be compromised by quality-deficient water supplies' (Department of the Environment, 2011: 10). The route to this incredibly limited conclusion is quite unclear given that likely negative financial impacts of remedial work on rural dwellers that rely on septic tanks are going to be quite significant. Even a limited knowledge of the context in this case would surely have merited a more extended comment on the potential negative impact on vulnerable and social excluded groups in rural areas, particularly if replacement waste water systems were deemed necessary. Equally, neither the 2012 RIAs of the Credit Guarantee Bill nor of the Microenterprise Loan Fund Bill make any reference to potential impact on vulnerable groups. It is noteworthy too that support for the RIA process has been largely transferred from the former Better Regulations Unit in the Department of the Taoiseach to the Departments of Communication, Energy and Natural Resources for 'economic sector regulation' and the Department of Jobs, Enterprise and Innovation for 'interaction of business and citizens with Governmental organisation, reducing red tape etc.' (Howlin, 2012). Neither of these departments is known for their particular knowledge of poverty or social justice issues, as evidenced in their lack of visibility in their Departmental Strategy Statements, nor for their capacity to support the undertaking of PIAs or even ensuring that others carry them out.

Considering the contribution of the National Anti-Poverty Strategy
It might be expected that the National Anti-Poverty Strategy (NAPS) announced by the then Minister for Social Welfare, Prionsias de Rossa, at the UN Summit on Social Development in Copenhagen in 1995 would be named by most informed commentators as a critical juncture in the evolution of a social justice capacity or ethos in the Irish case. However, amongst those interviewed in the preparation of this book, this was not the case. Instead, assessments of the NAPS, while agreeing about its potential relevance, are variously tinged with comments about its impotence, poor levels of political or administrative buy-in or a lingering sense of lost potential and opportunity. What the NAPS experience suggests is that even when a political decision is taken to advance a particular policy the likelihood of successful implementation is dependent not only on the existence of broad political support but also on the buy-in from senior officials. This is made even more complex when the policy to be implemented is cross-departmental and where a sponsoring minister has only limited ability to influence the 'silo' mentalities of other state institutions. These silo mentalities are seen as a considerable obstacle, particularly in building co-operation across government departments:

> The Departments work in silos and I mean I could see this in dealing with them from Combat Poverty ... they would deal with Combat Poverty, the Department

of Health would, the HSE would deal with Combat Poverty or Education, maybe reluctantly, but they wouldn't deal with Social and Family Affairs they weren't going to have a Principal Officer coming over from Aras Mac Diarmida to Marlborough Street[5] to tell them what to do, that just wasn't on. Whereas we could do it in Combat Poverty because we were an independent organisation and we could work with them separately. (O'Kelly, 2012)

Whether it is as a result of inadequate capacity building, lack of promotion or an absence of monitoring and follow-up, it is clear that the uptake of the National Anti-Poverty Strategy and of Poverty Proofing/Poverty Impact Assessment by the public administration system has been far from enthusiastic. The choices made to ignore the requirements of poverty proofing or to cosmetically engage with it, from the Cabinet, through central government departments and downwards to local government were all made in the certain knowledge that no negative consequences or sanctions would result. This does perhaps reinforce arguments to legally hardwire poverty proofing/PIA, thereby making it obligatory for all relevant policies to produce a comprehensive policy assessment. Clearly, the NAPS never gained the type of political and, more crucially, the administrative traction that would have been needed for it to achieve its ambitions. Deprived shortly after its introduction of its primary political sponsor, Prionsias de Rossa, the NAPS failed to secure the support of a range of champions that would have been necessary to see it implemented. However, there is no guarantee that even the longer term presence of a sponsoring minister would have been able to overcome the apparent administrative disinterest in the strategy and its poverty proofing/poverty impact assessment offspring.

The potential for individual agency

The role of individual agency and the potential for individual officials to make a contribution to achieving social justice objectives was highlighted in earlier chapters. Beyond the broader institutional questions the degree to which individual officials within the public administration system have potential and/or responsibility to address and champion social justice issues is an important area for consideration. This largely depends of course on the disposition of individual officials or group of officials but also relies on the extent to which a dominant, control centred ethical perspective restricts their capacity to operate with greater freedom and in a more deliberative fashion. This final short, local case study presents an example of how a group of officials – local authority and state agency – collaborated to deliver a different type of approach to collaboration and development within the context of an urban regeneration programme. While the focus in this case study is on the role of those within the public administration system, there is no doubt that the active participation of local residents and a range of community and voluntary sector organisations was also crucial to the success of the initiative.

Background

In 2004, Tralee Town Council decided to undertake the regeneration of an area of the town known as Mitchels/Boherbee. This is an area comprising approximately 700 houses, both local authority housing and privately owned. The population of the area included a mix of settled and Traveller residents and over recent times some issues have arisen to heighten levels of tensions within the area, both between settled and Traveller residents, including illegal wire burning and roaming horses and within the Traveller community itself. In its early stages, the regeneration project was envisaged as a primarily physical regeneration initiative, a focus reflected in the nature of the original 2004 masterplan and associated mechanisms for its delivery. However, this plan was revised and a new masterplan was completed in 2008. This current regeneration plan makes provision for a range of infrastructural, economic and social development projects, some of which have already been completed while others are still on-going. However, what is not easily visible within this or indeed any other planning document is the emphasis placed not only on physical regeneration but also on the process of regeneration and the central role of local residents within it. Those involved in the programme will readily admit that this focus on process was not where the project started (Scannell, 2010). Crucially, the interaction between staff of the Town Council, the RAPID programme in Tralee and the Community Work Department of the Health Services Executive (HSE) contributed to the development and delivery of a more holistic and empowering model of regeneration, one that neither receives nor seeks a media spotlight but which does deliver important outcomes for local residents.

While day to day responsibility for the management of the regeneration programme rests with the Town Council, the project is formally overseen by the Mitchels/Boherbee Regeneration Steering Committee, a committee comprising elected representatives within Tralee, community representatives chosen by the broader community and officials from Tralee Town Council and a number of other state agencies. The direct selection of community representatives onto the regeneration management structures contrasts with the experience of regeneration in Limerick City, in which all members of the overall regeneration board were centrally selected. In the Tralee case, the Regeneration Steering Committee is chaired at a senior level by the Kerry County Manager, indicating a high level of local authority commitment to the project. Below this a Community Participation Task Group (CPTG), supported by staff of the HSE Community Work Department, is in the first instance designed to facilitate community participation but in reality acts as a type of problem solving, clearing house to address any issues as they might arise on a more regular basis. As well as these more formal structures a variety of other informal fora dealing with issue or area specific needs are facilitated on an on-going basis.

Outcomes

At this stage a variety of tangible, physical outcomes have been delivered by the regeneration programme. Having recognised the need to move from a singularly physical regeneration masterplan in 2004 to one where community participation was heightened in 2008, inevitably the delivery of these tangible outcomes has been slow. This had been a source of some frustration in the area but whatever frustration has existed was well balanced by a sense of trust in the ability and intent of the regeneration programme to deliver. By 2013 a number of key infrastructure projects were delivered, including housing for older people, new low carbon housing, a district heating scheme and a new health centre. Others such as the provision of an integrated services centre, while slow to start, have progressed as intended. A number of social projects have also been implemented, including a Traveller Horse Project and the continued provision of a range of adult and further education programmes. However, planned economic projects have been slow to materialise, in part due to the impacts of the recession but also to the absence of an agency willing to champion economic development in the area.

Beyond the physical outcomes, however, the delivery of what could be called process results is one of the most enduring features of the regeneration programme. Underpinning this is a strong sense of shared vision and trust between most local residents and the Town Council. While substantial issues of mutual trust building exist between Travellers and the Town Council there is no doubt in this case that Council officials have devoted considerable amounts of time to building more open and constructive relationships. In short, the whole regeneration programme is premised on open and transparent communication. In the words of one local resident: 'If you've got something so say you can say it straight up to them' while another commented: 'I think they have been very transparent. Maybe we were very sceptical at the start that we were going on past reputations of the council, telling you one thing and doing another. I think they have been more than transparent on a lot of the issues' (Community Residents Focus Group, 2011). Another resident positively compared the regeneration experience with the past:

> This is the first time ever that the Council sat down with the people and spoke and discussed what was happening and listened to the people. We didn't make all of the decisions but we had as much a say as the council. It was the first time ever that they came together, they were always there if we needed them but this was the first time they asked the community what they want. (2011)

Evidently then there is a strong sense of Council officials being willing to listen and to be transparent with information, leading residents to have confidence in the nature of decisions being taken and their capacity to influence them. The willingness of officials to engage in a variety of formal and informal settings, a significant amount of which occurred beyond normal office hours is a key factor in building such confidence. And while challenges remain in building confidence across all elements of the community, a solid base has been laid. Beyond the issue of the relationships between the Town Council and local residents is the success of relationships between key state agencies involved. In this case, the earlier role of the RAPID programme and the HSE working with local authority officials is significant, mediating a movement from a purely infrastructural, product oriented programme to one in which the process of engagement was also seen as part of the regeneration ambition.

Issues arising

While a range of theoretical frameworks might be used to explore the Tralee case, it is appropriate to situate it within a democracy framework, in particular, deliberative democracy. Viewed in this way, the Tralee case resonates with many of the features of Empowered Deliberative Democracy (EDD), a theoretical construct that derives from practical efforts to deepen the democratic experience drawn from the United States, South America and India. Taking a look at the theory first, empowered deliberative democracy can be said to represent an attempt to more concretely address the institutional and democratic challenges posed by broader notions of participation and deliberation. It has three key features. Firstly, and particularly at the local level, democratic institutions should be concerned with the resolution of specific and 'tangible' problems. Secondly, it should seek to achieve the active participation of those directly affected by the problem and of relevant officials. Third, it should privilege the use of deliberative approaches to locate solutions (Fung and Wright, 2001). In emphasising the role of deliberation, it should be noted that EDD requires participation in deliberative decision-making, not just in powerless, non-decision-making, deliberative arenas, many of which may represent little more than post-decision legitimisation.

Alongside these statements of principles, three institutional design characteristics or properties are advanced. The first of these requires devolution from centralised administration to empowered 'local action units' which are 'endowed with substantial public authority' (Fung and Wright, 2001: 21), described elsewhere in the report of the UK Power Enquiry as 'co-governance' (Smith, 2005: 56). The second design feature balances the first, introducing the need for 'centralised supervision and coordination' to 'reinforce the quality of local democratic deliberation' by 'co-ordinating and distributing resources, solving problems that local units cannot address by themselves, rectifying pathological or incompetent decision-making in failing groups and diffusing innovations and learning across boundaries' (Fung and Wright, 2001: 22).

Clearly, the purpose of this feature is to encourage decentralisation while at the same time tempering the capacity for unrestrained and possibly ill-informed local action. The final design feature contributing towards an EDD ambition is the location of the state at the centre of the deliberative process, not at the margins. The objective in putting forward this design feature is to avoid leaving state institutions to go about their business while civil society organisations engage in a variety of external and quite separate activities. EDD architecture also emphasises the necessity for certain enabling conditions to be put in place. The EDD experiments point to a number of such conditions, the most signifi-cant of which is seen to be the balance of power between the participants in the deliberative process. The suggestion here is that if this balance is roughly equal, it is more likely that the deliberative process will work because readily available alternative means of decision-making do not exist.

The approach taken to regeneration in Tralee provides a positive exam-ple of public administration working in a deliberative way to advance social justice, broadly defined. Moreover, it provides an example of public officials carrying out their roles and responsibility in a justice conscious fashion. In the initiative described above there was no obligation on the officials to work in the way they did. Within the administrative system, full national funding support would have been provided for the original, infrastructure driven approach to regeneration devised in 2004, irrespective of a commitment or otherwise to the more process elements. However, individual agency amongst a number of likeminded officials directed a different approach. This is not to suggest that any one philosophical or theoretical construction of social justice informed the approach of those involved. Instead, underpinning the initiative was a shared desire to operate and communicate in a way that was, at its simplest, respectful and empowering.

The initiative displays many of the features of an EDD process. It was (is) clearly a locally motivated and designed effort to address tangible local problems in a way that strongly encouraged the participation of those affected by the problems and in a way that emphasised communication, dialogue and deliberation. It was not an externally driven initiative, prompted either by a national policy process or by an unexpected local crisis, as was the case in other more high profile regeneration initiatives, such as the Limerick Regeneration initiative. The Tralee case succeeded in creating respectful spaces where local residents could articulate their perspectives and could enjoy substantial levels of confidence that their perspectives would be taken on board. These spaces, facilitated by the legal personality of the local authority, constituted the local action unit. In this case though, with the exception of expenditure monitoring by the Department of the Environment, Community and Local Government, there was limited external monitoring of the initiative.

Crucially, the Tralee programme did locate the state at the core of the regeneration initiative and did not seek to bypass it in favour of a dedicated agency. While this may be a function of size in the Tralee case, it is also due to the fact that the regeneration impulse was locally driven, not nationally directed. However, even with the state at the centre of the process, officials have been willing to give up on some of their own power and control, thereby enabling more equal deliberation to take place, while still attending to their various political and management accountability requirements. In creating the necessary conditions for deliberation officials have:

- taken time to develop and share understandings and vision;
- devised processes that are informed by a commitment of respect, equality and openness;
- sought to build mutual confidence, even in circumstances where their confidence in some community members was seriously challenged;
- designed a process where they are accountable both to the local elected representatives and directly to local residents within the regeneration area;
- been action oriented;
- shown capacity for flexibility and openness to change;
- ensured that there is open and honest discussion between residents and local authority officials;
- enabled residents to have proper input into planning at every stage in the process; and
- facilitated residents to be informed of all developments.

At the same time they have not:

- expected people to participate in cosmetic process;
- privileged the views of those with particular technical expertise and instead have been willing to value different forms of communication and expression;
- undertaken consultation in situations where decisions had already been made or in reality could not be influenced;
- made promises that they cannot keep.

In producing these results there has been a visible breakdown of silos between a number of the state entities involved, in particular between the local authorities and the HSE. This has allowed a mix of perspectives, experiences and ideas to shape the initiative and has helped to plug any capacity gaps that might exist were a single agency to be responsible. It is clear too that the officials involved in supporting the process operated from a positive disposition towards meeting the needs of residents and were committed to a problem solving approach. So, rather than be perplexed by problems, they sought to identify innovative ways to resolve them and, within the bounds of administrative and political rules, displayed a preference for flexibility over rigidity; green tape over red tape; and collaboration over control. Most crucially though, this initiative illustrates how committed action by local officials can overcome the overall inertia within the public administration system towards social justice and citizen engagement. It is important that the system learn from and reward such initiative.

Conclusion

Through the three cases presented in this chapter a more detailed picture of how public administration engages with social justice issues begins to emerge. The more substantial, whole of government experience of the NAPS strongly suggests that public administration in Ireland has not enthusiastically embraced a social justice orientation. It demonstrates that there was ever only lukewarm support for a whole of government approach to addressing poverty and social exclusion, particularly if the impetus behind it is seen as marginal, politically or administratively or if the political impetus is short term. There is an argument to be made therefore that the NAPS did not live up to some of its early ambitions due in no small part to the unwillingness of public sector institutions to integrate it into their own departmental priorities. The agencification experience, represented by the case of the Combat Poverty Agency (CPA), further shows that while the state may establish agencies to supplement the operation of its mainstream administrative institutions, it will move to close them down if it doesn't like the messages coming from them, echoing some of the reported analysis of the Equality Authority. From a social justice perspective this creates a significant dilemma. If agencies are to play an advisory and policy support role, as in the case of the CPA, are they to do so only within the narrow parameters determined by officials whose understanding of and capacity in the area of social justice is limited? There would seem to be little value to having agencies in the first place if such limits are placed on their ability to bring different intellectual perspectives to bear on public policy.

However, despite the overall inertia and lack of social justice orientation within the public administration system suggested by the studies of the NAPS and the poverty proofing/Poverty Impact Assessment processes and by the closure of the CPA, the potential for individual agency emerges as something to celebrate. The case of Tralee shows how the contribution of a group of officials to work in an empowering, communicative and deliberative fashion can bring about real regeneration, not just in physical terms but in the capacity of the state to relate to its citizens. This smaller, localised example from Tralee offers a different perspective, one that shows how individual initiative, albeit institutionally supported, can make a real and significant difference. It proves that the world does not end when officials take time to talk openly to citizens and do so in a way that puts at least some of their power aside and which is solution, result and green tape focused.

Notes

1 The Community Development Programme (CDP) was set up in 1990 to fund locally based, owned and managed projects, designed to address poverty and social exclusion. The programme initially funded 15 projects and at its height in the mid 2000s supported more than 180 local initiatives in a variety of different communities.
2 This programme funded up to ten national anti-poverty networks and included organisations such as the Irish National Organisation of the Unemployed, the Community Workers Co-operative, the Irish Traveller movement and others.
3 Prionsias de Rossa was a Minister from the Democratic Left party in what was termed the 'Rainbow Coalition', which remained in power from 1994 to 1997.
4 In the context of the discussion on the closure on the CPA in the first case study, the NAPS experiences shows the degree to which the policy outputs of the CPA could influence public policy was, to a large extent, determined by the level of interest openness and disposition of the sitting minister and his/her officials.
5 Headquarters of the Department of Social Protection and of the Department of Education respectively.

8

Towards a social justice agenda in public administration

Introduction

The discussions presented thus far in this book converge into a single, power-ful, though insufficiently heard argument, namely, that social justice in Ireland or elsewhere cannot be achieved if the machinery of the state, the public administration system, does not explicitly place a commitment to social justice at its core. Irrespective of the strength of advocacy of civil society organisations or of the occasional impetus provided by individual political leaders, ambitions for social justice will always be undermined if public administration does not operate from such a commitment. While political leadership may on occa-sion offer this commitment, unless the impetus is of sufficient strength and is sustained and applied across the whole of government, this too may struggle to impact on pre-existing, embedded administrative cultures.

In Ireland there is little to suggest that there is anything even approaching an institutional commitment to social justice within the public administration system. This is not to say that public administration does not do things that contribute to social justice outcomes. Nor does it imply that individual officials or groups of officials may well undertake innovative initiatives and that many of them may be quite personally committed to a vision of a more just society. However, the experience is sporadic, episodic and unsupported by deeper institutional commitments, dispositions and capacity to pursue social justice objectives. This is evidenced by:

- the limited visibility of any significant systems level engagement with concepts of fairness, justice, equity, equality or inclusion, demonstrated in the analysis of departmental strategy statements and local government corporate plans;
- perspectives offered by current and former senior officials and prominent civil society leaders;
- widespread administrative disengagement from potentially the most

important political policy initiative to promote justice and address poverty, the National Anti-Poverty Strategy, and from the associated process of Poverty Impact Assessment;

- a more recent retreat from a variety of governance and civic engagement mechanisms, particularly from community development activities within disadvantaged communities;
- an unpicking of strategic elements of the social justice infrastructure under the guise of cost cutting, seen particularly in the demise of a number of key agencies, the disempowerment of others and in the undermining of important elements of social justice oriented civil society;
- a rise in New Public Management tendencies within public administration, with its emphasis on contracted and marketised service provision;
- an emphasis on technical, instrumental capacity building at the expense of transformative or relational capacities; and
- the absence of any visible leadership within public administration willing to champion the ideals of a more just society.

In seeking to explain the absence of a more visible social justice ethic in public administration, some may criticise the leadership provided by elected representatives. While there is some validity in this argument, as the significant role of senior officials in policy-making becomes more apparent locating responsibility with politicians does not stand up to scrutiny. Officials do not simply do the bidding of their political masters, they advise, they promote, they inform, they shape, both policy processes and policy outcomes. At local level their power is even more substantial. So, at a time when a commitment to social justice in Ireland is even more of an imperative, there is just cause for concern about how public administration institutions can contribute to renewing not only our economy but also our much damaged society. To address this concern, ten conclusions are offered for consideration in this final chapter.

Conclusion 1: it is necessary to articulate a broader, societal imperative for social justice
While arguments have been made that public administration can and should play a more active role in promoting social justice, there is a view that any public administration system simply mirrors the society it serves. Thus, if society and the political leadership it chooses are not committed to or informed by some level of shared values or beliefs in social justice, can public administration be expected to be any different? Of course the counter-argument to this is that public administration needs to be proactive, not just reactive, and should assume responsibility and leadership in shaping the direction of economic and social development. Nevertheless, there is merit is questioning the broader societal consciousness of social justice. Speaking to this issue, a number of sources

cited in earlier chapters proposed that there is a limited shared consciousness or understanding of social justice in Irish society and point to the absence of a sense of national solidarity, to an increased individualism and fracturing of communities and to a lack of a focus on social justice in the education sector, right from primary school, through secondary and into third level. Others observe a more nuanced understanding and point to the involvement of many Irish people in struggles against injustice and community activity, at home and abroad. There is some evidence that Irish people are conscious of injustice and the impacts it produces. For example, a 2010 Eurobarometer survey on poverty and social exclusion reported that 43% of respondents in Ireland believed that the reason people lived in poverty was because there was so much injustice in our society while a further 20% believed the cause was bad luck (European Commission, 2010a). Within popular debate, in the media and elsewhere, narratives of injustice and unfairness are regularly articulated, often accompanied by calls for state intervention to remedy perceived wrongs. However, what is justice for one may easily be seen as injustice for another.

This all points to a need for a more conscious exploration and elaboration of what social justice or a socially just society means in contemporary Ireland, with its attendant implications for public administration. An opportunity to enable such an exploration could have been offered by the Constitutional Convention, providing the space to explore the Constitutional provision for social justice and the admittedly impotent directive principles of social policy. However, as the Convention began its discussions in 2013, the relative mundaneness of its agenda becomes apparent. Thus, an alternative space or spaces needs to be created in which a more structured dialogue on the meaning of social justice in Ireland can be undertaken. In such a space, while we might not be able to achieve Rawls' ambition of thinking about social justice behind a veil of ignorance, we might well be able to begin to think about it in a more far reaching way and outside of a narrow, economically pre-determined and individualistic mindset. Consideration should therefore be given to establishing a National Commission on Social Justice with the objective of exploring some of the key elements of what social justice means in the Irish case. There is no doubt that such a Commission would encounter a wide range of views of what social justice is or is not, some of them contradictory. However, it would have the potential to begin to identify common ideals, strands and principles which could subsequently form the basis of Constitutional and/or legislative provision. It could also provide the basis for political parties and civil society organisations to clearly articulate their views on what social justice means to them. It could also enable underlying institutional elements, such as the role of public administration, to be examined. To ensure that the Commission operated with sufficient political neutrality combined with an appropriate level of political gravitas, it could be established under the auspices of the office of the President, building on the justice thematics articulated by the current and more recent presidents. Further, to ensure that its deliberations are adequately supported, a well-respected body such as the National Economic and Social Council could be tasked to act as the Commission secretariat.

Conclusion 2: reclaim public administration as a resource, not a liability

In one of a number of stimulating public interventions in recent times, President Michael D. Higgins (2012) laid down the following challenge:

> Public intellectuals are now challenged, to engage with the, often unstated, assumptions upon which taken-for-granted versions of our world are offered, often in the form of what it is suggested to be inevitable, rather than constituting any serious invitation to new understanding or, and even more important, compassion.

In the case of public administration the constituency of 'public intellectuals' of course covers a broad church, but includes those officials, commentators, academics, civil society leaders and politicians who are concerned to more deeply explore the future of public service in Ireland. Unfortunately, the voices of this cohort have been overwhelmed by much of the tone of popular and political conversations about public administration which have become almost predictably negative, fuelled by an emphasis on inefficiency, ineffectiveness, retrenchment, reducing costs and technical reform. Instead of public administration being seen as a national resource, we are approaching the point where it is almost exclusively portrayed as a national liability. However, like any resource, it needs renewal – not least a renewal of values and ethical assumptions, upon which deeper and more sustainable reform can be built. Unfortunately, there is limited evidence of thinking or deeper reflection on the nature of public administration, on its values, on its moral foundations or on how it contributes to Irish society. While some may consider such reflection a luxury in the current climate, postponing it is short sighted and may ultimately prove costly. At this point the challenge is to create spaces, intellectual and otherwise, to consider the role of public administration in Ireland, and, in particular, the role of public administration where social justice is core to its value systems and its operation. Table 8.1 outlines what this would look like and contrasts it with other possibilities for public administration where social justice is either subservient to other priorities, e.g. economic development, or is largely incidental to the functioning of public administration, being left instead to the intervention of non-state actors and/or the market. Each of these three contrasting possibilities will have quite distinct perspectives on variables such as: the role of the state; anticipated levels of government/public administration intervention; their underlying ideology of administration; their dominant ethical orientation; the principal value base; the nature of the disposition towards social justice; the institutional change imperative, if any and, finally, the public administration reform orientation.

Table 8.1 Contrasting possibilities of public administration and social justice

	Incidental	*Subservient*	*Core*
Perspective on the role of the state	Minimalist	Intermediate / activist (economic)	Activist – social and economic
Level of government / PA involvement	Low	Medium	High
Form of PA	New Public Management	Old public administration – Weberian hierarchy	New Public Administration
Dominant ethic	Discretionary	Control centred	Deliberative
Value base	Market values	Bureaucratic values	Democratic values
Capacity orientation	Oversight, regulatory	Technical, procedural, regulatory	Relational, transformative
Social justice disposition	Basic, emphasis on personal responsibility	Residual, targeted	Central, societal responsibility
Citizen engagement	Market / customer centred	Elite centred	Citizen centred
Institutional change imperative	Change impetus towards smaller state, reduced bureaucracy – increased reliance on market institutions	Democratic institutions are fixed and functioning as required. Little change impetus	Institutions may engender injustice and inequality – significant change needed
Reform orientation	Fixing dysfunctional public sector – applying a private sector reform framework	Technical reform, downsizing	Reassertion of public administration as a resource. Asserting values and public interest in PA

What emerges therefore is an understanding of a distinct form of public administration in social justice mode where:

- The state is activist and takes a leadership role, both in social and economic terms. It has moved beyond the intermediate role and rejects the idea of the minimalist state.
- Expectations of government and public administration involvement in the delivery of services are high, as opposed to other modes that seek to increase levels of delegation in varying degrees to civil society or private sector interests.

- The dominant ideology of administration is informed by New Public Administration which builds on the traditional Weberian notion of public administration but rejects the more market dominated orientation of New Public Management.
- The dominant administrative ethic is deliberative, emphasising on-going dialogue with citizens in a bureaucratic framework where system rules and regulations create 'green' as opposed to red tape. This does not mean an abandonment of controls, rules and regulation, simply a reordering of priorities.
- The value base is 'democratic', emphasising advocacy; compassion; confidentiality; individual rights, political awareness and the public interest, retaining, but not being dictated to by, values of efficiency and effectiveness and rejecting an inexorable slide towards blind acceptance of the values of the market.
- Capacity building is oriented towards transformative thinking and action and towards building the relational state, moving beyond the more narrow technical types of capacity building.
- A social justice disposition is central to the public administration rationale, rather than being subservient to exclusively growth oriented economic policies or premised on the primacy of individual responsibility.
- Public administration is citizen centred and facilitative of civic engagement as opposed to being exclusively elite centred or focused on the citizen as a client or a customer.
- The focus of institutional change is on enhancing institutional capacity and on recognising the need to address the role of institutions in creating injustice. By contrast, other modes of public administration will emphasise the downsizing of the state or will see its existing core institutions as needing little if any change.
- Finally, the nature of administrative reform in social justice mode will recognise administration as a resource and will seek to assert public interest values. Alternative perspectives will see reform more in technical terms or in terms of replacing dysfunctional public sector approaches with private sector norms and values.

Currently, it could be argued that Irish public administration as a whole lies someplace between the social justice as subservient mode and the social justice as incidental mode, with increasing pressure to embrace the latter. Clearly though, the public administration system is not homogenous and some elements may already operate with social justice as a core concern. For those that do not, the potential for social justice to be promoted as a more integrated and intrinsic part of their practice will inevitably rely both on internal motivation and on political and administrative leadership. However, it will also require external pressure, particularly for civil society organisations not only to advocate particular aspects of policy but also to focus on issues of institutional development and change.

Conclusion 3: express a commitment to a renewed and more meaningful form of governance

A key element of the social justice agenda for public administration is engagement with citizens and civil society, often expressed through commitment to different forms of governance principles and processes. While the global emphasis on governance as a means of addressing complex problems remains in place, in Ireland there is clearly a retreat from the practice of governance, particularly from the array of social partnership structures and processes created since the late 1980s. Whether this is purely politically motivated or whether it also reflects an administrative agenda is not always clear – there is undoubtedly an element of both. While accepting criticisms of some of the less positive, rent seeking elements of social partnership, the principle of engaging a wider number of voices in public debate on the development of public policy is more easily defended. However, as with the concept of social justice itself, a process of deeper reflection on the meaning and purpose of governance in Ireland is well overdue and could be informed by some of the more thoughtful examinations of governance in the global south.

One of these, which promotes the idea of 'humane governance', directly locates concerns about poverty, exclusion and inclusion at the core of governance, rejecting in the process: 'governance that is handed down from above by the elite' (Mahbub ul Haq Human Development Centre, 1999). And, despite being developed in a particular context, its architects contend that it offers a 'norm appropriate to all countries, not just South Asia. It remains an ideal even in mature democracies of the developed countries' (1999: 28). The Humane Governance approach calls for a three-pronged strategy to address the needs of: political governance, economic governance and civic governance. Good political governance, therefore, emphasises the rule of law, accountability and transparency and is designed to confront a view of the political economy that sees the state as 'captured by special interest groups; lobbyists and politicians eager to follow short sighted policies that will ensure re-election' (1999: 31). As such, it emphasises decentralisation of power and increased accountability, both for politicians and public officials thereby addressing the role of public administration. Moving beyond political governance, the recipe for good economic governance rejects a minimalist role for the state. It proposes that as well as being concerned with macroeconomic stability, the protection of property and the removal of market distortions, the state also has a responsibility to be 'concerned with investment in people and basic infrastructure, protection of the natural environment and a progressive and equitable fiscal system to promote economic growth with social justice' (1999: 31). Finally, good civic governance is concerned with realising the importance of civil society in governance, particularly those concerned with the protection of the rights of the poor and excluded as well as the promotion of good citizenship. All three dimensions are seen as being fundamentally interlinked and supportive of one another, 'Bound together by the principles of ownership, decency and account-ability, good political, economic and civic governance are equally integrated to form a governance framework that is both dynamic and progressive' (1999: 36). From this model of humane governance, it becomes readily apparent that governance processes cannot be seen exclusively as the means to achieve certain ends, even if those ends have a social justice dimension. Instead their very operation must be part of the social justice process itself. Recalling the distinct imbalances of power and priorities that were present in social partner-ship processes in Ireland, including the influence of public administration, there is at least some reason to believe that applying these principles of humane governance could have tempered or at least exposed to stronger scrutiny those priorities that dictated or indeed, distorted the decision-making process.

Conclusion 4: clarify the relationship between politics and administration
Asserting a stronger role for public administration in promoting social jus-tice occasionally encounters accusations of interfering with the politics/administration dichotomy. Here, the assumption is that policies to promote social justice should be determined only by elected governments and as such, may be subject to considerable fluctuation. This of course is a flawed argument. In the first instance, in Ireland at any rate, the Constitution provides clear sig-nals of a concern for social justice, albeit that the nature of the commitment is not justiciable and was toned down following advice from the Department of Finance and others during the drafting of the 1937 Constitution, as discussed in Chapter 3. However, this does not mean that the public administration system should not seek to act in accordance with the spirit of the Constitution, which at least went to some towards articulating a social justice/social policy agenda. On the contrary, it implies a duty for public administration to advise government and the Oireachtas on how social goals can be met 'The State shall strive to pro-mote the welfare of the whole people by securing and protecting as effectively as it may a social order in which justice and charity shall inform all the institutions of the national life' (Government of Ireland, 1937: 45.1). The system of public administration is clearly one such institution. For this reason, it is worth con-sidering the argument that it has not lived up to its Constitutional obligations and has instead been complicit in the creation of a social order where justice and charity as primary guiding principles have been largely forgotten.

Beyond the Constitution, the public administration system is further bound by a whole range of international human rights obligations to which the Irish state has committed itself. However, awareness of these obligations and the concepts that underpin them is far from adequate. Efforts to more effectively inform the staff of public-sector institutions about these commitments are being made by the Irish Human Rights and Equality Commission through the provision of a targeted training programme for officials and different levels of administration. However, the fact that the funding for the training programme is not provided by the state, but by a philanthropic donor, is itself revealing of a less than committed attitude to translating human rights commitment into administrative practice. Nevertheless, the existence of these Constitutional and treaty based commitments justifies an argument that public administration should play a stronger role in promoting social justice approaches and, accordingly, should provide more direct and proactive advice to government and to the Dáil, via the appropriate committees. More controversially perhaps, it also establishes a duty on public administration to act as a promoter and protector of social justice throughout the policy formulation and implementation cycle. Unfortunately, the unwillingness to embrace the innovative poverty proofing/poverty impact assessment process discussed in Chapter 7, does not inspire confidence in its willingness to do this but does not displace the obligation that exists. This of course brings us back to the earlier analogy of the passenger ship (citizens) being steered by the captain (political leadership) and rowed by the crew (public administration) towards the rocks (economic and social crisis). At what point can the crew be expected to inform the captain of the folly of maintaining a course destined for disaster, assuming of course that they even recognise the danger. If they do recognise the danger, does their obligation and loyalty lie with the captain, at all costs seeking to avoid any embarrassment in front of the passengers; or is it to the passengers. If the latter, does this require the crew to in some way to communicate the imminent danger, short of mutiny, and in a way that does not undermine the captain. In real terms, this represents the possibility of a conflict between of public administration's obligations in service to the government and its obligation in service to the nation and its citizens, as expressed through the Constitution and international human rights obligations. It is probable that such a conflict will only arise in exceptional circumstances, such as those that are presently occurring in Ireland. In this case however, the crew has kept rowing and seems to have been unknowing, unwilling or unable to communicate clear and audible warnings or to have those warnings listened to. This introduces the need to increase the visibility of the advice provided by officials to the political system as a means of tempering political excesses, either through Dáil Committees; publication of policy option papers by senior officials or presentation of policy options to a renewed governance process. Whatever route might be found will inevitably raise objections on the basis of undermining the democratic process. However, in certain circumstances, there is already an acceptance of the principle of administrative checks on democratic decision-making, not least in the refusal of successive governments to countenance the creation of real local democracy and evidenced in more recent restrictions on the power of local councillors to rezone land. Thus, the notion of public administration as simply subservient to the will of elected representatives becomes more attractively nuanced.

Conclusion 5: recognise civic engagement and a strong civil society as components of a healthy democracy

In Chapter 4 the relationship between social justice and civic engagement was established. This is not to say that civic engagement is exclusively a social justice issue, just that achieving social justice objectives requires attention to enabling the voice of all citizens to be heard, not just those with wealth, status or education. However, the gap between civic engagement theory and civic engagement practice is considerable and significant challenges are presented to live up to the rhetoric of participation. In Ireland, a recent Government White Paper Putting People First has added considerably to the rhetoric, but provided no weight of decision-making or firm impetus that might deepen local democratic participation.

Within any civic engagement context, public administration plays a crucial role: brokering or blocking access; facilitating or frustrating participation; enabling or emasculating voice; managing or manipulating relationships. However, little of the available evidence suggests that there is much appreciation of the democratic underpinnings of civic engagement, of the relationship between representative and participatory democracy and of the role of public administration in marrying the two. Equally, in practice, there is little evident valuing by government of the ideal of an independent civil society as a component of a healthy democracy. This contrasts with the clear recognition by the Irish government of the role of civil society organisations in countries many thousands of miles away, where it contends that:

> All groups in society must play their part in the development process. Citizens have a right and a responsibility to participate in and influence political decisions that affect their lives. These rights and responsibilities can be exercised through formal structures (e.g. voting in elections), and by organising themselves to demand better services from their governments. More broadly, they can demand more responsive and more accountable government. (Government of Ireland, 2006b)

Unfortunately, expressions of such clarity from the White Paper on Irish Aid are becoming rarer in the domestic environment. For all intents and purposes there appears to be unwillingness to see civil society as a fundamental component of the democratic infrastructure. As a result, there is a failure to rationalise and justify the expenditure of exchequer resources on civil society organisations on democratic grounds, particularly for those elements of civil society which are without independent resources and who seek to promote social justice. The growing reluctance to recognise the importance of funding social justice advocacy is symptomatic of the narrow vision for civil society prevalent within much of the public administration and political systems. Equally, there is little if any protection for civil society organisations from the whims of politicians or public servants who it seems can restructure, punish or reward less powerful civil society organisations with relative impunity. In Ireland, largely due to the low level of philanthropic funding, maintaining and enhancing the capacity of civil society, and therefore of democracy, relies heavily on the investment of state resources. The delivery of these resources needs to be structured in such a way that protects the autonomy of civil society organisations, within transparent accountability frameworks, but which do not unduly inhibit their capacity to provide open and sometimes critical commentary on the role of government and indeed of public administration. This may well require an independent funding mechanism to be created, possibly through a dedicated state agency that can sustain the level of ideational tension that is essential to democratic creativity and renewal.

Conclusion 6: build the capacity of public administration to lead on social justice

Many of those who write about public administration in Ireland have variously pointed to capacity deficits, in long term planning, policy co-ordination, civic engagement, pace of institutional and organisational change, leadership and consistency. On the other hand, some elements of public administration are seen as having made huge progress in building their competencies, not least the Revenue Commissioners, who are consistently ranked amongst the top tax collection bodies in the world. It is perhaps significant that the Revenue Commissioners have entered into collaboration with the third level sector in order to enhance the skills of its staff. While the main emphasis in the case of the Revenue Commissioners is on technical aspects of taxation, some broader elements of social administration are catered for, including a focus on the role of public administration in social justice. In general though, current plans for the reform of the public sector signal little concern to increase capacity beyond a range of management, technical and instrumental competencies, either in the training of existing staff or in the recruitment of external staff into the public service. At a more specific level, the absence of a focus on social justice competencies at all levels within the public sector is apparent, in particular, the weakness of transformative and relational capacity. This presents challenges at a number of different levels.

In the first instance, the distinct but related challenges of deepening knowledge and enhancing disposition around social justice call for attention.

The focus on knowledge seeks to increase exposure to different ideas and understandings of what social justice means and their possible implications for the public sector. At the same time, to make use of or to create openness to new knowledge will inevitably require changes in individual and institutional thinking on social justice, on the reasons for social injustice and inequality, on the role of state institutions in generating injustice and inequality and on accelerated processes of ideational, organisational and cultural change. Adjusting disposition will also require a particular focus on the role of senior officials in signalling the centrality of a social justice approach, an issue which is addressed further below. However, any discussion of knowledge and dispositional challenges raises the shadow of the perceived anti-intellectual bias that exists within the public sector and in politics. Addressing the complexities of social justice requires not only knowledge, but new ways of thinking and exposure to ideas and concepts that draw officials beyond the immediacy of their administrative realities. For those socialised in the realm of the practical, the instrumental and the applied, this can appear abstract, impractical and unnecessary. However, without creating the space and the imperative to reflect on established, possibly tired and sometimes discriminatory modes of thinking, the ability to stimulate transformative mindsets and to generate new and more effective solutions to old problems will be inhibited. There is no doubt that some in the public sector will dismiss out of hand the value of promoting deeper understandings of social justice, such as occurred with the National Anti-Poverty Strategy, but this innate conservatism will needed to be tackled at senior level if a commitment to social justice is to become more deeply embedded within public administration.

Having addressed the knowledge and dispositional elements, a comprehensive programme of skills development will subsequently allow increased knowledge and renewed disposition to be translated into more concrete social justice outcomes and outputs, for example, skills in the areas of programme and project design, poverty impact assessment, civic engagement, facilitation, communication, research, to name but a few. A second major challenge of course is how to deliver such a programme, particularly at a time when resources are scarce. At a practical level, increasing the capacity of existing staff could be pursued in a number of ways:

- The internal training units present in many government departments could be required and supported to directly address the challenge of raising awareness of social justice issues, including the delivery social justice oriented training programmes and curricula. The development of these training programmes could be achieved in partnership with civil society organisations and/or third-level institutions.
- New forms of learning partnerships could be developed with civil society

organisations and the third-level sector, including the option of intern-
ships for civil/public servants within civil society organisations and vice
versa.
- Comprehensive capacity building programmes could also be developed
for departmental staff in partnership with third level institutions, following the Revenue Commissioners' model.
- Specialist 'social justice' units could be established within public sector
institutions, with a particular focus on institutional capacity building.
Some of the specialised social inclusion units set up within local government may provide a model for this, though unfortunately these were often
staffed by people who themselves had no specialist knowledge or skills in
the area of social inclusion or social justice.

Beyond the focus on existing staff, the other obvious way to increase social justice capacity is to directly recruit social justice specialists into the public sector
at relatively senior levels. Thus, in the same way that the deficit in economic
planning capacity has been recognised and addressed, so too the capacity
deficits in the area of social justice should be acknowledged and remedied by
direct recruitment.

Finally, the task of building capacity for social justice presents particular
challenges for educational institutions that offer programmes to existing public
sector staff and potential public sector recruits. These institutions need to
consider the balance their programmes offer between more narrow, workplace
specific education and the type of broader intellectual development needed to
enable leadership in pursuit of a more just society.

Conclusion 7: actively build a stronger and more widespread disposition towards social justice within public administration

The relationship between disposition and social justice as it is addressed in this
book is not simply a question of whether someone is in favour or otherwise
of the pursuit of social justice objectives as a matter of public policy; it goes
deeper than this and encompasses a more fundamental conflict of ideas about
the nature and role of public administration itself and related questions about
the nature and practice of democratic decision-making. Going even further
beyond this, a focus on disposition targets understandings of justice and the
type of ingrained and arbitrary orthodoxies that may be more or less conscious
and more or less explicit, but which influence individual and institutional
behaviours. The contrasting case studies of the National Anti-Poverty Strategy
(NAPS) and the Tralee Regeneration programme in the previous chapter
illustrate the importance of individual and institutional disposition as a factor
in pursuing social justice outcomes. On one hand, in the NAPS, a combination
of institutional and individual dispositions allowed officials to pay less than

adequate attention to a whole-of-government initiative to address poverty and social exclusion, a disposition that weakened even further when the original sponsoring minister left political office. There is little evidence either of institutional drive to embed the Strategy or of sanctions on those who ignored some of its main components. On the other hand, in the case of the Tralee regeneration programme, a group of local authority and HSE officials, combining strongly citizen centred and social justice dispositions, quietly led an effective regeneration programme which has, in most cases, built strong trust and relations with the local community. This was not driven by a pre-existing institutional disposition, but neither was it impeded by it.

What is less clear from these case studies, and the NAPS in particular, is whether the failure to fully embrace the strategy was motivated simply by a lack of understanding or inadequate motivation, aided by an inability to break through institutional silos or whether it represents a more deeply ingrained opposition to social justice policies being rolled out across the public sector. From the views of most of those interviewed for this book it would appear to be the former: a lack of drive, of resourcing and an unwillingness to take ownership of a policy that emanated from one particular government department. However, there is a need to undertake further and more widespread research to assess this question more comprehensively. In the meantime, and alongside the capacity building elements discussed earlier, achieving a stronger social justice disposition presents a more immediate challenge to focus attention on articulating the value base and the moral foundation of Irish public administration. More specifically, it confronts public administration with the differences between the types of activist, democratic and citizen centred values associated with a New Public Administration or the type of minimalist, bureaucratic and customer oriented principles of New Public Management (NPM). If nothing else, a dialogue about these different perspectives would enable a more conscious and self-directed future to be chosen, rather than simply drifting further down the NPM route because no other alternative has been presented.

Conclusion 8: developing the relational state

As well as building the capacity to envisage a transformed society, the capacity of the state and public administration in particular to relate to its citizens presents an on-going challenge. The complexities of building the 'relational state' have already been addressed in Chapter 1, with some suggesting that, in practice, the mainstream infrastructure of the state may have an inherent inability to operate in relational mode and will find it particularly difficult to deal with 'difference, contingency and essential unpredictability' (Stears, 2012: 39). The logic of this argument resonates with the rationale sometimes advanced for the creation of state agencies in Ireland and elsewhere; namely, that agencies have a particular capacity to do things that mainstream government departments are unable to do and they can do them without the same bureaucratic restrictions. Effectively, state agencies can operate less in control or rules centred fashion and more in an entrepreneurial or deliberative mode, enabling them to build more effective relationships with a range of relevant stakeholders, often acting as a bridge between stakeholders and mainstream public administration. As such, agencies can be seen as adding considerably to the capacity of the activist state. For agencies established with a dedicated or partial social justice remit, the evidence of this is readily visible. For example, the Combat Poverty Agency, the Equality Authority, the National Economic and Social Forum, the National Economic and Social Council and others all created a particular capacity to reach out to often marginalised communities in a way that government departments could never hope to. At a sub-national level, many, if not all, local development companies fulfilled a similar role, engaging with communities that local authorities often had little contact with.

In more recent times however, much of this relational capacity has been abandoned in the generalised targeting of state agencies and their lazy portrayal as unnecessary and wasteful. To some extent it could be argued that this has been used as a means of curbing the role of some agencies, not least those with a social justice remit. This is most evident in the approach taken to the closure of the Combat Poverty Agency and the budget reductions imposed on the Equality Authority. Equally, the proposals to place local development companies more firmly under the control of local government runs the risk of diminishing much of their relational capacity and provides a convenient distraction to yet another failure to adequately address the devolution of power to local government in Ireland. In the short term at least, the pursuit of social justice objectives requires the relational capacity of the state to be increased and certainly not diminished, a role which experience suggests, is enhanced by the presence of dedicated state agencies as opposed to relying solely on the mainstream institutions of public administration.

Conclusion 9: monitoring the role of public administration in promoting social justice

It is one thing to put mechanisms in place to promote social justice ideas within public administration, but it is something else to know that these ideas are being pursued and that they are achieving a desired impact. One of the recurring themes in earlier chapters has been an acknowledgement of the limited ability within the public administration system to assess the impact of policy or indeed to even know that it has been implemented in the way that was intended. The experience of the National Anti-Poverty Strategy highlights in stark terms the need for stronger capacity to monitor and evaluate policy implementation, particularly in the realm of social justice. While this might in an ideal world might be undertaken by the Office for Social Inclusion, it is far from clear that the necessary capacity or motivation to do so exists. It could also be incorporated as an element of the Organisational Review Programme (ORP) process, though the frequency and capacity of this process may be limiting. Consideration needs therefore to be given to the establishment of some form of a publicly funded but independent Social Justice Observatory which would be specifically tasked with monitoring the contribution of public administration in addressing social justice issues, potentially highlighting innovative actions and exposing poor practice. This could in the first instance provide the basis to highlight and disseminate best practice but could also undertake more detailed reviews of social justice innovations.

Conclusion 10: recognising the centrality of the local

Finally, the particular importance of local level public administration has to be noted and its role in the promotion of social justice considerably enhanced. The local level, whether this is defined as a county or sub-county unit, is the level at which citizens most often encounter public administration, from a very young age within the education system or as adults through a range of different exchanges with local authorities, health services, the justice system and others. It is the level at which positive impressions and engagements are often generated or it can be the level where disillusion with public administration begins. For those who rely more heavily on welfare support from the state it is also the main level of interaction, one where their human dignity is either reaffirmed or where it is diminished. While local public administration has little if any control or influence on how national policy decisions are made, it has considerable scope to influence and shape how those policies are delivered, as evidenced by the Tralee regeneration case study. Moreover, its proximity to citizens offers the potential for more regular engagement, providing an opportunity to harvest valuable information on citizen concerns and the relevance of certain policies.

However, there are deficits to be addressed if local public administration is to play a stronger role in promoting social justice. A notable feature of local administration in Ireland, particularly within local government, is the absence of an established capacity to generate new ideas, reflect on past practices or identify new directions. This contrasts with experiences from the UK where a body such as the Local Government Association provides a much stronger 'thinking' capacity for local government, undertakes research, gathers perspectives, organises campaigns and reflects more regularly on the contribution of local government. While, the size and functions of local government in the UK are far more extensive than in Ireland, there remains nevertheless a need for a similar capacity to be developed in Ireland. In particular, the local level capacity to innovate around social justice, social inclusion or civic engagement is another area of weakness in local administration in Ireland. This again contrasts with the UK where the establishment of Fairness Commissions to address inequality in a number of local authorities – York, Islington, Tower Hamlets, Sheffield, Liverpool, Newcastle and Blackpool – points to a social justice oriented innovation, prompted from within the local authorities themselves rather than being dictated by central government. Specific consideration therefore needs to be given to how local public administration can play a more active and effective role in deepening the consciousness and practice of social justice. In the context of the recently introduced property tax, such consideration would appear timely.

The last word ...

These ten conclusions capture some of the perspectives on the role of public administration in promoting social justice in Ireland. It is not assumed that the thinking behind them or the proposals within them will find universal approval, agreement or that they will be easily delivered. However, for those who are interested in achieving a more just society in Ireland in these most challenging of times, they do present an entreaty, an intellectual challenge to conceive of public administration in a different way. Across the range, institutions concerned with the administration of the public sector, including the education sector, there has been a wholly inadequate level of reflection on the role, function and mechanics of public administration and how it addresses the priority of social justice. Is it acceptable at this point that such reflection continues to be seen as a luxury, something that has to await the resolution of the budget deficit or the resumption of higher levels of economic growth? Failure to reflect more deeply on administrative choices at this point in time may generate further systemic weaknesses and associated social costs down the line. This poses a particular challenge to the education sector to address its own responsibilities and to create spaces for deeper reflection and learning. It is of course recognised that such a process will be difficult and contested, potentially divisive as well as controversial. However it is needed now more than ever. In this regard, it seems appropriate to leave the final word on this to Barrington:

> At the moment it is perhaps only necessary to point out that great perplexities exist in all of these questions and that it is the task of those who study public administration to try to produce some sort of principles by which these problems could be tackled so that what we might call 'institutional development' can be got going. We have had too much hunting after fashion in fits and starts, and too little thought about how best to produce a gradually developing model of a system of government, coherently organised to meet the political, infrastructural, economic, social, and cultural needs of the people if the consensus on which the whole enterprise depends is to be maintained and enhanced. (Barrington, 1980: 28)

References

Aberbach, J. 2003. 'Administration in an Era of Change'. *Governance*, 16, 315–319.

Adams, J. 1902. *Democracy and Social Ethics*, New York: Macmillan.

Adshead, M. 2002. *Developing European Regions? Comparative Governance, Policy Networks and European Integration*, Harlow: Ashgate.

Adshead, M. and McInerney, C. 2008. 'Ireland's National Anti Poverty Strategy as New Governance'. *In:* Considine, M. and Giguere, S. (eds.) *The Theory and Practice of Local Governance and Economic Development*, Basingstoke and New York: Palgrave Macmillan.

Ahern, D. 2001. *Written Answers: Anti Poverty Strategy*, Dublin: Dáil Éireann.

American Political Science Association 2004. *American Democracy in an Age of Rising Inequality*, www.apsanet.org/content_2471.cfm accessed 18 October 2012.

Arnstein, S. 1969. 'A Ladder of Citizen Participation'. *JAIP*, 35:4, 216–224.

Association of Municipal Authorities of Ireland 2007. *Submission to the Green Paper on Local Government Reform*, www.docstoc.com/docs/30565189/Submission-by-the-Association-of-Municipal-Authorities-of-Ireland, accessed 1 December, 2012.

Atkinson, R. and Davoudi, S. 2000. 'The Concept of Social Exclusion in the European Union: Context, Development and Possibilities'. *Journal of Common Market Studies*, 38, 427–448.

Aucion, P. 1990. 'Administrative Reform in Public Management: Paradigms, Principles, Paradoxes and Pendulums'. *Governance*, 3, 115–137.

Bache, I. and Flinders, M. V. 2004. *Multi-level Governance*, Oxford: Oxford University Press.

Baker, J., Lynch, K., Cantillon, S. and Walsh, J. 2004. *Equality: From Theory to Action*, Basingstoke, Palgrave Macmillan.

Barber, B. R. 1984. *Strong Democracy: Participatory Politics for a New Age*, Berkeley: University of California Press.

Barnes, M., Knops, A., Newman, J. and Sullivan, H. 2002. *Participation and*

Exclusion: Problems of Theory and Method, Economic and Social Research Council, accessed December 2004.

Barrington, T. J. 1965. 'Administrative Purpose'. *Administration*, 13, 176–191.

Barrington, T. J. 1980. *The Irish Administrative System*, Dublin: Institute of Public Administration.

Barry, B. 2005. *Why Social Justice Matters*, Cambridge: Polity Press.

Begg, D. 3 July 2012. *Personal interview.*

Beresford, P. and Hoban, M. 2005. *Participation in Anti Poverty and Regeneration Work and Research: Overcoming Barriers and Creating Opportunities*, York: Joseph Rowntree Foundation.

Berghman, J. 1995. 'Social Exclusion in Europe: Policy Context and Analytical Framework'. *In*: Room, G. (ed.) *Beyond the Threshold: The Measurement and Analysis of Social Exclusion*, Bristol: Policy Press.

Berlin, I. 2004. 'Two Concepts of Liberty'. *In*: Goodin, R. E. and Pettit, P. (eds.) *Contemporary Political Philosophy (Reprinted from Four Essays on Liberty (1958) Oxford University Press)*, Malden, Oxford and Carlton: Blackwell Publishing.

Bohman, J. 1998. 'The Coming of Age of Deliberative Democracy'. *Journal of Political Philosophy*, 6, 400–425.

Box, R. C. 2005. *Critical Social Theory in Public Administration*, New York: M. E. Sharp.

Box, R. C. 2008. *The Case for Progressive Values*, New York: M. E. Sharpe.

Boyle, R. 2007. *Comparing Public Administrations: An Assessment of the Quality and Efficiency of Public Administration in Ireland Compared with selected European and OECD countries*, Dublin: Institute of Public Administration.

Boyle, R. 2009. 'The Changing Face of the Irish Public Service'. *In*: Mulreany, M. (ed.) *Serving the State: The Public Sector in Ireland*, Dublin: Institute of Public Administration.

Boyle, R. 2011. *Public Sector Trends 2011*, Dublin: Institute of Public Administration.

Boyle, R. and Humphreys, P. C. 2001. *A New Change Agenda for the Irish Public Service*, Dublin: Institute of Public Administration.

Boyle, R. and MacCarthaigh, M. 2011. *Fit for Purpose? Challenges for Irish Public Administration and Priorities for Public Service Reform*, State of the Public Service Series Dublin: Institute of Public Administration.

Bryer, T. A. 2007. 'Towards a Relevant Agenda for a Responsive Public Administration' *Journal of Public Administration, Research and Theory*, 17, 479–500.

Buckley, T. 30 October 2012. *Personal interview.*

Burchardt, T. and Craig, G. 2008. 'Introduction'. *In*: Craig, G., Burchardt, T. and Gordon, D. (eds.) *Social Justice and Public Policy: Seeking Fairness in Diverse Societies*, Bristol: Policy Press.

Burton, J. 2012. 'Written Answers: Regulatory and Poverty Impact Assessments'. Dublin: Dáil Éireann.

Burton, P., Goodlad, R., Croft, J., Abbott, J., Hastings, A. and Macdonald, G. 2004. *What Works in Community Involvement in Area-based Initiatives*, London: Home Office.

Cahill, F. E. 23 May 1937. *Letter from Fr. Edward Cahill to Eamon DeVelera*.

Callanan, M. 2007. 'Retrospective on Critical Junctures and Drivers of Change'. *In*: Callanan, M. (ed.) *Ireland 2022: Towards 100 Years of Self Government*, Dublin: Institute of Public Administration.

Cameron, D. 2011. *Speech on Big Society*, www.number10.gov.uk/news/pms-speech-on-big-society accessed 2 October.

Catholic Bishops Conference 1996. *The Common Good and the Catholic Church's Social Teaching: A statement by the Catholic Bishops Conference of England and Wales* www.catholic-ew.org.uk/Home/News/2010/Choosing-the-Common-Good/%28language%29/eng-GB accessed 22 September 2012.

Central Statistics Office 2011. *Census 2011. Profile 7: Religion, Ethnicity and Irish Travellers*, Dublin: Stationery Office.

Central Statistics Office 2012a. Earnings Hours and Employment Cost Survey Quarterly, www.cso.ie/px/pxeirestat/Statire/SelectVarVal/Define.asp?maintable=EHQ10andP Language=0 accessed 2 July.

Central Statistics Office 2012b. *Survey on Income and Living Conditions (SILC) 2010*, Dublin: Stationery Office.

Chambers, R. 2004. *Ideas for Development: Reflecting Forwards*, IDS Working Paper 238, Sussex: Institute for Development Studies.

Chappell, Z. 2012. *Deliberative Democracy: A Critical Introduction*, Basingstoke: Palgrave.

Chari, R. and Bernhagen, P. 2011. 'The Sunset over the Celtic Tiger'. *Irish Political Studies*, 26, 473–488.

Chubb, B. 1970. *The Government and Politics of Ireland*, Stanford, CA: Stanford University Press.

Clancy, P., Hughes, I. and Brannick, T. 2005. *Public Perspectives on Democracy in Ireland*. Dublin: Tasc.

Clarke, M. and Stewart, J. 1998. *Community Governance, Community Leadership and the New Local Government*, York: Joseph Rowntree Foundation.

Cohen, J. and Fung, A. 2004. 'Radical Democracy'. *Swiss Political Science Review*, 10, 23–34.

Cohen, J. and Rogers, J. 1997. *Can Egalitarianism Survive Internationalisation*. Working Paper 97/2, Economic Globalisation and National Democracy Lecture Series www.mpi-fg-koeln.mpg.de/pu/workpap/wp97–2/wp97–2.html accessed 13 February 2007.

Collier, D. and Levitsky, S. 1997. 'Democracy with Adjectives: Conceptual Innovation in Comparative Research'. *World Politics*, 49, 430–451.

Community Residents Focus Group 2011. McInerney, C., 'Re: Conclusions of Community Residents Focus Group', Tralee.

Comptroller and Auditor General 2000. *Report on Value for Money Examination: Training and Development in the Civil Service*, Dublin: Department of Finance.

Connolly, E. 2007. *The Institutionalisation of Anti Poverty and Social Exclusion Policy in Irish Social Partnership* Poverty Research Initiative, Dublin: Dublin City University / Combat Poverty Agency.

Cooke, G. and Muir, R. 2012. 'The Possibilities and Politics of the Relational State'. *In:* Cooke G. and Muir R. (eds.) *The Relational State: How Recognising the Importance of Human Relationships Could Revolutionise the Role of the State*, London: Institute for Public Policy Research.

Cosgrave, S. and KW Research Associates 2007. *The Voice of People in Poverty in Local Government Structures and Processes: A Study of Community Fora*, Dublin: Combat Poverty Agency.

Costello, J. A. 1952. *Restrictive Trade Practices Bill (195), Committee Stage*, Committee on Finance, Dublin: Dáil Éireann.

Dahl, R. A. 1985. *A Preface to Economic Democracy*, Berkeley: University of California Press.

De Rossa, P. 2006. Speech by Proinsias De Rossa MEP, 'Planning for an Inclusive Society', Talbot Hotel, Wexford: Wexford Area Partnership.

De Rossa, P. 11 September 2012. *Personal interview.*

Dellepiane, S. and Hardiman, N. 2011. 'Governing the Irish Economy: A Triple Crisis'. *In:* Hardiman, N. (ed.) *Irish Governance in Crisis*, Manchester: Manchester University Press.

Deloitte 2010. *Reconnect, Reorganise, Restructure: Reform of the Irish Public Sector*, Dublin: Deloitte & Touche.

Denham, S. 2012. 'Some Thoughts on the Constitution of Ireland at 75', Paper presented to the Royal Irish Academy Conference 'The Irish Constitution: Past, Present and Future', Dublin.

Department of the Environment, Community and Local Government 2007. *Local Government Act 2001: Code of Conduct for Employees*, Dublin: Stationery Office.

Department of the Environment, Community and Local Government 2011. *Regulatory Impact Analysis: Screening Report*, Proposal for Legislation Regarding Septic Tanks and Other On-site Wastewater Treatment Systems, Dublin.

Department of Finance 2012. *Medium-Term Fiscal Statement: November 2012*, Dublin: Government Publications.

Department of Jobs, Enterprise and Innovation 2012. *Regulatory Impact Analysis* www.djei.ie/publications/ria/index.htm accessed 8 December.

Department of Public Expenditure and Reform 2011. *Public Service Reform Plan*, Dublin.

Department of Public Expenditure and Reform 2013. www.databank.per.gov. ie/, accessed 6 January 2013.

Department of Social and Family Affairs 2008. *Report of Steering Committee: Review of Combat Poverty Agency*, Dublin.

Department of the Taoiseach 2009. *Revised RIA Guidelines: How to conduct a Regulatory Impact Analysis*. Dublin: Department of the Taoiseach.

Department of the Taoiseach 2012. *Social Dialogue* www.taoiseach.gov.ie/ eng/Work_Of_The_Department/Economic_and_Social_Policy/Social_ Dialogue/ accessed 8 December.

Devlin et al. 1969. *Report of the Public Services Organisation Review Group*, Dublin: Stationery Office.

Devolution Commission 1996. *Interim Report*. Dublin: Stationery Office.

Dooney, S. 1976. *The Irish Civil Service*, Dublin: Institute of Public Administration.

Dooney, S. and O'Toole, J. 1992. *Irish Government Today*, Dublin: Gill and Macmillan.

Doyle, P. 2009. 'Framing the Closure of the Combat Poverty Agency', MA dissertation, Dublin City University.

Dryzek, J. 1996. 'Political Inclusion and the Dynamics of Democratization'. *American Political Science Review*, 90, 475–487.

Dryzek, J. 2000. *Deliberative Democracy and Beyond: Liberals, Critics, Contestations*, Oxford: Oxford University Press.

Dworkin, R. 2011. *Justice for Hedgehogs*, Cambridge, MA: Belknap Press of Harvard University.

Edelenbos, J. 2005. 'Institutional Implications of Interactive Governance: Insights from Dutch Practice'. *Governance: An International Journal of Policy, Administration, and Institution*, 18, 111–134.

European Anti Poverty Network 2009. *Small Steps Big Changes: Building Participation of People Experiencing Poverty*, Brussels: EAPN.

European Commission 1992. *Towards a Europe of Solidarity: Intensifying the Fight against Social Exclusion, Fostering Integration*. COM (92) 542, Brussels: European Commission.

European Commission 2010a. *Eurobarometer 321: Poverty and Social Exclusion*, Brussels: European Commission Directorate General for Communication.

European Commission 2010b. *Eurobarometer Report 74.1: Poverty and Social Exclusion*, Brussels: European Commission.

European Commission 2010c. *The Social Situation in the European Union 2009*, Brussels: DG Employment Social Affairs and Equal Opportunities, European Commission.

European Commission 2010d. *Social Climate Report: Special Eurobarometer 315*, Brussels: European Commission Directorate General for Communication, European Commission.

European Commission 2011a. *Social Climate Report: Special Eurobarometer*

349, Brussels: Directorate General for Communications, European Commission.

European Commission 2011b. *Social Climate Report: Special Eurobarometer 370*, Brussels: Directorate General for Communications, European Commission.

European Commission 2012. *Social Climate Report: Special Eurobarometer 391*, Brussels: Directorate General for Communications, European Commission.

European Commission. 2013. *Social Protection and Inclusion: Common Indicators*, Brussels: DG Employment Social Affairs and Inclusion, http://ec.europa.eu/social/main.jsp?catId=756andlangId=en accessed 4 January.

European Union 2000. Charter of Fundamental Rights of the European Union, 7 December 2000, Official Journal of the European Communities, 18 December 2000 (OJ C 364/01), www.refworld.org/docid/3ae6b3b70.html, accessed 2 November 2012.

Evans, K. J. 2000. 'Reclaiming John Dewey: Democracy, Inquiry, Pragmatism and Public Management'. *Administration and Society*, 32, 308–328.

FitzGerald, G. 1986. Adjournment of Dáil Motion (Resumed), Dublin: Dáil Éireann.

FitzGerald, J. 2011. *Restoring Credibility in Policy Making in Ireland*, ESRI Working Paper 415.

Fraser, H. 1997. 'A Potentially Historic Development'. *Poverty Today*, Dublin: Combat Poverty Agency.

Fraser, N. 1990. 'Rethinking the Public Sphere: A Contribution to the Critique of Actually Existing Democracy'. *Social Text*, 25/26, 56–80.

Frazer, H. 24 May 2012. *Personal interview*.

Frederickson, H. G. 2005. 'The State of Social Equity in American Public Administration'. *National Civic Review*, 94, 31–38.

Frederickson, H. G. 2007. 'Social Equity in the 21st Century: An Essay in Memory of Philip J. Rutledge' *Public Administration Times*, 30, 11–19.

Frederickson, H. G. 2010. *Social Equity and Public Administration: Origins, Developments and Applications*, New York: M. E. Sharpe.

Fung, A. and Wright, O. W. 2001. 'Deepening Democracy: Innovations in Empowered Participatory Governance'. *Politics and Society*, 29, 5–41.

Gaventa, J. 2006. *Triumph, Deficit or Contestation? Deepening the 'Deepening Democracy' Debate*, IDS Working Paper 264, Sussex: Institute of Development Studies.

Goss, R. P. 1996. 'A Distinct Public Administration Ethic'. *Journal of Public Administration Research and Theory*, 6, 573–597.

Government of Austria 2011. *Standards of Public Participation: Recommendations for Good Practice*, Vienna: Austrian Federal Chancellery.

Government of Ireland 1937. *Bunreacht na hÉireann: Constitution of Ireland*, Dublin: Stationery Office.

Government of Ireland 1973. Ministers and Secretaries (Amendment) Act.

Government of Ireland 1996. *Better Local Government: A Programme for Change*, Dublin: Department of the Environment and Local Goverment.

Government of Ireland 1997a. Public Services Management Act, Ireland.

Government of Ireland 1997b. *Sharing in Progress: The National Anti Poverty Strategy*. Dublin: Department of Social Welfare.

Government of Ireland 2000a. *Programme for Prosperity and Fairness*, Dublin: Department of the Taoiseach.

Government of Ireland 2000b. *White Paper on a Framework for Supporting Voluntary Activity and for Developing the Relationship between the State and the Community and Voluntary Sector*, Dublin: Department of Social and Family Affairs.

Government of Ireland 2001. Local Government Act, Dublin: Stationery Office.

Government of Ireland 2003. *National Action Plan Against Poverty and Social Exclusion, 2003–2005*. Dublin: Office for Social Inclusion.

Government of Ireland 2005. *Guidelines on Consultation for Public Sector Bodies*, Dublin: Department of the Taoisearch.

Government of Ireland 1986a. Combat Poverty Agency Act Ireland, Dublin: Stationery Office.

Government of Ireland 2006. *White Paper on Irish Aid*, Dublin: Department of Foreign Affairs.

Government of Ireland 2007. *National Action Plan For Social Inclusion 2007–2016*. Dublin: Stationery Office.

Government of Ireland 2008. Social Welfare (Miscellaneous Provisions) Act 2008, Dublin: Stationery Office.

Government of Ireland 2011. *Government for National Recovery 2011–2016*, Dublin: Stationery Office.

Government of Ireland 2012a. *Putting People First – Action Programme for Effective Local Government*, Dublin: Department of the Environment, Community and Local Government.

Government of Ireland 2012b. *Third Report of the Organisational Review Programme*, Dublin: Department of Public Expenditure and Reform.

Government of Scotland 2005. *National Standards for Community Engagement*, Edinburgh: Communities Scotland.

Government of Scotland 2008. *Evaluation of the Impact of the National Standards for Community Engagement: A Report to the Scottish Government*, Glasgow: Clear Plan UK.

Gray, A. and Jenkins, B. 1995. 'From Public Administration to Public Management: Reassessing a Revolution?' *Public Administration*, 73, 75–99.

Hannum, K. 2012. *Social Justice: Why Are Some Faithful Tarnishing the Good Name of This Essential Catholic Value*? www.uscatholic.org/church/2012/06/social-justice-whats-tarnishing-its-good-name, accessed 27 November.

Hardiman, N. 2006. 'Politics and Social Partnership: Flexible Network Governance'. *The Economic and Social Review*, 37, 343–374.

Hardiman, N. and MacCarthaigh, M. 2008. 'Administrative Reform in a Liberal Market Economy', paper presented to the Conference on New Public Management and the Quality of Government, 13–15 November, Quality of Government Institute, University of Gothenburg.

Hardiman, N., MacCarthaigh, M. and Scott, C. 2012. *The Irish State Administration Database*, Dublin.

Harriss, J. 2007. *Working Paper 77 – Bringing Politics Back into Poverty Analysis: Why Understanding Social Relations Matters More for Policy on Chronic Poverty than Measurement*, Manchester: Chronic Poverty Research Centre, www.chronicpoverty.org/resources/working_papers.html accessed 6 February 2008.

Harvey, B. 2004. *Implementing the White Paper: Supporting Voluntary Activity – Report for the CV 12 Group*, Dublin.

Harvey, B. 2008. *Community Sector Funding: Report Commissioned by a Consortium of Anti Poverty Networks*, Dublin.

Health Service Executive 2009. *Framework for the Corporate and Financial Governance of the Health Service Executive: Codes of Standards and Behaviour*, Dublin.

Health Service Executive 2011. *Employee Handbook*, Dublin.

Healy, S. 25 May 2012. *Personal interview*.

Healy, S., Mallon, S., Murphy, M. and Reynolds, B. 2012. *Shaping Ireland's Future: Securing Economic Development, Social Equity and Sustainability*, Dublin: Social Justice Ireland.

Held, D. 1987. *Models of Democracy*, Stanford, CA: Stanford University Press.

Higgins, M. D., 2012. Remarks by President Higgins at the Conferral of Membership on him by the Royal Irish Academy, Dublin.

Hirst, P. 2000. 'Democracy and Governance'. *In:* Pierre, J. (ed.) *Debating Governance: Authority, Steering and Democracy*, Oxford: Oxford University Press.

Hoeller, P., Joumard, I., Pisu, M. and Bloch, D. 2012. *Less Income Inequality and More Growth – Are They Compatible: Part 1- Mapping Income Inequality Across the OECD*, Paris: OECD.

Hogan, G. 2012. *The Irish Constitution 1928–1941*, Dublin: Royal Irish Academy.

Howlin, B. 2012. Written Answers: Regulatory Impact Analysis, Dublin: Dáil Éireann.

Hughes, I., Clancy, P., Harris, C. and Beetham, D. 2007. *Power to the People: Assessing Democracy in Ireland*, Dublin: TASC.

Hynes, J. 3 July 2012. *Personal interview*.

Immergut, E. M. 1992. 'An Institutional Critique of Associative Democracy: Commentary on Secondary Associations and Democratic Governance'. *Politics and Society*, 20, 481–486.

Indecon 2008. *Review of County / City Development Boards Strategic Reviews and Proposals for Strengthening and Developing the Boards*, Dublin: Indecon International Economic Consultants.

Institute for Public Health 2011. *The Impact of Recession and Unemployment on Men's Health In Ireland*, Dublin and Belfast: IPH.

International Association for Public Participation. www.iap2.org/ accessed 21 Feburary 2011.

Irish Human Rights Commission 2010. Human Rights Guide for the Civil and Public Service, Dublin: IHRC.

Jayasuriya, K. 2004. 'The New Regulatory State and Relational Capacity' *Policy and Politics*, 32, 487–501.

Jensen, M. J. 2006. 'Concepts and Conceptions of Civil Society'. *Journal of Civil Society*, 2, 39–56.

Jessop, B. 2004. 'Multi-level Governance and Multi-level Metagovernance'. *In:* Bache, I. and Flinders, M. V. (eds.) *Multi-level Governance*, Oxford: Oxford University Press.

John Paul II 1993. *Veritatis Splendor*, Encyclical Letter.

Johnson, N. J. and Svara, J. H. 2011. *Justice for All: Promoting Social Equity in Public Administration*, New York: M. E. Sharpe.

Jones, E. and Gaventa, J. 2002. *Concepts of Citizenship: A Review*, Institute of Development Studies Development Bibliography 19. Brighton: Institute of Development Studies.

Jones, P. A. and Waller, R. L. 2010. 'A Model of Catholic Social Teaching: Assessing Policy Proposals'. *Catholic Social Science Review*, 15, 283–296.

Keoghan, J. F. 2003. Reform in Irish Local Government. *In:* Callanan, M., and Keoghan, J.F., (ed.) *Local Government in Ireland: Inside Out*, Dublin: Institute of Public Administration.

Keyes, J. 19 July 2012. *Personal interview.*

Kwon, H. 2005. *Transforming the Developmental Welfare State in East Asia*, Social Policy and Development Programme Paper 22, Geneva: United Nations Research Institute for Social Development.

Lane, P. 2011. *The Irish Crisis*, IIIS Discussion Paper 356, Dubin: Institute for International Integration Studies.

Laurent, B. 2007. 'Catholicism and Liberalism: Two Ideologies in Confrontation'. *Theological Studies*, 68, 808–838.

Layte, R. 2011. 'Should We Be Worried about Income Inequality in Ireland?' *ESRI Research Bulletin*, 2.

Lemass, S. 1946. Industrial Relations Bill (1946): Recommital, Dáil Debate, Dublin: Dáil Éireann.

Lemass, S. 1952. Restrictive Trade Practices Bill, (195) Committee Stage, *Committee on Finance*, Dublin: Dáil Éireann.

Levitas, R. 2004. 'Lets Hear it for Humpty: Social Exclusion, the Third Way and Cultural Capital'. *Cultural Trends*, 13, 41–56.

Lister, R. 1997. 'Citizenship: Towards a Feminist Synthesis'. *Feminist Review*, 57, 28–48.

Litton, F. 2012. An Overview of the Irish System of Government. *In:* MacCarthaigh, M. and O'Malley, E. (eds.) *Governing Ireland: From Cabinet Government to Delegated Governance*, Dublin: Institute of Public Administration.

Live Simply Network. 2012. *Catholic Social Teaching: Introduction and Principles* www.catholicsocialteaching.org.uk/principles/ accessed 21 September.

Luckham, R., Goetz M. and Kaldor, M. 1999. *Democratic Institutions and Politics in Contexts of Inequality, Poverty and Conflict*, Working Paper 104, Brighton: Institute of Development Studies.

Lukes, S. 1974. *Power: A Radical View*, London: Macmillan.

MacCarthaigh, M. 2008. *Public Sector Values*, CPMR Discussion Paper 39, Dublin: Institute of Public Administration.

MacCarthaigh, M. 2009. *The Corporate Governance of Commercial State-owned Enterprises in Ireland*, CPMR Research Reports, Dublin: Institute of Public Administration.

MacCarthaigh, M. 2010. *National non-commercial State Agencies in Ireland*, Research Paper 1, State of the Public Services Series, Dublin: Institute of Public Administration.

MacCarthaigh, M. 2012. *Organisational Change in Irish Public Administration*, Dublin: University College Dublin.

Macpherson, C. B. 1977. *The Life and Times of Liberal Democracy*, Oxford: Oxford University Press.

Mahbub ul haq Human Development Centre 1999. *Human Development in South Asia 1999: The Crisis of Governance*, Oxford: Oxford University Press.

Manley, J. F. 1983. 'Pluralism I and Pluralism II'. *American Political Science Review*, 77, 368–383.

Mann, D. 1999. 'The Limits of Instrumental Rationality in Social Explanation'. *Critical Review*, 13, 165–189.

Manor, J., Robinson, M. and White, G. 1999. *Civil Society and Governance: A Concept Paper*, Sussex: Institute of Development Studies.

Marinetto, M. 2003. 'Governing beyond the Centre: A Critique of the Anglo Governance School'. *Political Studies*, 51, 592–608.

Marini, F. (ed.) 1971. *Towards a New Public Administration: The Minnnowbrook Perspective*, Scranton: Chander Sharp.

Marks, S. P. 2005. 'The Human Rights Framework for Development: Seven Approaches'. *In:* Sengupta A., Negi, A. and M., B. (eds.) *Reflections on the Right to Development*, New Delhi: Sage Publications India.

McCarthy, D. 2009. 'Towards 2016: Challenges Facing the Public Service'. *In:*

Mulreany and Michael (eds.) *Serving the State: The Public Sector in Ireland,* Dublin: Institute of Public Administration.

McCarthy, D. 26 June 2012. *Personal interview*

McDunphy, M. 23 March 1937. *Memorandum by Michael McDunphy: Observations on First Circulated Draft.*

McElligott, J. J. 24 April 1937a. *Memorandum by James J. McElligott: Notes on Revised Drafts of Articles 42–44.*

McElligott, J. J. 1937b. *Memorandum from James J. McElligott to Maurice Moynihan: Observations on First Circulated Draft.*

McGauran, A. M., Verhoest, K. and Humphreys, P. C. 2005. *The Corporate Governance of Agencies in Ireland: Non Commercial National Agencies,* CPMR Research Reports, Dublin: Institute of Public Administration.

McGilligan 1946. Industrial Relations Bill (1946): Recommital. Dáil Debate. Dublin: Dáil Éireann.

McInerney, C. 2006. *Evaluating the Tralee Rapid Programme.* Kerry: Kerry County Council.

McInerney, C. and Adshead, M. 2010. *The Challenge of Community Participation in the Delivery of Public Services: Exploring Local Participatory Governance in Ireland,* Dublin: National Economic and Social Forum.

Meade, R. and O'Donovan, O. 2002. 'Corporatism and the Ongoing Debate about the Relationship between the State and Community Development'. *Community Development Journal,* 37, 1–9.

Meir, K. J. 1976. Representative Bureaucracy and Policy Preferences: A Study in the attitudes of Federal Executives. *Public Administration Review,* 36, 458–469.

Michalski, W., Miller R. and Stevens, B. 2001. *Governance in the 21st Century: Power in the Global Knowledge Economy and Society,* Paris: OECD.

Michels, A. and De Graaf, L. 2010. 'Examining Citizen Participation: Local Participatory Policy Making and Democracy'. *Local Government Studies,* 36, 477–491.

Moran, M. 2006. 'Social Inclusion and the Limits of Pragmatic Liberalism: The Irish Case'. *Irish Political Studies,* 21, 181–201.

Morgan, A. 2009. Social Welfare (Miscellaneous Provisions) Bill 2008: Second Stage (Resumed), Dublin: Dáil Éireann.

Mulgan, G. 2012. Government with the People: The Outlines of a Relational State. *In:* Cooke G. and Muir R. (eds.) *The Relational State: How Recognising the Importance of Human Relationships Could Revolutionise the Role of the State,* London: IPPR.

Murphy, M. 2002. 'Social Partnership: Is It the Only Game in Town'. *Community Development Journal,* 37, 80–90.

Murray, J. A. 2007. 'Services, Counsel and Values: Managing Strategically in the Public Sector'. *In:* Galavan, R., Murray, J. and Markides, C. (eds.) *Strategy, Innovation, Change.* Oxford: Oxford University Press.

Nahem, J. and Sudders, M. 2004. *Governance Indicators: A Users Guide*, New York and Luxembourg: UNDP and the European Commission.

Narayan, D., Chambers, R., Shah, M. K. and Petesch, P. 2000. *Voices of the Poor: Crying Out for Change*, New York: Oxford University Press for the World Bank.

National Academy of Public Administration 2012. *Standing Panel on Social Equity in Governance*, www.napawash.org/fellows/standing-panels/standing-panel-on-social-equity-in-governance/ accessed 18 October.

National Economic and Social Forum 2002. *A Strategic Policy Framework for Equality Issues*, Forum Report 23, Dublin: NESF.

NESC 2009. *Ireland's Five-Part Crisis:An Integrated National Response*. Council Report 118, Dublin: National Economic and Social Council.

Newman, H. 2011. *Independent and Interdependent: Sustaining a Strong and Vital Community and Voluntary Sector in Ireland*, Dublin: The Wheel.

Nolan, B. 2009. 'Income Inequality and Public Policy'. *Economic and Social Review*, 40, 489–510.

O'Brien, M. and Penna, S. 2007. 'Social Exclusion in Europe: Some Conceptual Issues'. *International Journal of Social Welfare*,17, 84–92.

O'Broin, D. and Waters, E. 2007. *Governing Below the Centre: Local Governance in Ireland*, Dublin: New Island.

O'Connor, S. 2001. *Review of the Poverty Proofing Process*, Dublin: National Economic and Social Council.

O'Donoghue, S. 2012. *Personal interview*.

O'Higgins, T. F. 1959. Debate on the Third Amendment of the Constitution Bill, 1958: Committee Stage, Dublin: Dáil Éireann.

O'Kelly, K. 11 December 2012. *Personal interview*.

O'Neill, J. 20 May 2012. *Personal interview*.

O'Riain, S. 2004. *The Politics of High-Tech Growth*, Cambridge: Cambridge University Press.

O'Riordan, J. 2011. *Organisational Capacity in the Irish Civil Service: An Examination of the Organisation Review Programme*, State of the Public Services, Dublin: Institute of Public Administration.

O'Sullivan, T. 2003. Local Areas and Structures. *In*: Callanan, M. and Keogan, J. (eds.) *Local Government in Ireland: Inside Out*, Dublin: Institute for Public Administration.

OECD 2008a. *Income Distribution and Poverty in OECD Countries*, Paris: OECD.

OECD 2008b. *Ireland: Towards an Integrated Public Service*, OECD Public Management Reviews, Paris: OECD.

OECD 2009. *Focus on Citizens: Public Engagement for Better Policy and Services*, OECD Studies on Public Engagement, Paris: OECD.

Offe, C. and Roge, V. 1997. 'Theses on the Theory of the State'. *In*: Goodin, R. E.

and Pettit, P. (eds.) *Contemporary Political Philosophy*, Oxford: Blackwell Publishing.

Office for Social Inclusion 2006a. *National Report for Ireland on Strategies for Social Protection and Social Inclusion: 2006–2008*, Dublin: Stationery Office.

Office for Social Inclusion 2006b. *Review of Poverty Proofing*, Dublin: Department of Social and Family Affairs.

Oldfield, K. 2003. 'Social Class and Public Administration: A Closed Question Opens'. *Administration and Society*, 35, 438–461.

PA Consulting Group 2002. *Evaluation of the Progress of the Strategic Management Initiative / Delivering Better Government Modernisation Programme*, PA Consulting Group.

Panel on the Independence of the Voluntary Sector 2012. *Protecting Independence: the Voluntary Sector in 2012*, London: Baring Foundation, Civil Exchange and DHA Communications.

Parkinson, J. 2003. 'Legitimacy Problems in Deliberative Democracy'. *Political Studies*, 51, 180–196.

Pateman, C. 1970. *Participation and Democratic Theory*, Cambridge: Cambridge University Press.

Pateman, C. 2004. 'Participation and Democratic Theory'. *In:* Blaug, R. and Schwarzmantel, J. (eds.) *Democracy: A Reader*, Edinburgh: Edinburgh University Press.

Pearce, N. 2012. 'Under Pressure: The Drivers of a New Centre-left Statecraft'. *In:* Cooke, G. and Muir, R. (eds.) *The Relational State: How Recognising the Importance of Human Relationships Could Revolutionise the Role of the State*, London: IPPR.

Pempel, T. J. 1999. 'The Developmental Regime in a Changing World'. *In:* Woo-Cumings, M. (ed.) *The Developmental State*, Ithaca and London: Cornell University Press.

Personal Communication: Business Sector Representative. February 2006.

Personal Communication: Community / Voluntary Sector Representative. February 2006.

Personal Communication: Farming Organisation Representative. February 2006.

Personal Communication: Trade Union Representative. January 2006.

Phillips, A. 2004. 'Democracy, Recognition and Power'. *In:* Engelstad, F. and Osterud, O. (eds.) *Power and Democracy, Critical Interventions*, Aldershot: Ashgate.

Pierre, J. 1999. 'Models of Urban Governance: The Institutional Dimension of Urban Politics'. *Urban Affairs Review*, 34, 372–396.

Pierre, J. and Peters, B. G. 2000. *Governance, Politics and the State*, New York: St. Martins Press.

Plant, R. 2004. 'Neo Liberalism and the Theory of the State'. *In:* Gamble, A. and Wright, T. (eds.) *Restating the State*, Oxford: Blackwell.

Pollit, C. 1995. 'Management Techniques for the Public Sector: Pulpit and Practice'. *In*: Peters, B. G., and Savoie, D.J. (ed.) *Governance in a Changing Environment*, Montreal: McGill-Queens University Press.

Private Interview. June 2012a. *Assistant Secretary*.

Private Interview. 2012b. *Retired Senior Civil Servant*.

Quin, B. 2003. 'Irish Local Government in a Comparative Context'. *In*: Callanan, M. and Keogan, J. (eds.) *Local Government in Ireland: Inside Out*, Dublin: Institute of Public Administration.

Rabbitte, P. 2012. *Written Answers: Legislative Programme*, Dáil Éireann Debates Vol 722, No. 2, Dublin: Dáil Éireann.

Rawls, J. 2001. *Justice as Fairness: A Restatement*, Cambridge, MA: Belknap Press of Harvard University.

Rhodes, R. 2000. Governance and Public Administration. *In*: Pierre, J. (ed.) *Debating Governance – Authority, Steering and Democracy*, Oxford: Oxford University Press.

Robinson, M. 2008. 'Hybrid States: Globalisation and the Politics of State Capacity'. *Political Studies*, 56, 566–583.

Roman, D. B. and Baybado, P. A. 2008. Theological Constants of Justice in Catholic Social Teaching. *Philippiniana Sacra*, 43 83–98.

Room, G. 1995. 'Poverty in Europe: Competing Paradigms of Analysis'. *Policy and Politics*, 23, 103–113.

Santiso, C. 2001. 'Good Governance and Aid Effectiveness: The World Bank and Conditionality'. *Georgetown Public Policy Review*, 7, 1–22.

Savoie, D. J. 1995. 'What is wrong with the New Public Management'. *Canadian Public Administration*, 38, 112–121.

Scannell, M. 10 December 2010. *Interview*.

Schumpeter, J. A. 2003. *Capitalism, Socialism and Democracy*, Abingdon: Routledge.

Shafritz, J. M. and Russell, E. W. 2002. *Introducing Public Administration*, (3rd Edition), Boston: Addison Wesley-Longman.

Shorthall, R. 2008. *Adjournment Debate – Departmental Agencies*, Dáil Éireann Debates, 661, 1, Dublin: Dáil Éireann.

Silver, H. 1994. 'Social Exclusion and Social Solidarity: Three Paradigms'. *International Labour Review*, 133, 531–578.

Smith, G. 2005. *Power Beyond the Ballot: 57 Democratic Innovations from Around the World*, London: Power Inquiry.

Sorensen, E. 1997. 'Democracy and Empowerment'. *Public Administration*, 75, 553–567.

Standards in Public Office Commission 2008. *Civil Service Code of Standards and Behaviour* revised edn, Dublin: Department of Finance.

Stears, M. 2012. 'The Case for a State That Supports Relationships, Not a Relational State' *In*: Cooke, G. and Muir, R. (eds.) *The Relational State: How*

Recognising the Importance of Human Relationships Could Revolutionise the Role of the State, London: IPPR.

Sullivan, H. 2002. 'Modernization, Neighbourhood Management and Social Inclusion'. *Public Management Review*, 4, 505–528.

Svara, J. H. 2001. 'The Myth of the Dichotomy: Complementarity of Politics and Administration in the Past and Future of Public Administration'. *Public Administration Review*, 61, 176–183.

Taskforce on Active Citizenship 2007. *Report of the Taskforce on Active Citizenship*, Dublin: Secretariat of the Taskforce on Active Citizenship.

Tsikata, D. 2004. 'The Rights-Based Approach to Development: Potential for Change or More of the Same?' *Institute of Development Studies Bulletin*, 35, 130–133.

United Nations 1995. *Report of the World Summit for Social Development*, 1995 Copenhagen, New York: United Nations.

United Nations Capital Development Fund 2003. *Local Government Options Study – Draft Report. UN Capital Development Fund*, New York: United Nations.

United Nations Economic and Social Council 2010. *Challenges to and Opportunities for Public Administration in the Context of the Financial and Economic Crisis*, New York: United Nations.

United Nations General Assembly 1948. *Universal Declaration of Human Rights*, Paris: United Nations.

United Nations General Assembly 1986. *Declaration on the Right to Development, A/RES/41/128*, New York: United Nations.

Van Wart, M. 1998. *Changing Public Sector Values*, New York: Garland Publishing.

Ventriss, C. 2010. 'The Challenge for Public Administration (and Public Policy) in an Era of Economic Crises … or the Relevance of Cognitivie Politics in a Time of Political Involution'. *Administrative Theory and Praxis*, 32, 402–408.

Villa-Vincencio, C. (ed.) 1987. *Theology and Violence. The South African Debate*, Johannesburg: Skotaville Publishers.

Warren, M. E. 1996. 'Deliberative Democracy and Authority'. *American Political Science Review*, 90, 46–60.

Watt, R. 19 July 2012. *Personal interview*.

Wilkinson, R. G. and Pickett, K. 2010. *The Spirit Level: Why Equality Is Better for Everyone*, London: Penguin.

Wisman, J. D. and Smith, J. 2011. 'Legitimating Inequality: Fooling Most of the People All of the Time'. *American Journal of Economics and Sociology*, 70, 974–1013.

Wolff, J. 2008. 'Social Justice and Public Policy: A View from Political Philosophy'. *In: Social Justice and Public Policy: Seeking Fairness in Diverse Societies*, Bristol: Policy Press.

Wooldridge, B. and Gooden, S. 2009. 'The Epic of Social Equity'. *Administrative Theory and Praxis*, 31, 2, 222–234.

World Bank 1997. *World Development Report: The State in a Changing World*, New York: Oxford University Press.

Wright, R., Borstlap, H. and Malone, J. 2010. *Strengthening the Capacity of the Department of Finance: Report of the Independent Review Group*, Dublin: Department of Finance.

Young, I. M. 2000. *Inclusion and Democracy*, Oxford: Oxford University Press.

Index

Note: 'n' after a page reference indicates the number of a note on that page. Page numbers in italic refer to figures/tables.

Leabharlanna Poiblí Chathair Bhaile Átha Cliath
Dublin City Public Libraries